The Moment of Racial Sight

The Moment of Racial Sight

A History

IRENE TUCKER

The University of Chicago Press
Chicago and London

Irene Tucker is associate professor of English at the University of California, Irvine. She is the author of *A Probable State: The Novel, the Contract, and the Jews*, also published by the University of Chicago Press.

The University of Chicago Press, Chicago 60637
The University of Chicago Press, Ltd., London

Printed in the United States of America

21 20 19 18 17 16 15 14 13 12   1 2 3 4 5

ISBN-13: 978-0-226-92293-5 (cloth)
ISBN-10: 0-226-92293-6 (cloth)
ISBN-13: 978-0-226-92295-9 (e-book)
ISBN-10: 0-226-92295-2 (e-book)

The University of Chicago Press gratefully acknowledges the support of the Humanities Collective, University of California, Irvine, toward the publication of this book.

Library of Congress Cataloging-in-Publication Data
Tucker, Irene.
The moment of racial sight: a history / Irene Tucker.
pages. cm
Includes bibliographical references and index.
ISBN 978-0-226-92293-5 (cloth: alkaline paper)—ISBN 978-0-226-92295-9 (e-book) 1. Race awareness—History. 2. Race in literature. 3. Kant, Immanuel, 1724–1804. 4. Mill, John Stuart, 1806–1873. 5. Darwin, Charles, 1809–1882. 6. Collins, Wilkie, 1824–1889. Woman in white. 7. Wire (Television program) I. Title.
GN269.T83 2013
305.8009—dc23   2012024767

∞ This paper meets the requirements of ANSI/NISO Z39.48-1992 (Permanence of Paper).

For Julian,
who teaches me funny phrases, and how to love

CONTENTS

ACKNOWLEDGMENTS

The Moment of Racial Sight: A History exhumes the fantasy that an individual might, in an instant, discern the likeness of all humans, the notion that the grounds of political equality might be discovered in a glance. The task of these acknowledgments is, happily, to mark a different reality: the building of a project by way of relationships discernible not in an instant, but in their endurance through time, friendships with people remarkably, notably, different from one another and from themselves, then and now.

David Clark was this project's earliest official (Chicago Press–appointed) reader, and his capacity to discern a streamlined argument in the draft he encountered was essential to the future of the book. I thank him for his early perspicacity, and for his subsequent detailed, appreciative, and, for me, revelatory description of my project. Two additional anonymous readers challenged me, in different ways, to produce a better, cleaner, clearer argument, and for this I thank them. Alan Thomas squired the book through the extended review process with the skill and aplomb I have come to depend upon, even as the ground of the academic publishing industry shifted beneath our feet. I thank him for his wise stewardship, and also, at the eleventh hour, for his good-humored generosity. Randy Petilos has been, as always, a virtuoso of efficiency and organization. Carlisle Rex-Waller edited my manuscript with a gentle and generous hand.

This book has benefited as well from being presented in chunks small and large, coherent and less so, to a variety of audiences. Thanks to the provocative questioners at McGill University, University of Notre Dame, University of California, Berkeley, Pomona College, University of Toronto, University at Buffalo (SUNY), Tel Aviv University, Haifa University, Ben Gurion University, and Brown University. Thanks especially to organizers Esther Frank and Marcie Frank, Sara Maurer, Mark Allison and Marisa Palacios Knox, Aaron Kunin and Larissa Tokmakoff Castillo, Rachel Ablow and Ruth Mack, Eitan Bar-Yosef and Chanita Goodblatt, and, finally, Jacques Khalip.

Cathy Gallagher and Elizabeth Abel observed the coming together of this book from a greater distance than they did my first book; nevertheless, the influence of both remains palpable in my scholarship and in the type of thinker and mentor I aspire to be. Isobel Armstrong was kind and generous when she did not need to be.

Only toward the end of this project, as I decided to write a chapter on *The Wire* and began work on it, did I discover the degree to which the city of Baltimore, with its uniquely stark intersection of race and medicine, provided the conditions of possibility for my argument. I am happy to have the opportunity to pay homage to Baltimore in all its charming eccentricity and not-quite-paradoxical urban intimacy. More particularly, the graduate seminars I taught in the English department at Johns Hopkins University were the earliest testing ground for the ideas that became this book, and I am grateful to all the participants for prodding me toward clarity and precision, even while displaying a rare intellectual adventuresomeness and openmindedness that inspire me to this day. Thanks especially to Jason Hoppe, Naomi Fry, Amit Yahav, Dan Stout, and Jason Potts. Michael Clune and Jason Gladstone generously invited me to join a conversation they were having about my piece on Mill and photography, and the questions they asked, as well their own important work on the representational specificity of photography, were crucial in helping me to articulate the relation of the Mill chapter to the rest of the project. Madeline Copp of the Eisenhower Library and Christine Ruggere of the History of Medicine Collection at Welsh Library of Johns Hopkins University helped me navigate the archives to discover the texts that came to be crucial to my thinking. Other Baltimore friends have been steadfast and loyal over the course of more than a decade, making Baltimore a home to which I can always return even as life has taken me elsewhere: Peggy MacKenzie, Susie Herrmann, Neil Hertz, Linda Delibero, Maud Casey, Mary Fissell, Jane Bennett, Tobie Meyer-Fong, and Kellee Tsai. Anne Eakin Moss and Ken Moss, along with Itzik and Aron, have been especially generous, repeatedly opening their home to me and to Julian, offering delicious food and great company to us both. Lisa O'Connell impresses again and again with her integrity and clear-sightedness, while Colene Bentley is always sensible and steady. Jennifer Culbert stayed my friend even during those times when I wasn't such good company and, in her loyalty, allowed me to know that I would be good company again in the future. Jonathan Goldberg and Michael Moon have been stalwart friends and colleagues over the space of two institutions and nearly a decade and a half. Although we no longer share a department or a city, and we can only break bread together at wide intervals, I am happy to look forward to many more years of shared meals, good gossip, and grand repartee.

Thanks to my teammates on the Unstoppables—Baltimore City softball champs many times over—for more than a decade of loyal friendship, and for helping me keep in mind the difficulty and necessity of this project. Special thanks to Joy (Peachies) Pride, Teresa Smiley, Hazel Prioleau, Tonya Griffin, Willamae Johnson, and Gloria Wilson (who offered helpful insights on life as a Maryland State Trooper, even as she uncomplainingly stretched for my errant throws to first).

To my fellow University of California, Irvine, travelers in the nineteenth century, Jerry Christensen, Jami Bartlett, and Andrea Henderson—who share with me a sense not only of the heterogeneity of our period but also of the capaciousness of what might count as nineteenth-century literary studies—I thank you for your intellectual generosity of spirit and for your imaginativeness. Also at Irvine, Jayne Lewis read large sections of the manuscript with her always discerning eye and with a nuanced sense of our converging aspirations. Plus, she is always game for adventure. Ann Van Sant helpfully provided a reading list to supplement my knowledge of eighteenth-century medicine. Rei Terada manages to be both responsible to and brilliant about the philosophical tradition she engages, and I was lucky to benefit from both. Carol Burke and Arlene Keizer are wise all the time and fierce when times call for fierceness. The two of them are my models of how to be department citizens. And for their friendship and good sense, I thank Daniel Gross, Eyal Amiran, Hilary Schor, and Laura O'Connor. Finally, thanks to Benjamin Bishop, Nasser Mufti, and Katherine Voyles, for providing the stuff of good conversations.

Alyson Bardsley makes me laugh with her acute and often unsparing critical eye, while Kim Drake makes me laugh with her laughter. Again and again, Simon Stern reveals impassioned erudition to be something other than an oxymoron. Cindy Franklin's regular Sunday afternoon phone calls, across time zones and oceans, have steadied me for decades now. Jane Garrity manages, with her newsy notes, to make the geographical distance between us fall away, while Jacqueline Shea Murphy offers the unshakeable familiarity of a forever friendship. Francesca (Pish) Royster inspires me by the force of her own wonderful work bringing together the past and the contemporary, the popular and the recondite—and there is still no one else who can as reliably make me laugh until I fall on the floor.

I learned a great deal from my conversations with Elaine Hadley about Victorian liberalism, while a well-timed encounter with Sarah Winter's work on Darwin and Saussure helped me to realize that I needed to think about Darwin for this project. I'm thankful to Sarah for all her help in doing that, as well as for her steady, serious, and kind wisdom. Ian Baucom showed me from a distance, in our almost-annual dinners and in his own wonderful work, how to look to new contexts for thinking of race and how to invent new genres to match. Though we have never shared a department affiliation, Tamar Katz has managed to keep up with the details of my life and work, both trivial and profound, for well over a decade now. I thank her for her groundedness, good humor, and well-timed outrage. Elizabeth Maddock Dillon and I have together navigated the vagaries of the profession; if vagaries there are to be, I was, and am, glad to have her good company. I have come to look forward to my semiannual dinners with Sharon Marcus, whose consummate professionalism takes the form of the generosity of being able to appreciate the virtue of work very different from her own. Eric Zakim and Yael Meroz have been friends from Berkeley to Durham to Baltimore-DC to Tel Aviv, and I'm pleased to have re-upped with them for another generation of friendship. Mark Goble and Elisa Tamarkin singly and together offer a knack for collegiality and good gossip, some of the best prose styles in the business, and now a reason for me to make the drive up the 5.

For their willingness to keep doing the hard work of friendship, across decades, continents, and lives, through divergences and reconvergences, I thank Renee Kottenhahn, Rob Wolf, Sharon Friedman, and Denise Wolf.

A sabbatical at the Tel Aviv English department in 2008–9 gave me the critical distance and fresh intellectual community not only to begin work on a new project, but, as it turned out, to revisit *The Moment of Racial Sight* and discover the ways in which it *wasn't* quite done. Ilana Etgar paved the bureaucratic way for me during my stay, helpfully negotiating with everyone from the science librarian to the border agent at Ben Gurion Airport. Hana Wirth-Nesher offered an inspiring model of how to build ethical institutions and generously welcomed me into her home. Amit Yahav helped me find my footing early on, introducing me to all the best fish restaurants in town, and her fierce intelligence made her a welcome sounding board for matters intellectual and political. Ayelet Ben-Yishai has a knack for turning a crisis into an occasion for great hilarity; I admire her both for her sense of proportion and her willingness, when necessary, to ignore its demands. Over the course of less than a year, Milette Shamir went from being a disembodied e-mail contact to a dear friend. I am grateful for her compassion, her capaciousness, and her quiet brilliance. Thanks, too, to Michael Zakim, Yael Sternhell, and Roy Kreitner for indulging me in the fiction that I could be an Americanist.

To the unexpected bounty that is my Ikar community, I am full of wonder and gratitude for creating a world in which rigorous thinking and ethical acting and transportive singing are all of a piece with one another. Thanks especially to Jaclyn Beck, Jeff Auerbach and Nancy Nieman Auerbach, Reuven Firestone, Ruth Sohn, Dvora Weisberg, Neil Scheindlin, Doug Petrie, Jonathan Diamond, Judy Kulick, Melissa Balaban, Adam Wergeles, Ann Bohrer, Lizzi Heydemann, Avi Havivi, Aimee Bender, Harmony Jupiter, Debbie Jaffe, Edye Schneider, Jeff Rake, Paulette Light, Adam Greenwald, Nomi Stolzenberg, Eve Wettstein Meyerson, Rebecca Rosenthal, Adam Arenson, Ingrid Steinberg, Sarah Benor, Mark Bunin Benor, Dev Brous, Larry Weber, Beth Edelstein, Ross Levinson, Nan Friedman, Lloyd Pilchen, Hillel Tigay, Rick Brous, Marcia Brous, Hanne Mintz, Wendy Light, Ivan Light, and my Food Justice peeps: Ross Berman, Kathy Kobayashi, Annie Lainer Marquit, and Marty Longbine. Especially special thanks to Sharon Brous and David Light for imagining such a thing into being.

Having the time to complete this book meant depending on others not only to keep my son, Julian, safe but, just as important, to make him feel loved. I am grateful to Debbie Murchison, Regina Grossman, Silvia Mosby, and Tiffany Bryan in Baltimore and to Nasrin Pez, Jaclyn Beck, and Ben Zaretsky in Los Angeles for turning the thorniness of being paid to love someone else's child into the accomplishment of new and dignified community and friendship.

Jonathan Grossman not only read every word of *The Moment of Racial Sight* many times over, both in its present incarnation and in discarded others, but with notable self-sacrifice, he also read nearly every e-mail, description, job letter, and fellowship application vaguely associated with the project. He convinced me, after years of trying, to give up my commitment to the sentence as a unit of composition and, in so doing, contributed more than anyone to whatever clarity of prose I have achieved. Above all, he continued to believe in the importance of this project, and to reassure me that I was right in believing in it, when many others were telling me otherwise. He is a mensch, and I offer him my gratitude.

Last, I want to thank my family: my aunt, Corinne Stone, who never fails to ask after my book and to offer whatever support is necessary to make the process easier; my sister Diane (aka Ossa Tallulah), whose serendipitous presence in Los Angeles has happily allowed us to discover, as adults, the pleasures of day-to-day friendship, and my sister Meredith (Ossa Rissa), who is sensible and funny and wise, up close and across a continent. My mother, Marcia Tucker, works very hard at loving me, not least in those moments when she does not entirely understand me, and gives her grandson Julian a sense of love that makes his world big and safe and unshakable. And finally, I dedicate this book to my wonderful, gentle, loving, funny, cello-playing, novel-writing boy, Julian Lev Tucker, who teaches me every day the delicacy and power of kindness.

Portions of chapter 2 originally appeared as "Macaulay's Paranoid Parliament" in the special Macaulay issue of *Nineteenth-Century Prose* 33, no. 2 (2006): 83–123. Copyright © 2010 The Johns Hopkins University Press. Portions of chapter 2 also appeared as "Paranoid Imaginings: Wilkie Collins, the Rugeley Poisoner, and the Invisibility of Novelistic Ekphrasis," first published in *Partial Answers* 8, no. 1 (2010): 147–67. Reprinted with permission from The John Hopkins University Press. Most of chapter 3 appeared as "Picturing Utilitarianism," *Criticism* 50, no. 3 (2008): 411–46. They are reprinted here with permission of their publishers.

Thanks to Rochelle Gerson of HBO and Dana Rashidi, assistant to David Simon, for their help in getting teleplays of *The Wire*.

INTRODUCTION

In the summer of 1998, editors at Random House Children's Publishing received an unexpected phone call. On the line was an official from the Combined Joint Information Campaign Task Force, an agency of NATO and the United Nations Peace Stabilization Force headquartered in Sarajevo, who wanted to place an order for some children's books. The book was *The Sneetches*, written in 1961 by Dr. Seuss (Theodore Geisel), and the order was a large one—some 500,000 copies—to be translated into Serbo-Croatian and shipped to Bosnia for distribution to children there. The idea for the book distribution, the official said, had come from a NATO soldier who had read the book as a child and remembered its message of racial tolerance, and who thought that such a message might help the children who had experienced the region's protracted civil war learn how to live with one another.[1]

So what exactly is the lesson of *The Sneetches?* Dr. Seuss tells a story not of one group of Sneetches but of two: those with stars on their bellies, who control not only the beaches, but access to frankfurter roasts and picnics, parties and marshmallow toasts, and refuse entry to the "plain-belly" Sneetches, who are "left out cold, in the dark of the beaches." The plain-belly Sneetches seem largely resigned to their fates as second-class citizens until the arrival of traveling salesman and "Fix-it-Up Chappie" Sylvester McMonkey McBean, who promises, for the price of three dollars a Sneetch, to send them through a contraption that will add stars to their bellies and make them indistinguishable from their star-bellied compatriots. When the star-bellied Sneetches come to McBean to complain of their loss of exclusive star-bellied status, he offers to send them through his Star-*Off* machine (at the increased price of ten dollars a belly). The story culminates in a predictable frenzy:

All the rest of that day, on those wild screaming beaches,
The Fix-it-Up Chappie kept fixing up Sneetches.
Off again! On again!
In again! Out again!
Through the machines they raced round and about again,
Changing their stars every minute or two.
They kept paying money. They kept running through
Until neither the Plain nor the Star-Bellies knew
Whether this one was that one . . . or that one was this one
Or which one was what one . . . or what one was who.[2]

As the tale concludes, the Sneetches, having come to recognize the arbitrariness of the marks of their differences, decide that "Sneetches are Sneetches / no kind of Sneetch is the best on the beaches." To the degree that the lesson of Dr. Seuss's narrative is that all people deserve to be treated respectfully, and to be granted equal access to a polity's institutions and resources, it is a lesson worth teaching, and not just in war-torn regions like Bosnia.

But I'm equally interested in another lesson *The Sneetches* seems to advance, one less about the liberal democratic ideals of political equality and social toleration than about the formal structure of racial differentiation. Here the narrative movement of Dr. Seuss's story is crucial: once we come to see the arbitrariness by which signs come to bear meanings that organize the referents differentially, we will affirm our commitment to equality. We ought to treat people equally, this account would have it, because we could ourselves easily have been different than we are. We could have been born with stars, though we were not, and inasmuch as the arbitrariness of the assignment of signs announces the arbitrariness of the distribution of value and social rewards marked by those signs, we as a society commit collectively to disregard the signs' distinctions as a way of neutralizing the arbitrariness of their distribution. In this regard, *The Sneetches* is significant not as a simplification but as an exemplification of contemporary conceptions of race, both popular and scholarly. The fact that a book written for children both reveals and critiques this structure of racial meaning, and that this book is exported as an instrument for advancing the cause of racial tolerance internationally, testifies to the pervasiveness of this understanding. The examples proliferate: in a television address on 11 June 1963 aimed at justifying his decision to command the Alabama National Guard to carry out a US district court order to desegregate the University of Alabama, President John F. Kennedy mused, "If an American, because his skin is dark, cannot eat lunch in a restaurant open to the public, if he cannot send his children to the best public school available, if he cannot vote for the public officials who represent him, if, in short, he cannot enjoy the full and free life which all of us want, then who among us would be content to have the color of his skin change and stand in his place?[3]

I want to suggest that virtually all critical analyses of race *as a category* continue to mark out their analytical fields and conceive of their political interventions as a relation between an arbitrary signifier and that which it signifies—that is, within a logic that is fundamentally linguistic. The arbitrariness of the racial sign structures the most familiar form of reparative politics as well, one made explicit by Kennedy's address: that the signs and significance of bodily difference are arbitrary generates the aspiration to a political equality measured by the interchangeability of citizen-subjects.[4]

The rhetoric by which this linguistic racial logic is most often expressed is the rhetoric of racial construction. In its most basic rendering, such rhetoric instructs us that for all their apparent obviousness and self-evidence, racial categories do not really exist: they are (merely) constructed, which is to say, without sound basis in biology. Thus, when Anthony Appiah traces W. E. B. DuBois's unwitting reversions to racial essentialism, Appiah himself feels compelled to remind us of the biologists' case for race's illusoriness:

> Apart from the visible morphological categories of skin, hair and bone by which we are inclined to assign people to the broadest racial categories—black, white, yellow—there are few genetic characteristics to be found in the population of England that are not found in similar proportions in Zaire or in China, and few too (though more) which are found in Zaire but not in similar proportions in China or in England.[5]

This stark form of the racial construction critique certainly carries a whiff of anachronism, and not simply because Appiah was writing in 1985, in the era of deconstruction, for publication in the locus classicus of the literature of race-as-sign, Henry Louis Gates's edited collection *"Race," Writing, and Difference*. The critique feels anachronistic because virtually no one buys the argument that racial differences are borne out in biology, so the argument against biology seems oddly beside the point.

But is it? I want to suggest that the racial "linguisticism" or structuralism I've identified in *The Sneetches* continues unabated in more subtle form: in the notion that analyses of race involve, first and foremost, the discovery of what racial signs *mean*.[6] Such signs, laden with meaning, are read through rather than read: the marks of such difference are understood to lie in the relation between a sign that one can easily recognize and the elusive, shifting, and often contradictory meanings that sign is made to bear.[7] We are thus repeatedly presented with histories by which blackness came to be associated with, say, primitivism or spiritual authenticity or violence so that we may discover the contingency of such associations. If the relation between the racial sign and the various meanings attributed to it can be shown to have a history, then surely it could have had—or could still have—a different history. Once race is understood as a kind of language, moreover, critiques of race of necessity take the form of theories of language. Conceived within this paradigm, historicizations of race inevitably turn out to be histories of racial meaning, while theories of race disclose, over and again, the variety of uses to which the arbitrariness of racial signification can be put.[8]

This assimilation of various racial histories to the general contingency of racial meaning has the added consequence of emptying out—which is to say, formalizing—the very notion of culture. Here, Appiah's conclusion is telling:

> The truth is that there are no races: there is nothing in the world that can do all we ask "race" to do for us. . . . What we miss through our obsession with the structure of relations of concepts is, simply, reality.
>
> Talk of "race" is particularly distressing for those of us who take culture seriously. For, where race works—in places where "gross differences" of morphology are correlated with "subtle differences" of temperament, belief and intention—it works as an attempt at a metonym for culture; and it does so only at the price of biologizing what *is* culture, or ideology. . . . What exists "out there" in the world—communities of meaning, shading variously into each other in the thick structure of the social world—is the province not of biology but of hermeneutic understanding.[9]

For Appiah, a notion of race grounded in real biological differences contravenes the idea of culture because it offers an account of the world in which individuals' behaviors, aspirations, habits, and failings are not consequences of, or even attributions to, deliberate acts of will but instead follow from the bodies those individuals inhabit. To affirm the salience of race is to commit to the notion that subjects have no control over the people they resemble or associate themselves with or over the worlds they imagine or construe. But if, in Appiah's account, race is "metonymic" for culture inasmuch as the former supplants the latter, his conception of culture as "not-race" likewise takes the form of a metonym: culture is (only) what stands in as an expression of the constructedness or contingency of the made world, that is, an expression of subjects' agency. In this way, the monolith of race generates the monolith of culture-as-construction as its critique, a vision that reduces the rich and varied ways of organizing worlds into recapitulations of a single story in which what matters is simply that people have acted one way and not another.[10]

That race and culture are, within this schema, not opposites but inversions of one another becomes especially apparent when we see the two unexpectedly converge in the racial sign itself. The existence of immediately discernible marks of difference is, by virtually all accounts, crucial to race's classificatory primacy. As Michael Omi and Howard Winant observe in their 1986 *Racial Formation in the United States*:

> One of the first things we notice about people when we meet them . . . is their race. We utilize race to provide clues about *who* a person is. The fact is made painfully obvious when we encounter someone whom we cannot conveniently racially categorize—someone who is, for example, racially mixed or of an ethnic/racial group with which we are not familiar. Such an encounter becomes a source of discomfort and momentarily a crisis of racial meaning. Without a racial identity, one is in danger of having no identity.[11]

For Omi and Winant, race subtends identities because it is the thing about people we can recognize in an instant—before we know what they do for a living, what their political affiliations are, how many children they have, what their friends are like. Such immediacy is, in Omi and Winant's telling, a consequence of the observer's deep familiarity with their culture's "racial etiquette," that is, "a set of interpretive codes and racial meanings which operate in the interactions of daily life."[12] The more self-evident the sign, the more complete the subject's acculturation. Immediacy of legibility stands as proof of the racial sign's utter conventionality: like the Sneetches who know exactly what a star on the belly signifies the moment they see it until the possibility of buying manufactured stars gives them pause, Omi and Winant's racial observers only come to reflect upon the conventionality of their racial habits and manners when their rules and valuations are disrupted.

But if, for Omi and Winant, the self-evidence of the racial sign is what marks it as pure culture, for Appiah, there is nothing to be said about the racial sign itself because it is pure nature: "Apart from the visible morphological characteristics of skin, hair and bone, by which we are inclined to assign people to the broadest racial categories . . . there are few genetic characteristics to be found in the population of England that are not found in similar proportions in Zaire or in China." The sorts of "genetic characteristics" that might direct people's behaviors or predict their aptitudes simply don't exist; for those "morphological characteristics" that do exist, their self-evidence testifies at once to their naturalness and to their meaninglessness, their fundamental irrelevance. If, as I have been suggesting, claims for the force of biological race and its constructedness are less departures from one another than inversions of a single paradigm, the convergence of these two contradictory accounts of the conspicuousness of skin, hair, and bone suggest a special role for these material qualities in structuring both the history and historiography of race.

For while the material stuff of race operates to hide the degree to which the constructionist critique of race rests upon a conception of culture that is at once without content and outside history, these marks of racial difference are able to do so only inasmuch as they remain curiously dehistoricized themselves. (The curious signifying trio of skin, hair, and bone gives way to the much more familiar primacy of skin color in *Color Conscious*, Appiah's 1996 coedited volume.)[13] Such marks function to absorb various histories into evidence of historical contingency in general, into culture as the metonymic extension of individual agency, only so long as they themselves are presumed to remain stable and unaltered over time. Immediately legible "morphological differences" can be at once the mark of biological immanence and evidence of a contingent racial meaning that has been thoroughly conventionalized only because racial histories are understood as *contents* variously ascribed to these signs, rather than shifting epistemologies encompassing the qualities and functions of the signs themselves. What if we were to consider the possibility that the very concept of an arbitrary, constructed racial sign—a stable signifier (skin color, stars) to which various shifting and contingent values come to be appended—might itself have a history?[14]

This study is premised upon the notion that there is such a history to be traced, and that it is worth tracing, not simply so that we can come to know that the material forms racial signs take are as arbitrary and contingent as their contents, but rather so we might discover what such arbitrariness—of the racial sign, of the model of racial identity made apparent by the sign—accomplishes. I will argue that, far from simply being the way race works, the concept of an arbitrary racial sign is consolidated relatively recently in the modern history of race theorized by Charles Darwin in his paired final works, *The Descent of Man, and Selection in Relation to Sex* (1871) and *The Expression of the Emotions in Man and Animals* (1872). For Darwin, who was famously reluctant to extend explicitly his theory of natural selection to human development, the notion of an arbitrary racial sign offered an instrument for making humans legible to one another from within a structure of an ecosystem that effectively rendered any local and internal point of view nugatory.[15]

But although *The Moment of Racial Sight* ends by uncovering the emergence of the notion of an arbitrary racial sign, it does not begin there. It starts one analytical step prior, with an examination of modern race's quality of immediacy and self-evidence. If, in the face of our knowing better, we still find ourselves perceiving racial differences with an instantaneousness that feels precritical, perhaps we ought to consider the possibility that the production of the experience of immediate and self-evident knowing is what race is doing—indeed, what it comes into being to do—rather than merely marking the depth of our acculturation or the inadequacy of our self-consciousness. Such a consideration demands that we turn from a history, or histories, of representation toward a history of epistemology, that we investigate the relation between what we know by way of race and how we come to know it rather than simply presuming the connectedness of the two. Such a shift in emphasis makes it possible to identify the kinds of epistemological problems the form of racial knowing solves and, in so doing, to suggest not only why such racial categories came into being when they did, but also why they continue to have a purchase on the ways in which we perceive and organize social relations and identities, notwithstanding our recognition of race's "constructedness." Accordingly, I begin *The Moment of Racial Sight* by asking why, in the final quarter of the eighteenth century, *skin* suddenly came to be privileged as the primary sign of racial identity. Immanuel Kant has long been identified as the first prominent European thinker to single out skin color in this way, and I consequently examine his essay on the topic, "On the Use of Teleological Principles for Philosophy" (1788).

In shifting my focus from what race means or represents to how it works to organize our ways of knowing other people and the world, I of necessity must enlarge the field of topics, disciplines, and technologies understood to be relevant to race. I anticipate that this enlarging will have a defamiliarizing effect. In shifting my attention away from the histories of discourses and institutional practices we already know to have been central to the conceptualizing of race—slavery and colonialism being the most salient—I mean not to minimize their significance but to account for the continued hold race has on our social imagination even in the wake of the historical dissolution of these practices. More concretely, this requires more than my examination of Kant's 1788 teleology essay in relation to his broader philosophical oeuvre, in particular the mid- to late-career critical philosophy for which he is best known. Understanding the broadened conception of race I am proposing entails looking beyond Kant as well. Read in the context of his late essay on the relationship between philosophy and medicine in *The Conflict of the Faculties*, Kant's emphasis on skin color suddenly becomes legible in the light of shifting medical paradigms of the human body. Such epistemological contextualizing, I will show, has the power to alter what we understand ourselves to know when we know racially, in the very gesture of making clear what function that knowing serves. To elaborate just a bit more upon the core example from my opening chapter: racial constructionism's rhetoric of otherness obscures the degree to which perceiving race involves, for better or for worse, experiencing individuals' likeness to one another rather than their difference.[16] Kant's racial skin, we shall see, turns likeness from an idea that must be discovered over time to something legible instantly; the mutually constitutive relation between Kantian race and the nascent discourse of modern anatomical medicine makes apparent how such instantaneousness might be useful in organizing the ways in which subjects see other people's bodies and their own.

I hope it is apparent, then, that the epistemological approach I am advocating involves broadening the intellectual and disciplinary contexts within which theories of race are analyzed. Although I begin and end *The Moment of Racial Sight* by exploring the writings of people who explicitly understood themselves, and were understood by their contemporaries, to be engaging modes of human categorization they called "race"—Kant in the opening chapter, Darwin and the production team behind *The Wire* in the final two chapters—the two intervening chapters attend to writers whose work seems, on the face of it, to have little to do with race. Understanding how race is but one important and useful structure within overlapping systems of knowing requires looking at systems of knowing that don't immediately announce themselves as racial but that nonetheless engage themselves in the epistemological project of race.

In chapter 2, I argue that the realist novel, in inviting readers to treat imperceptible verbal descriptions of characters' bodies as if they are witnessable phenomena, can be seen, like race, to attempt to turn a sameness that is elsewhere into something that can be seen. Wilkie Collins's 1859 novel *The Woman in White* places the question of how readers come to feel as if they can see characters who only exist in words at the center of its concerns. By this novel's accounting, characters' legibility rests on readers' capacity to imagine them to be like people those readers have seen, even as the plausibility of that imaginative association itself depends upon the not-quite-visible aspect of the characters in question. But even as Collins's novel identifies the generic practices of description by which we come to feel that we can see characters immediately as if they are before us, it places a story of how one character comes to be interchangeable with another at the center of its plot. Insofar as this turns likeness from a momentary vision to a process, *The Woman in White* undermines the racial logic of instantaneity. As I will argue in detail, both the novel's reflection upon its own descriptive logic and its plot of interchanged bodies can be seen to bear the marks of a historically contemporaneous event: the 1856 trial of the notorious Rugeley Poisoner, William Palmer, a physician charged with murdering his patients under the guise of medicating them. Seizing upon the particular illegibility within anatomical medicine of the processes of dying (and getting well) as his alibi, William Palmer managed to employ the intricacies of anatomical medicine that animated Kant's theorization of a notion of race built around differences in skin color the stuff of popular conversation. It is this case that provides the immediate historical framework for linking the process of seeing race to the process of seeing fictional bodies. This historical context also allows us to recognize the ways in which the process of seeing racialized bodies comes to be linked to midcentury anxieties about the vulnerability of the body to unseen forces within, and the ways in which such vulnerability threatened to compromise the capacity of the body to function as a structure ensuring the legibility of identity over time.

My third chapter examines how, in midcentury England, the instantaneous legibility that I argue is definitive of racial seeing comes to be a subject of political contention in its own right. John Stuart Mill has long been recognized as an important advocate for the political rights of minorities against the "tyranny of the majority," and contemporary legal theorists such as Lani Guinier have drawn upon Mill's writings in making the case for electoral systems that replace "winner-take-all" governance with models of shared, rotating authority. While these models of rotating governance have much to recommend them, they are not quite Mill's. Reading Mill's political writings in relation to his writing on poetry and in relation to contemporaneous writing about the just-invented technology of photography offers a significantly different understanding of the stakes of Mill's political vision: Mill is interested less, we shall see, in the mechanisms by which already established publics and political collectivities express themselves than he is in the process by which such collectivities come to be formed and recognized. For him, the fundamental problem of political representation is not figuring out how to allow various factions to speak their piece as they hammer out political resolutions but figuring out what sort of commonness—and what sort of political entity—can exist if political debate is structured around identifiable moments of conclusion, instants of agreement and resolution that, having been achieved, are institutionalized. Mill is invested in positing a world of full and ongoing reflexiveness—a world, that is, in which all social and material relations are understood to have been deliberately created through debate and agreement. But this commitment to argumentation as the fundamental ground of social cohesion turns out, by his own reckoning, to commit him as well to imagining a world in which individuals are constrained by their belated inhabitation of a world created by others. Bodily likeness stands as a manifestation of this constraining belatedness. The possibility of abstract vision enabled by photography allows Mill to imagine both that individual bodies might house different and differently organized perceptual capacities from one another and consequently that these particularized perceptual modes might serve as the mechanisms by which individual subjects free themselves from the burden of other people's past judgments regarding the best way to inhabit and organize a world.

Having begun to make the case for the project of understanding race as an epistemology, I want now to acknowledge some of the limitations—and yes, the dangers—of such an approach. First, the limitations. While I have offered my methodology as a salutary corrective to a predominant discourse of racial construction, I would be the first to admit that over the past decade and a half, there has been a great outpouring of important scholarship that circumvents this constructionist model altogether. I am thinking, just to take a few prominent recent examples, of writing ranging from Saidhiya Hartman's and Jacqueline Goldsby's work on lynching, Brent Edwards's work on black cosmopolitanism and, more recently, jazz performativity, to Elizabeth McHenry's work on nineteenth-century African American literary societies.[17] Such scholarship does not understand its task to be discovering what race means, or the processes by which it refers, or the sorts of qualities it purports to name or describe. Rather, this work is dedicated to offering accounts of how individuals and populations designated as members of a particular race come to envision the possibilities and limitations for acting in the world. And certainly, such positivism, in declining to accord race a stability or descriptive force beyond its immediate context, could be said to count as a theory of race: race is nothing more—or less—than the ways in which people use, recognize, or impose the term at any given moment. Generally speaking, I conceive of my work as a supplement to, rather than a commentary upon, this body of scholarship. Yet it is a supplementarity of a very specific order. Even the complexity of describing such positivism—by what principle are the uses, recognitions, impositions to be brought in relation to one another?—hints at the ways in which pragmatist historicizations of race, taken to their logical conclusion, offer discrete, thick cultural descriptions in place of something like a history of race. Stated plainly, the discontinuity of such formations is hardly anodyne, as the controversy surrounding Kenneth Warren's brilliant and provocative *What Was African American Literature?* surely attests. For Warren, "African American literature" *was* but is no more. The "collective enterprise we now know as African American or black literature . . . gained coherence as an undertaking in the social world defined by the system of Jim Crow segregation," and insofar as this literature was produced by "black writers [who] knew that their work would in all likelihood be evaluated instrumentally, in terms of whether or not it could be added to the arsenal of arguments, achievements and propositions needed to attack the justifications for, and counteract the effects of, Jim Crow," it can be said to have ended with the formal dismantling of legal segregation that was the triumph of the civil rights movement.[18] The resistance to Warren's declaration that African American literature comes in and out of existence in the space of just over half a century bespeaks both the analytical and political downsides of an embrace of such historicism. It is difficult to see how the refusal to engage race as a category beyond its immediate discursive or institutional context can help but foreclose the possibility of seeing how a given history of racially designated individuals and populations extends, interrupts, or supplements previous or coincident treatments, leaving us instead with a kind of opacity of historical immanence.

The danger of the kind of work undertaken in *The Moment of Racial Sight* is that it runs the risk of being construed as an effort to minimize or ignore the punctual atrocities and daily outrages of political, economic, social, and institutional disempowerment that have been perpetrated over the past three centuries by recourse to categories of race. After all, racial categories are most often invoked not merely to characterize differences, but to organize these differences into hierarchies of value. The racial constructionist analysis that offers the histories of various meanings and associations of particular racial signs in order to demonstrate that they might have been otherwise does so not because difference itself is bad, but because many hierarchies of difference are. Insofar as such work reminds us of these outrages by specifying them, and rages against the outrage not of difference but of discrimination by refusing to let it fade from view, such scholarship performs valuable work.

But it is not—has not been—enough. A good deal of the personal impetus behind the analysis of *The Moment of Racial Sight* has been my sense that the insight that racial meanings might have been different in the past has done little to alter how they are in the present, or more generally, to diminish the force and immediacy with which we continue to perceive race. Doubtless, much of this recalcitrance can be attributed to the relative powerlessness of cultural criticism, or for that matter, of the small adjustments of personal ideology, against the power of entrenched political, economic, and institutional structures, or the ongoing effects of past discrimination. But part of the reason for the stubborn persistence of race is that we have been asking the wrong questions, or at least not all of the right ones, when we turn our attention to the category. It is my hope that readers will respond to this study not simply by asking what this all has to do with slavery and colonialism but will find themselves thinking as well about how race is buttressed by ways of knowing the world that do not appear to have anything to do with race—our very understanding of the ways we inhabit, recognize, and control our bodies.

In recognition of the danger of misconstruing my approach and the persistence of race in our understanding of the world, I conclude this study by moving from the eighteenth and nineteenth centuries into the twenty-first, to analyze what is arguably one of the most ambitious grapplings with the politics of racial seeing and the racial organization of bodies in recent decades: the HBO series *The Wire*. First broadcast between June 2002 and March 2008, *The Wire* scrupulously details the interlocking institutions—both legal and illegal—of the majority-black city of Baltimore. More fundamentally, *The Wire* examines racial seeing as a set of practices of institutionalization. As I hope this introduction has begun to make clear, this project is animated by one of the abiding paradoxes of the modern conception of race: that what would seem to be a theory of the fundamental and unchanging inequality of human beings coincides historically with the most comprehensive set of efforts to argue for the equality of all humans—the Enlightenment. I attempt to make sense of this paradox by showing how that paradigmatic thinker of the Enlightenment, Immanuel Kant, theorized skin-based race as a structure by which the idea of likeness, of universal equality, could be transformed from a political and philosophical ideal into something capable of being perceived empirically, witnessed. In this regard, modern race ought to be understood as more than a concept that, like many others, is subject to institutionalization. Instead, modern race should be seen as a mode of institutionalization in and of itself, as an attempt to materialize a set of ideas and ideals. *The Wire*'s great insight, I will argue, lies in its grasp of the profound connection between race as a kind of institutionalization by means of the body and the various institutions of race, and for this reason, an analysis of that work, visual rather than textual, serves as a fitting conclusion for my study.

While it might be objected that *The Moment of Racial Sight* attempts—unwisely—to analyze race without analyzing racism, I want to make the case for a different construal of the project. In essence, the "racism" of race can be understood to have two aspects. First, it functions by linking certain (denigrated) meanings or associations to recognizable marks of racial difference and offering those associations as justification for the inequities of access to political, institutional, social, and economic resources. But the racism of race can also be seen to lie in race's function as a mechanism by which raced subjects are deprived of the recognition of salient qualities of individuality and instead are understood to be "just like" those exhibiting the same racial marks: once likeness becomes something that one must see empirically in order to believe, it of necessity becomes delimited, a register of difference as well. *The Moment of Racial Sight* aims to extricate these two aspects of race from one another so as to begin to produce a more nuanced—and, ideally, a more politically powerful—account of their interrelations.

Thus when I argue, as I do in my chapter on Kant and anatomical medicine, that we begin to notice and to care deeply about the color of other people's skin at the moment in history we understand our bodies to be both fundamentally like other people's bodies and capable of functioning, for good and for ill, outside our knowledge or control, I am not suggesting that racial categorization is not so bad as we thought it was or that it ought to be uncritically celebrated as an expression of some deep-seated commitment to universalism. If my account begins to make sense of the tenacity of racial ways of knowing—seeing racially is fundamentally bound up with how we understand ourselves as modern embodied subjects—I hope it will also impel new directions critical and political analyses might take: What are the benefits and what are the costs of understanding our political commitments to equality to emanate from, or reflect, an essential likeness of human bodies? Must likeness be something that we can perceive or experience? What forms of racial politics or modes of sociability would follow from our recognizing a link between our reliance on others to know ourselves comprehensively and our habits of racial recognition?

Come let us begin.

ONE

Kant's Dermatology; or, The Racialization of Skin

If, as we now know, the nineteenth century was to abound with fantasies of racial origin, Robert Willan, writing in the earliest years of that century, offers a fantasy of racial beginnings only a dermatologist could love. This fantasy, such as it is, commands little more than Willan's glancing attention in the massive 1809 *On Cutaneous Diseases*, a volume that at once consolidated theretofore scattered writings on skin diseases into something like a professional body of knowledge and established Willan himself as the nominal founder of the nascent medical specialty of dermatology.[1] More pressing is his design, laid out in the treatise's introduction, "to fix the sense of the terms employed, by proper definitions" and "to constitute general divisions or orders of the diseases, from leading and peculiar circumstances in their appearance: to arrange them into distinct genera; and to describe at large their specific forms, or varieties."[2] Willan's narrative of racial beginning is subsumed within his naturalist taxonomizing. He produces his tale as one instance among dozens of cases of icthyosis, a skin disorder "characterized by a permanently harsh, dry, scaly, and, in some cases almost horny texture of the integuments of the body, unconnected with internal disorder" (151).

Willan draws the case of Edward Lambert, icthyosis sufferer, from the written record, physician Henry Baker's 1755 *Philosophical Transactions*:

> [Edward Lambert] is now forty years of age; a good-looking, well-shaped man, of a florid countenance, and when his body and hands are covered, seems nothing different from other people. But except his head and face, the palms of his hands, and bottoms of his feet, his skin is all over covered in the same manner as in the year 1731, which therefore I shall trouble you with no other description of, than what you will find in Mr. Machin's account,

> only begging leave to observe, that this covering seemed to me most nearly to resemble an innumerable company of warts, of a dark brown colour, and a cylindric figure, rising to a like height, and growing as close as possible to one another, but so stiff and elastic, that when the hand is drawn over them they make a rustling noise. . . .
>
> . . . But the most extraordinary circumstance of this man's story, and indeed the only reason of my giving you this trouble is, that he has had six children, all with the same rugged covering as himself. . . . It appears therefore past all doubt, that a race of people may be propagated by this man, having such rugged coats or coverings as himself: and if this should ever happen, and the accidental original be forgotten, 'tis not improbable they might be deemed a different species of mankind: a consideration, which would almost lead one to imagine, that if mankind were all produced from one and the same stock, the black skins of the negroes, and many other differences of the like kind, might possibly have been originally owing to some such accidental cause. (155, 156–57)

If fantasy is limned by a kind of contextual mobility, Willan's dermatological version is determinedly earthbound. What we are invited to take away from the history of Edward Lambert is the importance of remembering the "accidental original," but as I shall contend, the lesson of the "accidental" is not simply an insight about the fundamental contingency of racial signification. For Willan, I suggest, remembering this accidental original is at least as much about knowing that "Psoriasis and Lepra differ from Ichtyosis, in being but partially diffused, and in having deciduous scales" (151). That is, Edward Lambert's story offers an account of the origins of racial difference precisely because it appears as a case within an elaborate descriptive taxonomy of skin and also because, as I shall explain, that taxonomy works to consolidate an emergent specialty of dermatology within a newly conceived field of anatomical medicine. To discover that the history of racial difference is inextricable from the history of writing about, examining, and treating skin is hardly to discover that racial signs are nothing but skin—skin, and therefore not signs. Rather, such a discovery suggests that, at the end of the eighteenth century and early part of the nineteenth, race comes to stand as a form of knowledge, to make visible individuals and the relations among them, specifically because the primary sign of racial difference in this period is the skin.

But while I make a case for understanding the development of Willan's taxonomy of skin disease and the coincident emergence of a modern, skin-centered model of racial difference as conceptually linked phenomena, I want to make clear from the outset that I am not simply suggesting that we ought to understand Willan's division of skin diseases and the racial division of humans into peoples to be linked by straightforward homology. Rather, it is the particular capacity of the skin both to body forth effects of a prior cause and to function as an immediately visible sign at one and the same time—a dual capacity manifested by Willan's taxonomy—that renders skin the locus at which an older conception of humoral, system-based medical knowledge is supplanted by a newer anatomical model of the body. It is this special status of skin as a kind of switching point in the history of the medicalized body that makes it an especially useful sign by which perceptions of human likeness and particularity are organized. Willan describes the skin conditions he organizes according to their "appearance," both the way they look at any given moment and the process by which they emerge and develop (the process of their appearance). This doubled sense of appearance evokes a model of skin that is both immediately apprehensible and temporally diffuse, and the promise of skin, as Willan would have it, seems to lie in its capacity to reconcile apparently contradictory states. Skin's peculiarly doubled aspect in the earliest years of the nineteenth century is partly the expression of its positioning as a meeting point of two different paradigms of the body, and in that regard, skin ought to be understood less as an object of knowledge in and of itself than as a structure for organizing knowledge. It is as a structure of knowledge that skin comes to solve certain problems that haunt Enlightenment thinking across a variety of disciplines and discourses.

There is a certain literal-mindedness in suggesting that the genealogy of modern race might be found within a history of skin. But if such literalism is understood to be a corrective to the sort of analysis that would see skin as a sign within the system of meaning that is race, then I do mean this project to be an intervention in the name of literalism. As I argued in my introduction, the particular marks of racial difference have generally been treated as either too natural or too cultural for analysis: Kwame Anthony Appiah sets aside the "visible morphological categories of skin, hair and bone" and, having done so, insists that there is nothing left "real" about race, while Michael Omi and Howard Winant argue that the force of these marks lies in their organization of a "racial etiquette." These two accounts stand not as opposites or critiques of one another but as inversions, and their structuring centrality has meant these morphological categories have generally been treated as things to be read through rather than analyzed in their own right. The problem of race is understood to be the problem of an overburdened signifier; skin color, facial features, texture of hair are eminently evident, entirely visible physical qualities that ought ideally to be evacuated of significance beyond the merely descriptive.[3] Even projects that work at the edges where the evidence of racial difference disappears—writing on passing is the most obvious example of this—implicitly assume the logic of racial self-evidence as the norm; the disappearance of such difference is argued powerfully to reveal the arbitrariness of the racial sign. Conceived within this paradigm, historicizations of race inevitably turn out to be histories of racial meaning, while theories of race disclose, over and again, the variety of uses to which the arbitrariness of racial signification can be put. Insofar as the significance of race lies in what it means, to read race knowingly rather than literally is to remain within a fundamentally linguistic racial logic.

Having been taught repeatedly that skin color doesn't really mean what various cultures have come to say it does, we fail to notice that there is nothing inevitable about the fact that skin *in particular* comes to bear meaning, however unfounded that meaning might be, nor is it inevitable that such signs should come to seem self-evident by means of visible perception. Even when the processes by which certain relations come to be understood in racial terms are taken as the object of analysis—the study of the racialization of slavery is an obvious case in point—the attachment of racial value to particular aspects of human bodies is understood to function as an alibi for, or rationalization of, interests whose meanings lie elsewhere. The assignment of inferior status to black Africans sold as slaves is conceived, for example, as a means of justifying interests that are primarily economic.[4] Once the particularity of skin as the sign of race can be shown to have a history, rather than standing as a mark of historicity or contingency in general, the histories that matter for making race need no longer be limited to those that are about what we already know race to be about, those social, economic, and political relations that racial signs at once name and hide.

This approach also allows us to understand the precritical, immediate feel of racial thinking, the peculiar doggedness of the epistemology in the face of our knowing better as something other than a form of irrationality. The constructionist, linguistic notion of race describes a racial logic and that logic's critique in a single stroke: the immediacy and self-evidence of racial knowledge is understood to be a consequence of the naturalization of racial meaning, and the force of race can be undone by revealing the naturalized sign to be merely conventional. What such an approach assumes is that race is fundamentally of a piece with a variety of other cultural phenomena that appear self-evident only because those who apprehend their meanings have forgotten that they might have been otherwise. Such an approach fails to admit the possibility that perhaps the instantaneity and self-evidence of racial knowledge is not simply evidence of a generalized forgetting of race's constructedness but actually describes what race does: renders people instantly and immediately knowable.

Once race is no longer presumed to function primarily as a structure of meaning, the terms within which we analyze it are likely to shift as well. Rather than ask how race has come to mean what it does, or show the degree to which the attributes we associate with a given racial sign came to be linked to that sign by happenstance or malign intent, we might ask what are the sorts of epistemological, political, or social problems race in its particular material forms comes into being to solve. If race is conceived as a response or a solution to a set of historically specific problems, then it might continue to be "useful" even as its logic is revealed to be constructed or historically contingent. The persistence of racial perception would then stand as evidence of that usefulness, rather than as a mark of irrationality or bad faith. Such an analysis would suggest as well that our habits of perceiving race are likely to be linked to and imbricated within social, discursive, and epistemological formations that at first glance seem to have nothing whatsoever to do with race.

Kant's Time

During his lifetime and throughout much of the nineteenth century, Immanuel Kant was recognized as being the first thinker to isolate and privilege skin color as the primary marker of racial difference, as well as to theorize such a privileging. Charles Darwin, for one, lists Kant within the otherwise still familiar catalog of natural historians—Linnaeus, Buffon, and Blumenbach are some of the others—whose accountings of human difference influenced his own theory of race in *The Descent of Man*. Because the current tendency is to read Kant's oeuvre primarily through his theorization of the aesthetic in his *Critique of Judgment*, his writing on race has often been overlooked entirely, or at least read in isolation from the body of his more well known work. By advocating a certain literal-mindedness in reading race, I mean to show the ways in which racial perception can be seen to have emerged as a method for negotiating some of the tensions internal to modern Enlightenment and post-Enlightenment models of subjectivity, including Kant's. Because Kant's analysis of the subject is so systematic, his writing becomes a particularly rich site for discerning these tensions. Because systematicity is a central element of his account of how subjects know the world and are themselves knowable, these tensions, if never fully articulated, can nonetheless be seen to animate and direct Kant's oeuvre, particularly his late writing, even as they offer a framework for understanding fundamental contradictions of the Enlightenment writ large.

In this spirit, I want briefly to outline two of the radical transformations enacted by Kant's critical philosophy, as well as to suggest, first, why the presumptions undergirding the knowing described by his philosophy might be threatened by Kant's experience of his own process of dying, and second, how his articulation of a skin-based notion of racial difference might be seen as an effort to respond to such threats while keeping intact the fundamental structures of his philosophical system. I address all of these issues in greater detail below. Here I simply offer a map in broad strokes of the relations I see animating Kant's thought, in terms that illuminate its engagements with various other contemporary efforts to render humanness legible, including modern anatomical medicine and racial perception. My account draws shamelessly on Jay Rosenberg's wonderfully lucid *Accessing Kant.*

Kant's critical philosophy breaks with the early analytical tradition out of which it emerges in at least two significant and interrelated ways. First, Kant's writing insists upon shifting emphasis from a project of knowing the material world to knowing the limits of the capacity to know that world. This new form of knowing conceives of the existence of the material world—what he terms the "noumenal"—as a precondition for thought and thus adduces the existence of that world from the evidence of that thought. We know something exists because we can have thoughts about it. The reverse is true as well: the fact that subjects can have thoughts about a real, ongoing, and necessarily interconnected world stands as evidence of the existence of those subjects.[5] For Kant, such mutuality of constitution of necessity has a temporal element as well. While skeptics like Hume worried that we can have no way of being certain that the images we perceive exist beyond the moments we perceive them—and in that sense no way of knowing whether they exist outside our heads, our fantasies—for Kant, establishing the realness of both the world and the subjects who know that world depends upon establishing the persistence of both through time. But the problem, for Kant, is this: although our many perceptual encounters occur successively, the simple fact that we must see one image before we see another tells us nothing about the temporal state of the perceived items in and of themselves. Here is where the mutually constituting relation of subjects and the object world Kant terms the "transcendental deduction" is crucial. Imagine, for a moment, a book on a shelf. Although we cannot, strictly speaking, experience the spine, the front and back covers, and the inside pages of that book at the same time, we nonetheless know the spine, covers, and pages to be part of the image we have of the book. They are all essential—in Kantian terms "necessary" or "lawful"—qualities of the book. How do we come to know this about books? We know because we experience a book's spine, covers, and pages successively, as we pull the book off the shelf and turn it over in our hands. And how do we synthesize these successive experiences of disparate elements into the unitary thing we know as a book? We do it because we experience ourselves as persisting over time. It is our persistence as subjects that enables us to knit together the different elements, to know, even if we can't quite experience, that they are all parts of the same thing. Our same persistence as subjects allows us to experience the covers and spines and pages of many books over time, and to understand those elements to be part of what makes a book a book, even as we understand the water stains or yellowed edges we encounter on some to be contingent, non-necessary qualities. And how do we experience our own persistence as subjects though time? We know we persist because we are able to experience the unchanging and essential qualities of the book.

So we can assemble all of the separately experienced elements of a book into a book because we persist over time, and we come to know we persist over time, that we are unitary selves, because we experience the unchanging thing that is the book. And so, too, do we assemble our experiences of the world as a thing that exists outside us. As Rosenberg puts it: "The conditions according to which the experienced world is constituted as an intelligible synthetic unity—that is, the conditions that entitle us to represent it as one mathematically lawful natural world—*are at the same time* the conditions by which an experiencing consciousness is itself constituted as a unitary self—that is, the conditions that make it possible for each of us to think of himself as one self-aware subject of many experiences."[6] But while a sense of our own persistence is a necessary condition for our understanding of the book as an object, it is not sufficient. For in order for us to see a book, we not only need to understand the back cover and the inside pages as part of the same object despite the fact they can only be perceived successively, we also need to know that other images we perceive as part of the same succession—the bookshelf itself, say—ought not to be synthesized along with our images of the cover and pages. We include some images we experience successively and exclude others because we have an idea of a book. In order for us to have such an idea, we need, Rosenberg explains, "Not just a sequence of representations, but the representation of a sequence."[7]

We need a concept of time itself, and that concept needs to be "mind-independent"—that is, existing outside the sort of mutually constituting relations of sequentiality that link our experience of our own duration as subjects to our experience of the duration of the synthesized book. Such a notion of time allows us to understand the various elements of a book as not simply sequentially apprehensible images, but as images that constitute a book because they are caused or intended, which is to say, organized according to an idea. It is this quality of being caused or intended that allows us to distinguish between the kind of thing we are seeing when we see a book's cover and the kind of thing we are seeing when we see a water stain on that cover. We do not extract the concept of cause from experience; rather, a notion of causation is the precondition for experience. In this context, as throughout his critical philosophy, Kant reasons backward, offering a description of the way things are as proof of conditions of possibility: we could not have experiences if causation were not true. Experience presupposes causation because both our continuity as subjects over time and the connectedness of our various images of the world to one another rest upon the presumption that the world acts in regular and lawful ways, that its various elements are the predictable effects of causes rather than simply random and unrepeatable accidents. Because we discover the presence of causation by way of the regularity and lawfulness of the world, it effectively does not matter when the causation takes place. All causation is effectively ongoing, made manifest by the world's persistence and consistency.

But here is the crucial issue: in thus placing specific mechanisms of causation beyond the reach of knowledge, Kant also excludes the possibility of examining change that is itself lawful. His system requires, in other words, that we treat all versions of change like the water stain—as something that can happen to an object in the world, rather than a fundamental quality of that object. Kant engages this conundrum surrounding the legibility of lawful change—including, most pointedly, the aging and dying of the human body—in the third essay of *The Conflict of the Faculties*. In this piece, a comparative examination of medical and philosophical knowledge, Kant's incapacity to think philosophically—in accordance with his critical method—as he is dying leads him to consider the ways in which the lawful changefulness that is the dying process might not be assimilable to the methodology of his critical philosophy.

Kant's second departure, which I will discuss only briefly for now, concerns the use to which philosophical knowledge can be put. He conceives of epistemology and ethics as thoroughly intertwined philosophical projects and frames the ambitions of philosophy accordingly. Philosophy can assume the roles usually accorded to state institutions or conventions of sociability because the forms of knowing it articulates imply a framework for relating to other people as well. To know is to recognize the lawfulness of the world, to distinguish its essential from its contingent aspects, and to treat people and things ethically is to treat them in ways that recognize and affirm those lawful, universal aspects. But Kant's sense of the coincidence of the epistemological and the ethical is predicated upon what I have already described as the constitutive limitedness of knowing. In ways that will become apparent as my discussion progresses, the capacity for philosophy to assume the authority of ensuring lawful behavior—its capacity, that is, to take on the roles of institutions and the rules of social behavior—itself depends upon treating citizen-subjects as though they can and must live forever.

I will be arguing that Kant's invention of race is animated by the challenges posed to his critical philosophy in both its epistemological and ethical registers by the sort of changefulness that cannot simply be relegated to the realm of the contingent. As articulated in his 1788 essay "On the Use of Teleological Principles in Philosophy," Kant's model of race links differences in skin color to "seeds" all humans possess deep within their bodies that render them fit for inhabiting all climates. Possessed universally, such seeds are part of what defines human lawfulness. At the same time, the seeds manifest themselves differently depending upon where various individuals, capable of living anywhere, have actually chosen to migrate. Race, as Kant figures it, is thus able to indicate at once lawfulness (the capacity to live anywhere) and change (the particular act of migration), rendering these qualities noncontradictory and instantly apprehensible. Differences in skin color mark humans—all humans—as the effects of some cause, their capacity to live anywhere as bodied forth by their specific acts of migration, rather than standing as an ever-shifting and thus contingent and dismissible mark of a changing place of habitation. Moreover, it is not simply Kant who attributes to skin the quality of registering lawfulness and chance at once. I conclude the chapter by returning to where we began, to Willan and his treatise on dermatology, where, we shall see, the yoking together of chance and lawfulness is revealed to undergird his vision of the emergent field.

Kant's privileging of skin introduces a conception of race that might be termed "modern" in its insistence that race is a quality of an individual that is at once essential and unchanging. In this regard, Kant's model marks a striking departure from older, "humoral" conceptions of human variety that understood skin color to be simply one manifestation of a complex of intertwined bodily and characterological attributes—temperament and health were some others—that were the consequences of forces operating both within bodies and in their surrounding environments and consequently were understood to change as those internal and environmental forces changed. Inasmuch as the humoral model of the body made no hard-and-fast distinction between the qualities of the body associated with identity and those associated with the relations of health and sickness—given the changeability of all bodily states, any distinction seems impossible to maintain—we ought not be surprised that Kant's revisionary essay on race is written at a moment in which the fundamental tenets of medicine are being radically reconceived. With the final decades of the eighteenth century came the theorization and institutionalization of modern "anatomical" medicine, a model of medicine premised on the principles that human bodies are fundamentally like one another and that disease is located within organs in the interiors of bodies, inaccessible to direct observation by doctors and patients alike. Skin becomes the site around which a premodern humoral conception of the human body and its illnesses, with its presumption of a porous boundary between bodies and their environments, is transformed into a modern anatomical model of the body and its diseases that locates the defining likeness of bodies deep in their interiors, blocked from observation by the surface of the skin.

I am not simply suggesting that, in the closing decades of the eighteenth century, race comes to be legible in the skin because skin's function and significance is unstable and thus vulnerable to redefinition. The case I want to make is a positive one: the paradigm of anatomical medicine is structured around a deep and fundamental incoherence, and modern, skin-based race comes into being as a structure for resolving this incoherence. Rather than being the consequence of historical transition and instability, then, race turns out to represent a drive *toward* stability. It is precisely this stabilizing function that helps account for race's peculiar staying power, helps account for why it is that we find ourselves noticing race even when we know we should know better. Historians have long puzzled over why it is that the same complex of discourses known as the Enlightenment that ventured the revolutionary claim that all humans are by their very nature equal was also the era in which differences in skin color came to be understood as indelible evidence of essential differences in human capacity. As George Frederickson puts it, "What makes Western racism so autonomous and conspicuous in world history has been that it developed in a context that presumed human equality of some kind."[8]

The emergence of "race science" in the early decades of the nineteenth century replaced a monogenetic, biblically founded theory of human origin (all humans are human by virtue of being created by God) with a polygenetic account (different races ought to be seen as different, independently developing species that can be hierarchized according to degree of development). This supplantation of monogenic by polygenic is typically treated by intellectual historians as a baffling and benighted regression.[9]

Consider the perplex with which Nancy Stepan opens her intellectual history of "scientific racism," in her 1982 *The Idea of Race in Science*: "A fundamental question about the history of racism in the first half of the nineteenth century is why it was that, just as the battle against slavery was being won by abolitionists, the war against racism in European thought was being lost."[10] Stepan, looking away from the eighteenth century toward the nineteenth, doesn't so much explain the turn from Enlightenment universalism to the multiple-origin stories of scientific racism as she redescribes it as a failure of ideological conviction. Frederickson, for his part, identifies a dialectic by which racial hierarchies are introduced as an intellectual structure for making sense of inequalities that only begin needing explanation once equality is the presumptive norm.

> If a culture holds a premise of spiritual and temporal *inequality*, if a hierarchy exists that is unquestioned by even its lower-ranking members, as in the Indian caste system before the modern era, there is no incentive to deny the full humanity of underlings in order to treat them as impure or unworthy. If *equality* is the norm in the spiritual or temporal realm (or in both at the same time), and there are groups of people within this society who are so despised or disparaged that the upholders of the norms feel compelled to make them exceptions to the promise or realization of equality, they can be denied the prospect of equal status only if they allegedly possess some extraordinary deficiency that makes them less than fully human. It is uniquely in the West that we find the dialectical interaction between a premise of equality and an intense prejudice toward certain groups that would seem to be a precondition for the full flowering of racism as an ideology or world view.[11]

Where Stepan offers a paradox and Frederickson a dialectic, I mean to argue that the racial models of thinking that came into being in the last quarter of the eighteenth century operate not in spite of or as a kind of dark historical underside of Enlightenment universalism, but rather as an effort to bring together two not entirely compatible principles of the era: a commitment to universal equality and a commitment to the truth of evidence drawn from empirical observation. The strange persistence of racial thought despite our knowing better may be attributable less to the failure of Enlightenment ideas than to their fulfillment.

Beyond Humors: Distinguishing Race and Medicine

In analyzing the centuries immediately preceding Kant's and Willan's writings, the difficulty of elaborating the relations governing medical and racial concepts of human variety lies less in identifying the points of overlap than in discerning their distinctions. Until the last quarter of the eighteenth century, when anatomical medical knowledge firmly supplanted a humoral conception of health and disease, the same environmental and humoral mechanisms that could disrupt the finely tuned and ever-shifting equilibrium of humors within the body to produce illness also had the power to determine the range and combination of skin color and bodily features that constituted what natural historians of the era would have referred to as "human variety." What is key to understanding the nature of the link between pre-anatomical conceptions of illness and "preracial" notions of human difference is recognizing that the humoral dynamics that drive both systems do not maintain any hard-and-fast distinctions between the forces that operate within the individual body and those that operate outside it. The mixture of blood, phlegm, black bile, and yellow bile determining not only one's immediate condition of health but also one's more general temperament could be affected, either deliberately or unwittingly, by the proportions of heat, cold, wetness, or dryness in the environment. These same environmental forces worked to produce the bodily characteristics by which geographically proximate peoples might be grouped together: Africans, for example, were understood to have dark skins and excitable dispositions that manifested the hot, sunny, and wet environment in which they lived. The skin thus functioned both as the point of interchange and contiguity between the interiors of individuals and their environments and also eventually operated as the site around which the discourses of medicine and racial difference came to be distinguishable from one another. While histories of medicine have devoted a great deal of critical energy to documenting the late-eighteenth-century turn from humoral to anatomical medicine, and historians of race have identified the significance of the disjunction between environmentalist conceptions of human difference and the biologized racial science that emerged in the early decades of the nineteenth century, very little work has been done to think through the deep logic of the differentiation of the medical and the racial, particularly how the history and meaning of racial difference might be newly understood in the context of this splitting off from medical knowledge.[12]

In order to explore the implications of this nexus, I would like to review briefly the history of thinking about human difference in the years leading up to the dissolution of the humoral paradigm. Skin color became firmly established as the primary signifier of racial difference only in the final decades of the eighteenth century. This localization of racial difference in the skin was the culmination of a new interest in the genesis of particular skin tones that intensified over the course of the century; by century's end, more than forty studies speculating on the origins of such difference had appeared. Prior to this, within the humoral paradigm, "complexion" referred to an inhabitant's temper or disposition; skin color was only one aspect of complexion.[13] The climatic model of human variety became less and less plausible as slavery and colonial exploration brought people into environments different from those into which they were born, without the resulting change in skin color that humoral models of human variety would have predicted. (The force of this colonial context became particularly apparent in Kant's debate with the German explorer Georg Forster, which I discuss in detail below.)[14]

The transformation in medical thinking that split off the science of treating bodies from the practices of apprehending their varieties isolated skin by elaborating a collection of institutional and scientific practices that turned the relations of interior and exterior into an object of investigation itself. The final decade of the eighteenth century and early decades of the nineteenth mark the heyday of what historians of medicine have retrospectively come to call anatomical medicine, or "Paris medicine," the collection of institutional, pedagogical, diagnostic, and therapeutic reforms by which the working of a modern anatomical body comes to supplant the systemic, humoral conception of health and the body theorized most comprehensively by Galen. The transformations in medical knowledge and institutional organization that took place during this period were understood by both the contemporary medical practitioners who brought them about and by the historians who have analyzed them since to be efforts to translate the revolutionary, democratizing energies of the political realm into the sphere of institutionalized medicine. Where surgeons' engagements with the mucky interiors of human bodies had long subjected them to the social opprobrium leveled at body handlers like barbers and gravediggers, over the course of the 1790s, physicians and surgeons began to be educated in the same institutions, using a common curriculum. Patient care, which had theretofore taken place in the privacy of patients' homes or in physicians' quarters, now moved largely into urban hospitals and clinics. Finally, medical knowledge came to be seen as located less within a corpus of received texts than as emerging from clinical encounters with sick patients.

But it would be a mistake to understand these changes as generated primarily by a shift from a quasi-scriptural textual authority to a modern scientific empiricism. Rather, the range of new practices—including, but not privileging, the diminished authority of received texts—can be more comprehensively understood as being both predicated upon and working to produce the fundamental reconception of the body. Where the humoral body was one in which "health" and "sickness" were not fundamentally discrete conditions, but rather variable positions on an individualized spectrum (harmonious or disharmonious and endlessly adjusting and adjustable states of heat, cold, wetness, and dryness), disease in the anatomical body was localized in particular organs, with the external symptoms of otherwise inaccessible malfunctioning interior organs confirmed by the evidence of lesions made visible after death by the process of autopsy.[15]

Just as these bodies functioned differently, the authority by which they might be known differed. Since the humoral body was one in which sickness and health represented states of equilibrium and disequilibrium, medical "knowledge" was irresistibly narrative, with patient as likely as physician to possess the authority to tell the sickness's story and thereby to diagnose.[16] Writing in a 1792 memoir, the artisan James Lackington recalled an incident in which he took ill after traveling in a coach: "I was so very cold, that when I came to the inn where the passengers dined, I went directly to the fire, which struck the cold inward, so that I had but a very narrow escape from death." Both sickness and cure involved the delicate manipulation of heat and cold; both patient and physician might dedicate themselves to such manipulating.

The most crucial change underwriting the shift from a humoral to an anatomical paradigm involved the shift from the thoroughly particularized body presumed by humoral medicine to an abstract standard body within anatomical medicine. Where, under a humoral logic, each individual body was constituted according to its own particular proportions of humors that determined the particular measure by which its sickness or health might be gauged, anatomical medicine understood all bodies to be operating according to the same mechanisms and designed its diagnostic procedures accordingly. We can best understand the force of the shift and its significance for the history of the legibility of bodies by tracing the emergence of anatomical medicine's central diagnostic process—the autopsy. While scholars have long assumed that autopsy could only emerge as a technique of scientific and medical investigation once religious scruples concerning the sanctity of the body began to fade, in an important recent book, *The Body Emblazoned: Dissection and the Human Body in Renaissance Culture*, Jonathan Sawday argues that the notion of the "decriminalization of autopsy" has been misunderstood to refer to the agents rather than the objects of autopsy. Autopsy became available as a tool of science only when it ceased to be a government-sanctioned technique for punishing criminals. In England, the 1752 Murder Act sanctioned "penal dissection" as a specific form of punishment to be carried out after a criminal had been executed, designed to intensify the punishment meted out to the worst criminals beyond the sanction of mere death:

> The overt context for the passage of the 1752 Act was a response to a perceived break-down in law and order on the part of the authorities. What was needed, it was felt, was a punishment so draconian, so appalling, that potential criminals would be terrified at the fate which awaited them in the event of their detection. Clearly, simple execution was not enough. . . . Dissection was to be understood as a specific alternative to the other form of public display encouraged by the authorities—the gibbeting of the corpse after death.[17]

Only in the second half of the eighteenth century, with the elimination of the public display of the corpse and the linked development of a system of differentiated, graduated punishments did the practice of autopsy become sufficiently detached from the violence of state punishment to be capable of establishing itself as a legitimate form of disinterested scientific investigation.

For my purposes, what is crucial about Sawday's history of early modern autopsy is the shifting conception of bodily particularity implicit in the movement from punishment to science. For autopsy to function as a method of punishment, the dead body must be conceived as eminently particular, and its particularity understood as part and parcel of its continuity with the actions and experience of the living criminal. Inasmuch as it intensifies the punishment, the autopsy differentiates the particular criminal's corpse from the corpses of other people by marking the special heinousness of that criminal's past acts. The distinguishing of punishment and autopsy, on the other hand, is predicated upon the pointed separation of the state of an individual's life and the state and treatment of his or her body after death. This disarticulation of living and dead bodies invests the information gleaned from the autopsy with scientific validity. Only when the posthumous investigation of the dead body takes place with an indifference toward the quality of the life that preceded it—when one corpse becomes interchangeable with another—can the information generated be presumed to illuminate bodies that have withstood different sorts of lives.

This punitive prehistory of medical autopsy casts light upon what is new and significant about the theory underwriting anatomical medicine and the mode of authority possessed by the physicians who practiced it. With the gradual emergence of an anatomical notion of the body, according to which the disease that manifests itself as lesions on organs buried within the body cavity becomes directly visible only after the patient has died and been autopsied, the skin functions as the structure blocking the immediate perception of disease. While skin might be assumed in this account to limit and constrain the physician's powers, its relation to anatomical authority is in fact far more complex. For doctors operating within this emergent anatomical paradigm did indeed lay claim to the power to diagnose patients' diseases while those patients remained alive, and they did so on the premise that the sick patient's organs were sufficiently identical to the already autopsied organs of another patient who had died. (Such a premise depends, of course, upon the withdrawal of the dead body as a site of state-sanctioned punishment.) This controversial new notion of a standard body undergirded the physician's authority to make judgments about the state of a patient's imperceptible, largely inaccessible, internal organs by correlating external symptoms of disease to the lesions found on internal organs of already dead and autopsied patients.

The shift to a diagnosis based on the evidence of an abstract standardized body undermined the patient's own diagnostic, even perceptual, authority. Where patients operating within a humoral body logic possessed as much right to diagnose and transform their physical state as the doctor who was audience to their individual narratives, patients became doubly deauthorized within the anatomical paradigm. Tucked deep within the body cavity, diseased organs are hidden from the sick patient's view by the skin of the body's surface; laid out on an autopsy table, such organs are visible to the physician while the patient whose disease has suddenly been made visible is, in a word, too dead to care. Anatomical physicians' authority thus depends upon their occupation of a point of view structurally prohibited to the patients whose bodies serve as their evidence—depends, that is, on foreclosing the body to the experience of those who inhabit it. Only with the emergence of anatomical medicine can patients begin to worry that they might be wracked by a disease, like cancer, and know nothing of it. Under a humoral logic, such self-opacity had been unthinkable.

Nor does the exclusivity of its authority exhaust the standardized body's conceptual strangeness. While the diagnostic usefulness of the standardized body supposedly rests on the claim that all bodies, living and dead, are fundamentally like one another, such a body can equally plausibly be understood to be constituted out of the sick and autopsied bodies' irreducibility to one another. In anatomical medicine, bodies become usefully comparable to the degree to which they are not the same, since it is only because one body is sick and the other one dead that the dead body can provide information about what is likely to be going on within the inaccessible depths of the sick body. This difference between sick and dead bodies can be understood to name anatomical medicine's fundamental therapeutic goal: to keep the sick body from becoming dead. The physician's unique authority is forged out of this very irreducibility, drawn not from the observation of any particular material body, but constituted by the imputed likeness between a given sick body and an endless series of "standard bodies" that can be asserted only insofar as particular relations of likeness and difference among actual bodies cannot be directly observed. The anatomical body's constitutive opacity to itself is an opacity literally located in the skin, and it is this opacity that ratifies the anatomical physician's authority. The skin prevents the physician from directly observing the organs within and, by blocking the observation of particulars, becomes the sign of the bodies' likeness to one another and, at the same time, the evidence that the judgment of such likeness is not the result of direct observation. The standardized body of anatomical medicine is not, it would seem, an empirical object. Wholly identifiable neither with the patient's diseased body nor with the autopsied corpse, the standardized body of anatomical medicine is a construct of necessary laws generated out of the comparison of bodies whose very comparability is made conceivable by the assertion of lawfulness, regularity of function, and predictable networks of causation.

The circularity of this anatomical medical logic is what constitutes such medical knowing, like Kant's transcendental deduction, as both diachronic and transcendental. A standardized body comes into being because the empirical evidence that generates that knowledge is neither observable at any single moment nor separable from the abstraction that is its consequence. But this circularity also means that the diachronicity implicit to the comparison—bodies are sick before they are dead—must be bracketed analytically, even though it is the pathological development of disease, the relation of cause and effect, that makes the evidence of the dead body relevant to the sick body, that links the two bodies.

This fundamental tension within the logic of anatomical bodies, the tension between the essentially synchronic lawfulness of the bodies and the diachronic progress of disease, manifests itself in the form of a deep and persistent tension between physicians' authority to diagnose (to engage with the likeness of sick and dead bodies) and their authority to take therapeutic measures like medicating (to engage with the changes between sick and dead bodies, the process of healing and dying). The early history of anatomical medicine is animated by this fundamental tension. As I discuss in greater detail below, 18-century medical practitioners frequently noted that while their diagnoses of patients drew on knowledge they had gleaned from studying autopsied bodies, their choice of treatments was of necessity a trial-and-error affair, since the causal relations of both the progression of a disease and its treatment by way of medicine are hidden from observation. It is the explicitness with which this tension is engaged that offers Kant a framework within which to explore the identical tension within his critical philosophy. This coincidence of concerns becomes most evident in the third essay of his *Conflict of the Faculties,* where a work that announces its plans to examine the institutional relations between the faculties of philosophy and medicine transmutes before our eyes into Kant's meditation on his own aging and dying. Conceived within this temporally complex evidentiary dynamic, skin announces and renders instantly perceptible the standardness of the body it edges and enfolds, a standardness that is inextricable from the body's status as an analytical effect.[18] In seeking to transform the limitations of what can be known (the interior of the body hidden beneath the skin) into something that can be seen (the skin of the standardized body), anatomical medicine lays out its analytical horizon of aspiration as the point at which seeing an object and seeing that object's resemblance to other objects takes place at one and the same instant.

Kant: Skin Deep

Subtitled "On the Power of the Mind to Master Its Morbid Feelings by Sheer Resolution," the third essay of *The Conflict of the Faculties* is structured as a letter to Professor Cristoph Wilhelm Hufeland of the University of Jena in response to Hufeland's recently published *Macrobiotics; or, The Art of Prolonging Human Life.* Kant criticizes Hufeland for his faith in the power of "regimen" to extend individuals' lifetimes. In taking aim against regimen, Kant positions himself as a critic of the humoral bodily paradigm, for which the category of the regimen was crucial.[19] For Kant, Hufeland's insistence on the power of regimen to prolong lifetimes is less significant as a claim about therapeutic efficacy than it is as an account of the organization and limits of medical knowledge. As Kant explains, for Hufeland, the development of "the art of prolonging human life" is predicated on the presumption that the degree to which an individual enjoys life is a reliable gauge of that individual's health. Such a presumption leads Hufeland to imagine, wrongly, that individuals might fulfill their two most ardent desires at once: "to have a long life and to enjoy good health during it."[20] Kant counters by insisting that to imagine one can fulfill both desires simultaneously is fundamentally to misrecognize the nature of one's knowledge:

> [A man] can *feel* well (to judge by his comfortable feeling of vitality), but he can never *know* that he is healthy. The cause of natural death is always illness, whether one feels it or not. There are many people of whom one can say, without really wanting to ridicule them, that they are always *sickly* but can never be *sick*. Their regimen consists in constantly deviating from and returning to their way of life, and by this they manage to get on well and live a long, if not a robust life. I have outlived a good many of my friends or acquaintances who boasted of perfect health and lived by an orderly regimen adopted once and for all, while the seed of death (illness) lay in them unnoticed, ready to develop. They felt healthy and did not *know* they were ill; for while the cause of natural death is always illness, *causality* cannot be felt. It requires understanding, whose judgment can err. . . . Hence if he does not feel ill, he is entitled to express his well-being only by saying that he is *apparently* in good health. So a long life, considered in retrospect, can testify only to the health one *has enjoyed*, and the art of a regimen will have to prove its skill or science primarily in the art of *prolonging* life, (not enjoying it). (181)

Hufeland's confidence in the efficacy of regimen, by Kant's account, is a confidence predicated on the notion that patients can know their state of health or sickness as they experience it.[21] While he does not name it as such, Kant launches his objections to Hufeland from within what is clearly an anatomical paradigm: a patient's sense of her own health as she experiences it can only be apparent, felt rather than known. ("Seed" [*keim*], Kant's figure for disease that is inaccessible because it is located within the body's interior, is one he also adopts in his theory of race, a repetition that underscores the association of his analyses of race and medicine.) The causality of disease that produces sickness cannot itself be felt, but must rather be known by some means other than direct perception. As is the case within anatomical medicine, here knowledge of one's actual state of health is retrospective: "A long life, *considered in retrospect*, can testify only to the health one has enjoyed." Anatomical medicine's crucial point of "retrospection" is, of course, the autopsy, where the diseased organs that have "caused" the newly dead patient's demise are suddenly made knowable to the anatomizing doctor and where the patient, barred from witnessing the evidence of his own autopsy, can even in retrospect testify only to his own *feelings* of "enjoyment."[22]

Kant's grappling with the capacity of regimen to prolong the individual life span clearly signals his interest in using anatomical medicine's critique of a humoral epistemology to illuminate the workings of a philosophical project in which knowing takes place by way of a delineation of its limits, and the discovery, via those limits, of the regularity and lawfulness of the world. But the particular terms by which he understands such an illumination to take place only become apparent when we examine the framework within which he introduces his medical discussion. Kant is explicit about naming his frame as such: while his critique of Hufeland's notion of regimen comes in the form of a letter to the author of *Macrobiotics*, Kant opens the essay by explaining how he has come to write this letter:

> The fact that I am only now, in January of this year (1798) writing to thank you for the gift of your instructive and enjoyable book "On the Art of Prolonging Human Life" which you sent me on 12 December 1796, might make you think that I am counting on a long life in which to reply. But old age brings with it the habit of postponing important decisions (procrastinatio)—just as we put off concluding our own lives: death always arrives too soon for us, and we are inexhaustible in thinking up excuses for making it wait. (175)

With this passage, Kant presents his readers with two analytical frameworks within which to understand his invoking the prolongation of the lifetime and its obverse, the process of dying. First, the impulse to prolong one's life ought to be seen as a form of postponement: it is like the procrastination that has allowed Kant to let nearly two years pass between his receipt of Hufeland's book and his writing to acknowledge that receipt. In analogizing the impulse to put off death to the procrastination that leads him to put off writing the thank-you note, Kant suggests that what links the two species of postponement is their common engagement of an abstract temporality, the sequentiality by which we might assemble spine, covers, and pages into an image of a book. But if we might be tempted to understand the general fact of the analogy linking procrastination to putting off death to rest simply upon this abstraction of time, I suggest that the peculiar form Kant's analogy takes prevents such a reading.

The evident strangeness of Kant's analogy lies in the reversal of the expected relations of tenor and vehicle: where we might have anticipated the relatively easily effected act of postponing decisions to stand as a model for the desired but less easily brought about goal of putting off death, instead, the more difficult—indeed, in Kant's view, impossible—trick of postponing one's own death is made the model for the seemingly more trivial procrastination regarding one's decisions. In highlighting the impossibility of the analogy as it is presented—we recall that Kant openly proclaims his skepticism about the life-prolonging power of Hufeland's regimen—Kant would seem to insist that the order in which analogical relations are presented matters. Tenor and vehicle are, by this account, nonreversible. In positing and then immediately withdrawing an analytical reversibility predicated upon entirely formal relations of likeness, the passage here suggests that the material differences of the objects generating the idea of likeness in some way remain present in that idea. Abstract sequence gives way to a passage of time structured by the subjects and objects doing the passing.

Kant thus seems to offer a specific argument about the way analogy ought to be understood to operate and, by extension, the way in which such an understanding of analogy might be seen to function as a model for his critical method, which, after all, rests upon the discovery of essential relations of likeness. Inasmuch as the tenor and vehicle that pick out likeness are not interchangeable, thinking lawfully—discovering relations of likeness—involves not simply having an idea of the abstract qualities these objects have in common, but rather knowing those qualities as they exist in the objects through whose relations they are known. To learn the lesson, or the law, of the relation between putting off death and putting off decisions is to give up the idea that we might ever be able to think such a lesson apart from the conditions that have allowed us to learn it.

In insisting upon the links between thinking analogically and thinking about postponement, Kant's analogy defines likeness as a kind of postponement, not simply a disregard of change implied by the abstract lawfulness of an interchangeable tenor and vehicle, but rather, as an active putting off of change created by the deliberate act of putting one analogical term in place after another. But the fact that Kant figures such deliberate putting off of change by means of the ordering of analogical terms also means that such a project of postponement will be only temporary (as indeed the term "postponement" implies). The recognition of lawfulness that begins with a local and identifiable act of ordering will at some point come to an end—

most definitively at the point at which death, unlike decision making, can no longer be put off.

Having described the willful arresting of change formally by way of the building of his analogy, Kant goes on a few pages later to register the collapse of such postponement as a collapse back into the particularity of dying, the now-singular term no longer tethered to its analogical brace. Nor does Kant confine his association of dying with the untenability of analogy to an isolated moment of framing: his description of his efforts to think philosophically as he himself is dying takes the form of the juxtaposition of two terms whose disintegration makes uncertain their relations to one another. Sliding repeatedly back and forth between offering a narration of his own experience and an account of an unspecified "patient," Kant recalls the effects of his contracting "catarrh accompanied by distress in the head." "The result of it," he remembers, "was that I felt disorganized—or at least weakened and dulled—in my intellectual work; and since this ailment has attached itself to the natural weaknesses of my old age, it will end only with life itself" (205). Describing the patient, Kant details the decline:

> This pathological condition of the patient, which accompanies and impedes his thinking, in so far as thinking is holding firmly onto a concept (of the unity of ideas connected in his consciousness) produces the feeling of a spasmic state in his organ of thought (his brain). This feeling, as of a burden, does not really weaken his thought and reflection itself, or his memory of preceding thought; but when he is setting forth his thoughts . . . the very need to guard against distractions which would interrupt the firm coherence of ideas *in their temporal sequence* produces an involuntary spasmic condition of the brain, which takes the form of an inability to maintain unity of consciousness in his ideas, *as one takes the place of the preceding one* [emphasis added]. In every discourse I first prepare (the reader or the audience) for what I intend to say by indicating, in prospect, my destination, and, in retrospect, the starting point of my argument (without these two points of reference a discourse has no consistency). And the result of this pathological condition is that when the time comes for me to connect the two, I must suddenly ask my audience (or myself, silently): now where was I? where did I start from? This is a defect, not so much of the mind or of the memory alone, as rather of *presence of mind* (in connecting ideas)—that is, an involuntary *distraction*. (207)

What is most striking about Kant's description in this passage is the way it is thought itself that fails to remain unchanging. Kant presents this collapse of thinking under the pressure of a failure of self-consistency in two different variations, third and first person, as a lack of coherence of temporal sequence. While the consistency that at once announces and constitutes thought is initially described in temporal terms, as the capacity to "indicate, in prospect, my destination, and, in retrospect, the starting point of my argument," it is also present, at least by negation, as a seamless oscillation between subject and object, the mutual constitution of subject and world that is Kant's transcendental deduction. Kant here evokes the dynamic of his critical method, as subjects and the object world they know constitute one another, thoughts becoming things as one idea taking the place of another produces a "unity of consciousness.

But where the collapse of the analogy between postponing death and postponing decisions appeared to undermine the claim that there might be a "mind-independent" temporality capable of canceling the differences between how embodied subjects die and know, Kant now evokes rhetorically the logic of anatomical medicine's "standardized body" in his effort to reinstate such an abstract temporality. Kant would seem here to present the same descriptions twice, first as a set of symptoms plaguing an unknown "patient," then again as an account of his own symptoms. It's worth noting that he offers no explanation at all of the relation governing the two sets of descriptions, simply passing from one to the other without remark. Absent such explanation, readers encountering the two points of view, couched in the rhetoric of pathology, are likely to engage in something resembling medical diagnosis: Are "brain spasms" and "distraction" different names for a single condition? What would be the sort of evidence by which one might make such a judgment?

Even as the passage describes thinking rendered incoherent by change, by its failure to remain self-consistent or to engage self-consistent objects over time, it also presents the description of an object (the unspecified patient) and a subject (the dying philosopher himself) who bear a striking likeness to one another.[23] Here both the extent of Kant's borrowings from anatomical medicine and the usefulness of the paradigm for allowing him temporarily to circumvent the problem of thinking about lawful change become apparent. Kant sets forth a relation of likeness—the resemblance of the brain-spasm-plagued patient and the dying philosopher—even as the terms of the likeness in question, a shared loss of the capacity for coherent thought brought about by their respective change or decline, would seem to render the recognition of such lawful resemblance unavailable to patient and philosopher alike. Like his anatomical medical contemporaries, Kant posits a standardized body, a lawful resemblance, as a means of making subjects and objects legible even in the face of their failure to remain consistent with themselves—even, that is, in the face of their own dying.

But if Kant's unacknowledged oscillation between first and third person, between diagnosed object and dying subject, announces his borrowing of the diagnostic methods of anatomical medicine in order to transform what is changing and hence illegible into a set of lawful relations, anatomical medicine's diagnostic logic ought to clue us in to what Kant accomplishes by *not* specifying the precise relation between his own incapacity to keep his thoughts straight and the brain spasms of the unnamed patient. We recall that one of the fundamental distinctions between humoral and anatomical paradigms of medical knowledge lay in who precisely had access to such knowledge. Where within a humoral logic, patients, privy to their own deliberate regimens as well as their inadvertent encounters with heat and cold, were understood to have at least as intimate knowledge of their own bodily states as their physicians, anatomical medicine's standardized body, conceived as a complex composite of an inaccessible sick body and an autopsied corpse, was knowable only to the physician who occupied neither sick nor dead body. In adopting the logic of anatomical medicine as part of his effort to extract lawfulness—and thus to rescue his critical method—from the unpredictably shifting and hence illegible thought processes he experiences in his own waning months, Kant both does and does not hew to anatomical medicine's complex structure of point of view. By juxtaposing without remark the fragmentation of his own attempts at sustained argumentation and the brain spasms of the unspecified patient in such a way as to imply their fundamental interchangeability with one another and thus their lawfulness, Kant suggests that the perspective from which such lawfulness can be discerned is neither his nor that of the spasmodic patient. On the other hand, because the "object" whose changefulness would threaten the analytical claims is philosophical thinking itself—what turns out to change here are Kant's thoughts as he is thinking—Kant cannot leave the thinker unspecified. The recognition of lawfulness that characterizes and indeed constitutes such thinking must be identifiable with the dying Kant's own thinking, if it is to rescue such thinking from the threat posed by its own fragmentariness and unsustainability. What the passage dramatizes, then, is not simply the irreconcilability of Kant's critical philosophy and the knowledge of lawfully changing objects but also the impossibility of recognizing this irreconcilability from within critical philosophy itself. As it is unable to be argued for, such an irreconcilability can be rendered discernible only by way of the sort of rhetorical demonstration offered here. By choosing the structure of the anatomical body as the framework within which to make apparent the lawfully rational mind's incapacity to account for its own decline, moreover, Kant suggests that we can come to understand what it this that critical philosophy cannot teach us only insofar as we recognize the degree to which our thinking minds must depend upon the continued life of the bodies they inhabit.[24]

It might be objected that this reading relies upon something too intensely personal and contingent (the psychological crisis Kant experiences on contemplating his own imminent death) to make an argument about the status of lawfulness in Kant's critical philosophy more generally, as well as about his philosophical system's engagement with the culture at large. But in fact while my account recognizes the reality of Kant's psychic pain, it in no way depends upon it. What matters here is not that Kant experiences a psychological crisis as his death approaches but that such a crisis manifests itself as an epistemological problem. Only with the advent of anatomical medicine and the new centrality of autopsy for constituting and rendering legible standardized bodies does death come to count as a pointedly *epistemological* state. But if Kant's rhetorical solution here—the creation of a readerly point of view able to comprehend the likeness of speaker and patient by remaining distinct from both—helps temporarily avert both psychological and philosophical crises, such a solution cannot outlast the textual relations that create it. Kant's efforts to present the recognition of lawfulness not solely as a mode of thinking but also as a foundation for ethics, as a structure for regulating and evaluating behavior in the relations between first person and third person, between ethical subjects and the people with whom they share the world, produce a condition in which this tension demands to be teased out.

Institutions of the Body

In the passage from the third essay of *Conflict,* Kant offers an oscillation between first and third person, a demonstration of the likeness of his own degenerating thought process and the failure of a patient to maintain unity of consciousness that is meant to function as a kind of compensation for his incapacity to track his own thoughts, to know for certain that what he begins thinking about is the same thing he ends up thinking about. It ought to come as no great surprise, then, that Kant's use of such a technique as a means of obscuring the challenges posed to the lawfulness of thinking itself comes under pressure when he introduces the possibility of using it as a means of determining the proper relation between first and third person—that is, as an ethics regulating the relations of subjects and objects.

We might pose the question this way: When the likeness of subjects and objects is asserted in order to make an otherwise unstable and incoherent subject legible to itself, how does this affect the ways in which the recognition of lawfulness might function—or fail to function—as a guideline for determining the proper ways that subjects ought to treat objects?

I suggested earlier that the ambitiousness of Kant's critical philosophy lies in the notion that an epistemology that recognizes the likeness of other people, their fundamental humanness, necessarily guarantees their ethical treatment. For Kant, the unity of epistemology and ethics means that philosophical thinking might assume the regulating role of institutions of state, or more precisely, that state institutions might be relegated to regulating the sorts of relations left undescribed by philosophy. Kant takes up the question of the relations between philosophy and institutions most trenchantly for our purposes in two essays, in his short piece "An Answer to the Question: What Is Enlightenment?" (1784) and in a more extended way, in the middle essay of the *Conflict*, on the relation of philosophy and law. It is in this latter essay that we come to see the ethical consequences of Kant's assertion of the likeness of other people as a *compensation* for the fundamental illegibility of a changing self.

For Kant, predictably, the measure of an institution's proper organization lies in the degree to which it can be seen to recognize the lawfulness of the relations it organizes. What is less predictable is the way he understands institutions to be capable of instantiating and helping to constitute such a recognition. We recall from our discussion of the transcendental deduction that Kant understands lawfulness—likeness—to be a manifestation of a pervasive and universalized intentionality. Even when we cannot see them, we know spines to be part of what makes a book a book—what makes a given book like other unseen books—while water stains are not, because spines are necessary for enabling books to do what they are intended to do, and water stains are not. Inasmuch as Kant understands lawfulness to announce intentionality, he sees institutions as operating to render such intentional lawfulness legible by making apparent the gap between any kind of local, individualized, and therefore non-universal intentions or desires and whatever condition is understood to be an effect of lawful intentionality. As we have already seen, for Kant, the registration of lawfulness is necessarily diachronic; consequently, the forms of institutional organization that instantiate such lawfulness not only must make apparent that the conditions that characterize a given social organization are the effects of something other than local causes, intentions, or interests, but must manifest such universal causation over time. This context makes sense of Kant's decision to open the second essay of the *Conflict* with an excursus on what constitutes properly philosophical prophesying, that is, knowing over time.

Kant draws a contrast between the prophesying of the minister-prophets of the ancient Jewish theocracy and the republican constitutionalism that emerges in France during the Revolution, a mode of government he understands to be essentially, if not obviously, prophetic. The fact that the Jewish prophets predict the demise of their state in advance of its collapse reveals nothing about the Jewish state or the nature of Jewish subjects, either individually or collectively, since the priests who make the predictions also control the institutions of state necessary to bring the predicted ends about. A correct prediction about the condition of the Jewish state prior to the moment such a condition comes into being does not generate any insight into the essential qualities characterizing that state because the priests who claim the capacity to prophesy—who lay claim, that is, to a knowledge of the future based on an understanding of the essential and hence ongoing qualities of the state—are also the functionaries who contingently possess the authority in the present that enables them to bring about that future state. So long as the people who predict the future are the people with the institutional power to bring about the predicted conditions, such predictions reveal the interests of the predictors, not any essential (because unchanging) qualities of the state. Knowledge about the future condition of such a state is thus essentially knowledge of its present, contingent relations.

An era of political revolution might at first seem an odd context within which to discover either properly philosophical prophesying or the sorts of political institutions that reveal the essential humanness of their citizens. Odd, until we consider the ways in which revolutionary times reverse the defining qualities of theocratic prophesying. For Kant, the contingency of the relations between revolutionary present and revolutionary future and the tenuousness of any specific institutional forms highlight the discontinuity between the forces whose interests battle for dominance at any given moment and the eventual outcome. In times of revolution, prophets are no longer assured the institutional power to realize their visions. The irruption of revolution introduces a gap between local intention and effect and, in so doing, marks the universality of that effect. In this sense, the 1789 Revolution operates as the model for the constitutional republicanism that might otherwise appear its thoroughly contingent outcome, insofar as both the Revolution and republicanism share a common structure of causation, one that forcefully separates the intentions and interests of individual agents from a discernible outcome. As Kant puts it, the Revolution's philosophical prophesying is characterized by its yoking of an intense partiality ("a universal yet disinterested sympathy for the players on one side against those on the other" [153]) with a willingness to allow other people to be agents of bringing about the sought-after goal (an absence of "the least intention of assisting" [157]). That someone else can be entrusted with the task of bringing about one's own political goals offers irrefutable evidence of the disinterestedness of those goals; one can hand the task off if one is no more likely to benefit from its accomplishment than one's surrogates are. Republicanism offers a theory of government and institutional form by which intensity of investment and an embrace of surrogacy do not contradict but rather reinforce one another. Surrogacy—or, as it is more commonly termed, representativeness—thus stands as evidence of the lawfulness of both the ends carried out by means of such an institutional mechanism and the citizens who effect and are affected by its actions.

Kant's intimation of a resemblance between the fragmented thoughts of a brain-addled patient and the cognitive wanderings of his own death-pressed self is haunted, we recall, by a not fully articulated ambiguity concerning the points of view from which change and lawfulness are enacted and recognized. To the degree to which Kant's discussion of revolution and republicanism renders explicit the relations between first and third person, between those subjects who frame goals and the people who act to realize those goals, such a discussion serves to bring to the fore critical philosophy's latent contradictions. As with Kant's analysis of his own pathological thinking, the problem here is one of point of view. Surrogacy would seem to testify to the disinterested and hence universal lawful quality of a given set of conditions inasmuch as it demonstrates the framing subject's goals and intentions to be not merely her own. But surrogacy can function as a guarantee of the disinterest and therefore the freedom of the individual subject only as far as the surrogates themselves are constrained in their behaviors. They must act to fulfill goals conceived by others in order to guarantee that those goals do not speak only to the desires of their framers or, what is not quite the same thing, only as far as the issue of their own interests, intentions, and desires is bracketed. Just as the confused "thinkers" of Kant's description of his cognitive decline are conceived alternately and contradictorily as objects barred from lawful thinking and subjectivity by the shifting incoherence of their consciousness and as subjects capable of recognizing the two thinkers' likeness to one another, here surrogates must be understood as functioning from two points of view at once. On the one hand, surrogates are understood to be acting from the perspective and at the direction of someone else, and they thus lack the full range of freedom that constitutes the lawfulness and essential humanness of the human. On the other hand, they must be understood to possess the capacity for freedom and self-direction characteristic of subjects, since it is only this capacity for intending that enables such surrogates to demonstrate that the effects they bring about are not merely the outcome of the local interests and intentions of the subjects who would direct their action. Whereas Kant's use of the hybrid first and third person allows him to finesse this contradiction in the brain-pathology passage—sometimes the narrator is identical with the confused thinker who cannot remember what he is arguing from one point to the next, while sometimes he is distinct from the subjects he describes and thus capable of discerning the likenesses between them—in the discussion of republican surrogacy, the contradiction emerges in full force.

Kant addresses this tension as it manifests itself in an institutional context most explicitly in "An Answer to the Question: What Is Enlightenment?" In this essay he advances an idiosyncratic version of the opposition between public and private uses of reason. As part of his effort to reconcile the logic of surrogacy or representativeness with the model of subjectivity he lays out in his critical philosophy, Kant designates "private" reason as the "often . . . very narrowly restricted" reason made use of by civil servants in the fulfillment of the tasks and duties assigned to them—in essence, surrogates' reason: "Now a certain mechanism is necessary in many affairs which are run in the interest of the commonwealth by means of which some members of the commonwealth must conduct themselves through an artificial unanimity, to public ends, or at least restrain themselves from the destruction of these ends." Public reason, for Kant, is the use of reason by scholars—as opposed to government bureaucrats or surrogates—which is to say, reason unhindered by the demands for obedience or responsibility to the immediate functions of the polis. Where an officer of the government might legitimately be compelled to obey unquestioningly the orders of his superiors without such automatic obedience counting as a constraint upon his private use of reason, the same person "nevertheless does not act against the duty of a citizen if he, as a scholar, expresses his thoughts publicly on the inappropriateness or even injustice" of taxes or military service or some other form of governmentally compelled behavior.[25]

For Kant, the questions of surrogacy and institutions are crucial to his Enlightenment project not simply because they offer a structure through which the essentially epistemological project of recognizing the lawfulness of subjects and objects can be made an ethics, but also because they in some sense name or gesture toward the perils of attempting to establish a program for enlightenment. Given that Kant characterizes the "the self-incurred immaturity" of a not-yet-enlightened subject as "the inability to make use of one's own understanding without the guidance of another" (58), any effort to produce a program that would direct other people toward enlightenment runs the risk of reinforcing the very conditions of dependency it is designed to ameliorate. The question of institutionalization that Kant takes up in the second essay of the *Conflict* is thus a question at the heart of the Enlightenment project itself, since even enlightened leaders or institutional structures can produce the opposite in their constituents if those leaders and institutions do the work of understanding in ways that relieve their constituents of the responsibility to think for themselves. So while the *Conflict* implies that surrogacy might be a reliable measure of social or institutional disinterest, surrogacy also dangerously resembles the sort of dependence on the reason of others that Kant characterizes as immaturity in "What Is Enlightenment?"

Given his criticism of the theocratic prophesying of the ancient Jewish state, it follows that for Kant state institutions can be assumed to guarantee the free action of their citizens not simply when there exist two distinct registers of public and private in which reason might be exercised, but when the different sorts of reason are exercised by a single individual alternately inhabiting different roles. Both elements of Kant's formulation are crucial because, taken alone, the division of reason into public and private functions merely redescribes without solving the problems associated with surrogacy. Surrogacy, in that case, functions as a guarantee of the disinterest and hence the freedom of the individual subject at the expense of the surrogates' own freedom. The surrogates themselves are constrained in their behaviors. The demands of freedom and disinterest are made noncontradictory only when they take place in the same individual—more precisely, only by taking place in the same body. Only when the mode of reason that a given individual employs is not predictable in advance is the freedom characteristic of the philosopher-scholar's public use of reason effectively extended to the functionary's more circumscribed employments. A government clerk need not be understood to be constrained by the demand that he carry out policies formulated by someone else so long as he feels himself free to go home at the end of the day and think through the wisdom of those policies, or imagines that, at some point in the future, he might himself become a policymaker. Only, that is, when the constraints of private reason are understood as a deliberate choice, an exercise of freedom rather than the effect of compulsion, can such reason both testify to the disinterest of the subject whose goals are being fulfilled and at the same time operate as the expression of the surrogate's freedom.

Given that the structure of surrogacy represents an attempt to imagine the recognition of lawfulness as the grounds for the civil and ethical recognition of others, the solution of "What Is Enlightenment?" to the formal problem of surrogacy implies that the crucial locus of human likeness is less the relations among different individuals than it is the persistence of the essential qualities of a single subject through time, a likeness sustained across that individual's successive inhabitations of public and private roles. Where Kant is able, in that essay, to finesse the question of the proper relation between first and third persons, between subjects and surrogates, by rendering the precise nature of the links rhetorically ambiguous, reading his much more explicit discussion of surrogacy through the prism of the passages involving anatomical medicine allows us to see an aspect of his conception of human lawfulness that might otherwise go unnoticed. Insofar as an ethical republicanism is one in which all conceivable forms of reason, both public and private, can be enacted in turn by the same subject, such a subject must be supposed to be capable of living forever. Kant's discussion of surrogacy makes apparent, in other words, that human mortality is not simply bracketed but must be actively suppressed by Kant's conception of lawfulness.[26] It goes beyond a need not to engage the fact that humans die. In order to embrace the logic of an ethical republicanism in which the same individual can enact all the possible positions of subject and surrogate, Kant must posit that humans live eternally.

Moreover, insofar as it suggests that the problems of republican surrogacy associated with institutions might be averted by conceiving of the exercise of public and private forms of reason not as positions inhabited by different people but instead as roles serially inhabited (and thus freely chosen) by a single individual, Kant's writing on surrogacy would seem implicitly to install the body in the place of institutions of state. In this account, it is not institutions but the bodies of the individual subjects that organize and regulate the relations among freely reasoning philosophers who conceive an end and the surrogates who bring such an end about. Such bodies both identify the enactments of public and private reason as serial iterations of a single subject and assure that those enactments remain expressions of freedom by remaining unpredictable to both the subject and those outside that subject. A body thus conceived secures the subject's freedom to choose to think in a mode befitting a philosopher or a functionary only so long as its workings remain partly opaque to the subject as well as to those outside. The impossibility of knowing precisely how one's body comes to do what one directs it to do offers evidence in the present for the possibility that one might choose to act differently in the future, that one might choose to think (and perhaps act) as a surrogate rather than as a citizen. Insofar as such a body never dies, however, it ought to be understood less as the actual material body of an individual than as the construct that is anatomical medicine's standardized body, the likeness of living and dead bodies that itself need never die or change. Since the body that undergirds the movement between public and private reason is not asked to offer evidence of anything more particular than its eternally ongoing identity with itself, it is capable of escaping the incoherences attending the legibility and treatment of disease in the anatomical body.

Or so it would seem. While Kant's narration of his own efforts to think lawfully over the course of his own dying suggests his belated recognition of the way in which his critical philosophy presumes that his subjects live forever, his account of his dying is equally valuable for the way in which it helps illuminate what is *not* addressed in the discussion of revolution and republicanism in the second essay of the *Conflict*. It is this set of suppressions, I want to argue, that allows us to see the ethical limitations of an institutional organization of surrogacy that depends upon the presumption of the eternal life of its citizens.

As we recall, Kant argued that revolution provides the context for understanding the likeness of humans as a collective social practice and not just an account of identity. Revolution offers this revelation because it is a moment in which intention, interest, and outcome bear an especially tenuous connection to one another. Only so long as those who conceive of a future end are not, in an era of revolution, in any way assured of the authority to bring such ends about can the relation between the moment of framing a future end and the actual condition arrived at be understood to reveal the lawful qualities of the human rather than the fleeting interests of the few. When Kant suggests that revolution provides the context for discerning the disinterest of thinking because it affords "spectators . . . in this game of great revolution" the opportunity for expressing "universal yet disinterested sympathy for the players on one side against those on the other" (153), he implicitly defines disinterest as a relation to an unknown future outcome. I would argue, however, that Kant's notion of revolutionary history is haunted not only by the obvious if unnamed referent of the French Revolution, but by this referent's unnamable specter—the Terror. The Terror must be suppressed, that is, because it names not only the collapse of a specific political process of transformation, but also the abandonment of political process as a relation to a future goal, the abandonment of future-directedness as the measure of disinterest. Whereas Kant imagined that political subjects might demonstrate their disinterest by cleaving fervently to a particular political position while contenting themselves with allowing others to realize that position, the threat posed by the Terror is precisely that people will be punished, their bodies will be made vulnerable, by the very fact of having allied themselves with one position, faction, or party as opposed to another. If treating the relations of republican citizenship and surrogacy as if they are serial iterations of a single subject who cannot die would seem to circumvent the problems associated with acting at the behest of other people, what this body cannot do is underwrite a disinterest measured and adjudicated in the present. In this regard, Kant's late discovery that the lawful subject of his critical philosophy is a subject who cannot die matters because it reveals his system's commitment to a disinterest, a lawfulness, that is measured as a relation to a future moment. In the context of the Terror, the costs of such a commitment become clear: if a mob displeased with a certain subject's expressed but not-acted-upon political position determines to exact punishment for that position, then it is not disinterest but rather the most stark and unmediated form of *interest* for that subject to hope that some surrogate will be elected to receive the punishment that is being meted out. When the choice is between my pain and yours, now, the subject with a body is deeply—and superficially—interested.

Autopsy's Gerontological Critique

I have been arguing that the Terror disrupts, and in disrupting effectively reveals, the essentially futural measure of disinterest. Only so long as citizen-subjects inhabit bodies that register these subjects' continuity over time can a willingness to be the instrument for achieving political goals conceived by someone else be a sign of both the disinterestedness of those goals and those citizen-subjects' own political freedom. But because a futural measure of disinterest is made apparent around bodies that are simultaneously vulnerable and opaque in the present, the challenge posed to Kant's critical method by the Terror is not only ethical but epistemological as well: the challenge wrought to Kantian understanding, that is, makes itself apparent in the form of an ethical crisis. The vulnerability of actual bodies in the present limits the degree to which the general structure of bodily legibility—a present opacity tied to the promise of future legibility—can operate to undergird disinterest. Such vulnerability highlights the way in which Kantian lawfulness presumes, not a timeless, but rather a future existence of subject and object alike.

This founding presumption, revealed, goes a long way toward answering the question with which my examination of Kant began: What can Kant's critical philosophy tell us about subjects and objects that by their very nature must die? Inasmuch as this philosophy functions as an ethics predicated upon a notion of disinterest that is always futural and thus dependent upon the concept of a lawful subject who lives forever, the answer is clearly, nothing at all. If I cannot die, I must do whatever it takes to assure that I do not—even if it means choosing me over you, choosing one exemplary, lawful humanness over another, at the point of a bayonet.

But if admitting the Terror to our calculus makes apparent the incapacity of citizen-subjects' actual bodies to ensure those subjects' function as both exemplars and mechanisms of political disinterest, it also serves to point up the degree to which Kant's ethics depends on something very much like the not-quite-material "standardized body" of anatomical medicine. Such a concept of the body, at once announcing its lawfulness and incapable of dying, describes precisely what Kant envisions when he imagines that subject citizens acting by way of and as surrogates to bring about their rationally conceived political goals might do away with political institutions. Citizen-subjects and their surrogates must be at once formally identical to one another and distinct, in the same way that the sick body of the patient and the autopsied dead body brought into relation by the paradigm of anatomical medicine must be identical to one another and distinct. It is only because citizen-subjects and surrogates are understood to be identical to one another that the citizens' employment of the surrogates to bring about the citizens' own goals doesn't count as instrumentalization. It is only because citizen-subjects and surrogates are understood to be different from one another that their juxtaposition can be made to matter by standing as evidence of the disinterestedness of the political ends. Similarly, it is only because a patient's sick body is understood to be identical to a dead body that an autopsy can reveal something about the patient's unseen interior. It is only because sick bodies and dead bodies are understood to be different from one another—sick bodies are not yet dead—that their juxtaposition can be made to matter by preventing the sick body from being dead. And if such Kantian subjects must inhabit the not-quite-real standardized body of anatomical medicine, it therefore follows that the complex epistemological questions that clustered around the standardized anatomical body as it established itself as the new paradigm of medical knowledge over the course of the late eighteenth and early nineteenth centuries might reveal important things about Kant's own work. The process of dying particularly troubled claims for the anatomical body's standardness. Because skin functions as the surface on which symptoms might appear, because it is the structure that makes interiors of bodies inaccessible to direct observation, and finally because it is the sign by which the standardness or lawfulness of the body becomes instantaneously perceptible, uncertainty over how the body's alterations should be read tended to manifest itself in the form of debates surrounding the legibility of the skin.

In order to show the ways in which Kant's development of a skin-based notion of race might be seen as an attempt to resolve fundamental tensions surrounding the relations of lawfulness and change within his work, I want to take a few moments to examine the ways in which the tension between anatomical medicine's diagnostic and therapeutic claims structured the early and more recent histories of the profession. The tension becomes most apparent, we shall see, in the checkered disciplinary history of the medical subspecialty that takes the process of dying as its explicit object of knowledge—gerontology. But the question of the place of the dying process within anatomical medical authority also gets posed by way of a series of local skirmishes over when and how in the movement from being sick to being dead patient's bodies become legible, and how dying might or might not interfere with such legibility. It is with these skirmishes I will begin.

Sawday's cultural history of autopsy leads us to key the supplantation of humoral medicine to the transformation of autopsy from a technique of punishment to a mode of scientific investigation. But not surprisingly, both the process by which the physician's observations came to displace the authority of the patient's testimony regarding her own symptoms and the process by which autopsy came to be understood as a central diagnostic technique in a generalized practice of clinical observation depended upon the emergence of a variety of scientific techniques for gaining limited access to patients' interiors. Access would offer evidence, it was hoped, to reinforce the findings uncovered by autopsy. As early as 1761, the Viennese physician Leopold Auenbrugger articulated his doubts about the reliability of patient testimony, which he found frustratingly inconsistent. Neither the accounts of symptoms provided by patients nor the external signs of illness offered evidence by which various types of diseases might be differentiated from one another. Auenbrugger argued that the sounds he elicited from the body by means of his own method of tapping the body cavity and listening to its quality of resonance provided a much more reliable index of malfunction.[27]

Even when autopsies were understood to generate qualitatively new kinds of information, many opponents of the practice maintained that it was at best useless and at worse deleterious to the goals of clinical observation. While Thomas Sydenham was among the first physicians to synthesize case histories of individual patients into descriptions of the typical course of given diseases and can thus be understood as pioneering the principle of the standardized body that underwrites anatomical medicine, he was nonetheless a fierce and vocal opponent of autopsies. Anatomical investigation, he argued, diverted physicians' attention "from history and the advantage of diligent observation of these diseases, of their beginning, progress and ways of cure."[28] So long as the science of autopsy presumed the identity of sick body and dead body, the process by which a sick body comes to be dead—the process of dying—must be analytically excluded. Accordingly, critics of autopsies rely upon this analytical opacity to argue that most anatomical defects discovered during autopsies were the natural results of decomposition after death or were the effects of the treatments administered to mitigate the illness. Even advocates of the practice worried that the lesions made visible by autopsy might represent the effects rather than the cause of death, evidence of decomposition rather than the standardness of the body. Paul-Joseph Barthez (1734–1806), who assumed a chair on the medical faculty at Montpellier in 1760, conceded autopsy's practical limitations: "Practical anatomy is useful, but it has many inconveniences. Dissecting bodies only reveals the end point of the effects of the disease, and does not permit us to know the first lesions that it has produced. Indeed, often, it does not let us know the end point."[29] Even as late as 1802, four years after the passage of a 1798 law swept away the last vestiges of the religious prohibition against autopsy by mandating that corpses be made widely available, Guillaume Dupuytren, recently appointed "chef des travaux anatomiques," cautioned the assembled members of the École de Médecine against extending the explanatory claims of pathological anatomy without warrant: "Avoid attempting to assign the proximate cause of death; the causes of certain lesions of organs may be expected to be different from the primary disease process."[30] For someone like Barthez, the constitutive paradox of anatomical medicine meant that therapeutics could at best be "a corpus of rationalized empirical knowledge." In his view, although the logic of anatomical evidence dictated the impossibility of knowing how a remedy worked, physicians might nonetheless build a store of case histories that would allow them to predict the probability of a specific treatment's success or failure.[31] However much the epistemology of anatomical medicine in this period rests upon a body standardized by the copresence of sick and dead bodies, the process by which the former becomes the latter—dying itself—cannot, within an anatomical logic, be standardized.

A recent history of medicine has suggested that the effects of this fundamental theoretical incoherence have continued to make themselves felt in the uneven history of the development of medical specializations, specifically, in the divergent histories of pediatrics and gerontology. We recall that in the third essay of the *Conflict*, Kant frames his narration of his intellectual decline, his sudden incapacity to constitute a temporality of logical sequence, by means of a strikingly gloomy conclusion: "The result of [my catarrh in the head] was that I felt disorganized—or at least weakened and dulled—in my intellectual work; and since this ailment has attached itself to the natural weaknesses of my old age, it will end only with life itself" (205). Kant evokes anatomical medicine's therapeutic paradox in a phrase: once the process by which a disease unfolds becomes the focus of analysis, the course of a disease can no longer be distinguished from the senescence of an individual life. If the notion of a standardized body requires the bracketing of the process of dying, Kant makes clear why this exclusion is so fundamental: the changefulness of dying threatens to render all embodied subjects irreducibly particular and in so doing to make incoherent any effort to differentiate between the normal and the pathological. Both pediatrics and gerontology delimit their areas of expertise in terms of developmental (physiological) states. Consequently, both specialties would seem to evoke the paradox I have been outlining, insofar as they lay claim to a general anatomical medical authority predicated upon the absolute distinction between the pathology that is disease and normal physiological development while at the same time carving out a portion of expertise regarding pathologies in terms of physiological categories. But David Armstrong has shown that, while pediatrics successfully established departments in all British medical schools, a recognized place in the curriculum, and separate higher examinations, "the very idea of geriatrics remain[s] an essentially contested concept."[32]

This historical discrepancy, I want to suggest following Armstrong's analysis, is largely the consequence of the way in which the process of dying that gerontology effectively stakes out as its area of expertise exists in fundamental tension with the structure of authority of anatomical medicine. While both pediatrics and gerontology seek to synthesize seemingly mutually exclusive paradigms, the two specializations do not function entirely analogously. I argued earlier that the concept of the standardized body that underwrites anatomical medicine must of necessity exclude the process of dying since the autopsied organs can only be presumed to reveal the state of the live patient's inaccessible interior so long as the process of dying by which the diseased organs become the dead organs is understood to be evidentiarily irrelevant. In Armstrong's account, what makes gerontology particularly problematic is the difficulty entailed in distinguishing between the "normal" physiological process of aging and dying and the pathological advance of disease. The specific nature of the relationship between the two processes is opaque insofar as both inevitably end in death. That is, the narrative of decline as a natural and inevitable period in the physiological profile of a life undermines the authority of anatomical medicine, with its emphasis on a notion of pathology, understood as a deviation from a not-quite-embodied standard body. The physiological and the pathological represent conflicting theoretical constructs to account for a single set of bodily changes.[33]

While pediatric medicine likewise begins by confounding mutually exclusive explanatory models—is bedwetting evidence of a bladder disorder or a yet unachieved state of physiological maturity?—the trajectory of pediatric development functions to pry apart the physiological and the pathological. Recall Kant's lament: "Since [my] ailment has attached itself to the natural weaknesses of my old age, it will end only with life itself." The difference between death caused by disease and death that is the consequence of "old age" turns out to be no material difference at all. By contrast, though the child who wets her bed because of a misshapen bladder might, at age three, be indistinguishable from the child who wets her bed because she hasn't yet learned how not to, there is little chance that those two children will be equally indistinguishable at the age of six. In the pediatric model, the fact that the end point of the trajectory is not predictable in advance—the child may learn to sleep through the night or she may remain plagued by the symptoms of her misshapen bladder—means that only that point of measurement need be taken into account in deciding which explanatory model, the physiological or the pathological, accurately characterizes the situation at hand. While the physiological and the pathological might begin by looking alike within the pediatric context, the outcome retrospectively sloughs off the explanatory model that turns out to have been inappropriate. With the geriatric narrative, by contrast, the fact that both the physiological and the pathological trajectories produce the identical outcome (death) means that the process by which the outcome is arrived at never becomes irrelevant, even as it is occluded in the constitution of the standardized body upon which the authority of anatomical medicine rests. With the geriatric narrative we get endless distinction without difference, the proliferation of entirely particular deathward courses whose particularity is part and parcel of both their resistance to analysis and their resistance to being checked.

Effectively, then, we can understand the pediatric and the geriatric to constitute two competing readings of the structure of anatomical knowledge. Inasmuch as the geriatric brings the process of dying to the center of its analytical purview, it makes clear the way in which the anatomical physician's knowledge, synthesized out of the limits of self-knowledge of both skin-enfolded patient and implacable corpse, renders disease visible at the cost of making it neither caused nor curable. The pediatric, by contrast, presents the process by which anatomical knowledge is made knowledge, the steps by which the changes of the body happen as a datum that can, as a matter of course, be cast off, made altogether irrelevant to what doctors can know and what patients can be told.

But what if pediatrics were understood not simply to be avoiding the outright contradiction between physiological and pathological notions of dying? What if we were to understand the early and untroubled incorporation of the pediatric specialization into modern medical practice to stand as evidence of positive work that pediatrics might be accomplishing in shoring up the authority of anatomical medicine against its fundamental theoretical incoherences, which threaten to leave both the process of dying and the possibility of healing entirely outside anatomical medicine's analytical purview? Where gerontology has established only tenuous and sporadic recognition as a medical specialty as a consequence of the way it presents two irreconcilable constructions of the evidence of dying, pediatrics has become ensconced within anatomical medicine, I believe, precisely because it details a practice by which physiological and pathological accounts of the body might be distinguished and rendered noncontradictory. Pediatric medicine provides a methodology by which the moment of determination of an unpredictable outcome—the child has a bladder dysfunction (disease/pathology) or the child has grown out of her bedwetting (physiology/development)—also provides the occasion for erasing the failed account. Once the pediatrician discovers the child to have been suffering from a bladder disorder rather than a developmental lag (or vice versa), not only is the alternative explanation discarded, but even more significantly, the casting off of alternatives becomes a way of casting off causation as a process altogether. Always conceived in present-perfect aspect (children are discovered "to *have been* suffering"), pediatric medicine constitutes a practice by which contingency (causation) is made to appear as if it can be recognized and resolved in a single instant in the present. To the extent to which the uneasy evocation of the specter of the Terror we find in the second *Conflict* essay bespeaks the present and immediate threat posed by an unpredictable and marauding mob on the very anatomical body whose opacity promises to underwrite the Kantian subject's disinterest, the pediatric method becomes the articulation of a political fantasy by which embodied subjects can be created anew in all their contingent vulnerability and can also be spared at every instant.

In essence, then, pediatrics articulates the desire for a version of development, causation—or in the conceptual language of the third essay in the *Conflict*, the time of the life span—that is begun and completed in an instant, a version of contingency that can simultaneously both underwrite the anatomical body's operation as the ground of disinterest and demonstrate that body to have been spared the vulnerability attendant upon contingency. The fantasy at the heart of the critical method would seem to be the notion that philosophical understanding, insofar as it allows subjects to see the lawfulness of the material world and renders them lawful by virtue of having done so, becomes the practice by which people can experience themselves making death irrelevant, as if by escape, over and over again. But just as the suppression of the Terror within Kant's narrative makes apparent the ways in which his critical method, dependent on a wholly futural index of likeness, must presume a subject capable of living eternally, the philosophy that names the pleasure of experiencing oneself as at once caused, intended, and perpetually invulnerable to the contingencies of the external world by virtue of the fact of one's humanity turns out to be a specifically pediatric fantasy. This is a fantasy in which the particularity of one's condition inevitably gives way to an unbounded futurity of likeness, a transcendental maturity forever before one. And just as the pediatric can be seen to codify, in the figure of professional practice, a kind of forgetting that would render growing up and getting well one and the same, so too does critical philosophy's promise of a perpetual birth into standardness turn on forgetting the utter predictability of getting old.

At its most untroubled, anatomical medicine would seem to promise that the inescapability of a sick body's ultimate future might be circumvented by the promise of the eternal life of existence as a lawful standard. This logic provides a template by which the futural measure of Kantian disinterest, and hence of the Kantian subject's lawfulness, can be made immediately and endlessly present. I suggest that we read Kant's racialization of the skin as a mighty—and ultimately perilous—realization of this fantasy by transforming skin from the structure that organizes the diachronicity of anatomical medical knowledge into an object of knowledge itself. The skin is crucial as much for the ways in which it structures the temporality by which knowledge is created and apprehended as for the ways in which it creates the possibility of perceiving, by way of the senses, relations of likeness, of standardness. In order to understand the local contexts through which a racialized notion of skin came to seem a solution to these instabilities within various forms of Enlightenment universalism, I want briefly to examine, first, Kant's own accounting of the relation between race and critical philosophy and, second, some debates concerning the development of contemporary medical technologies designed to make patients' interiors visible while they were alive.

Beyond the Humors: Kant's Race

Published in 1788, "On the Use of Teleological Principles in Philosophy" is historically revelatory about race precisely to the degree that it approaches its topic sidelong.[34] For the Kant of this essay, race matters particularly because it is not a topic of interest in and of itself, that is, because it emerges as a solution to a philosophical problem that seems on the face of it to have little to do with the category. Indeed, Kant opens the piece by explicitly invoking the difficulty of reconciling knowledge of specific causes and knowledge of the world, a difficulty that, I have been arguing, dogs his critical philosophy throughout:

> If we understand by *nature* the sum total of everything that exists determinately according to laws and by *world* (as nature properly so-called) these things together with their supreme cause, we can attempt to investigate nature following two different methods. The first of these methods is called *physics*, the second *metaphysics*. The method of physics is *theoretical* and employs only such purposes as can be known to us through experience. By contrast, the method of metaphysics is *teleological* and can employ only a purpose established by pure reason for its end. (37)

While we come to know nature theoretically—that is, by inductively experiencing the regularity of various impressions produced by nature's discrete elements—we can only assemble these discrete elements of nature into a unitary "world" by way of "metaphysics," or "teleology." To know something teleologically, we recall, is to assert the necessary existence of some cause—of causation in general—from the fact that we as unitary subjects can have thoughts about a unitary world. As Kant goes on to remind us a few lines later, the sorts of causation we discover theoretically and teleologically remain fundamentally distinct from one another: "No appeal to teleology or practical purposiveness can make up for the deficiencies of theory. We always remain ignorant about efficient causes even when we are able to make plausible the appropriateness of our assumption by appealing to final causes, be they from nature or from our will" (37). In other words, theory or induction can never give us definitive knowledge about specific or "efficient" causes, for we can never know for certain that the next example we encounter of an object or impression, or the next iteration of the actions of an object we have already encountered, will not be different or behave differently from those we have encountered before. And teleological knowledge is of no help in shoring up theory's epistemic vulnerabilities. The fact that we can assemble the elements of nature into a knowable world—we know ourselves as subjects who experience over time because we understand the various elements we encounter as predictably behaving parts of a unitary whole, and vice versa—only allows us to conclude that both the world and we unitary subjects have been caused, not that we have been caused by some specifically knowable mechanism. We can know that we and the world have been caused, just not how. And in both its structural unity—its status as a system of mutually interconnected parts—and the elusiveness of its specific mechanisms of causation, Kant's world resembles nothing so much as an anatomical body: "Now the concept of an organized being is the concept of a material being possible only through the relation of all that which is contained in it existing reciprocally as ends and means (as, in fact, every anatomist, as physiologist, also presumes when considering such beings)" (51).

It is precisely this distinction between theory and teleology, or nature and world, Kant suggests, that differentiates his account of human difference from that of the humorally inspired conception of Georg Forster, the politician-anthropologist and Kant critic. Here the apparently disparate inquiries of Kant's essay begin to edge toward one another: race suddenly emerges, in Kant's account, as an attempt to bridge the two forms of causation described by theory and teleology. Race is not a thing to be discovered in the world so much as a way of thinking about what has taken place in the world, an account of how the world as we know it has come to be caused:

> What is a *race*? The word certainly does not belong in a systematic description of nature, so presumably the thing itself is nowhere to be found in nature. However the *concept* which this expression designates is well established in the reason of every observer of nature who supposes a conjunction of

> causes placed originally in the line of descent of the genus itself in order to account for a self-transmitted peculiarity that appears in different interbreeding animals but which does not lie in the concept of the genus. The fact that the word race does not occur in the description of nature (but instead, in its place, the word *variety*) cannot keep an observer of nature from finding it necessary from the viewpoint of natural history. (40)

In Kant's telling, Forster's recent critique of him, an October 1786 piece in the *Teutschen Merkur*, stems from the humoralist's failure to apprehend the force of the distinction between "natural description" (an essentially theoretical account of human difference) and Kant's own "natural history" (an essentially teleological account).[35] In positing forms of human "variety" that are the consequences of the particular conditions of the environment at a given moment, Forster the humoralist offers "natural description," multiple and discrete comings-into-being of qualities that need not reproduce themselves. Forster's natural description cannot offer evidence of a singular, unitary humanity—phlegmatic individuals are the products of the cool, damp north, while the sanguine hail from the warm and moist equatorial regions—and it requires the presence of direct witnessing to be generated, witnessing that proves the existence of a given phenomenon at that moment only. (Because the qualities found within an individual need not be reproduced in the next generation or even sustained over a lifetime, the existence of such qualities can only be testified to by direct witnessing.) By contrast, Kant argues, natural history is concerned "with investigating the relation between certain present properties of the things of nature and their causes in an earlier time in accordance with causal laws that we do not invent but rather derive from the forces of nature as they present themselves to us, pursued back, however, only so far as permitted by analogy" (39). The alternative logic of natural history within which Kant seeks to locate race is one in which a subject need not be present to witness causal sequences since it understands prior causes to be discernible in the evidence of present relations of difference.

I suggest that in isolating skin color as the foundation of his teleological account of the human—by focusing on this difference as the primary evidence of causation—Kant does not simply affirm the tenets of his critical philosophy or, for that matter, of the anatomical medicine he identifies as that philosophy's analogy and implicit cause. Rather, he offers skin-based race as a means of closing the gap between the teleological and the theoretical and, in so doing, of making the specific mechanisms of causation both legible and legible in an instant. Kant builds his case against

Forster's humoralism and in support of his own idiosyncratic narrative of the origin of differences in skin color by pointing out Forster's failure to account for the particular ways in which populations with different skin tones are geographically arrayed. Forster's supposition "that the skin color of all these peoples—from southern Europe to the tip of Africa—can be proportionately calibrated to the climate of the land, changing from brown to black and back again to brown" is belied by the fact "that one does not find the same supposed gradations of skin color among the peoples living on the west coast of Africa, where nature instead makes a sudden jump from the olive-skinned Arabs or Mauritanians to the blackest Negroes in Senegal without going first through the intermediate rung represented by the Kassernians" (45). The failure of Forster's humoral mechanism to square with the empirical facts on the ground matters because the practical difficulties of interpreting such dermatological evidence demonstrate a fundamental theoretical misapprehension. In Kant's view, Forster's efforts at correlating skin color with locale in order to show how skin color is a direct effect of environmental forces are inevitably stymied by the difficulty of distinguishing the inherited elements of skin tone from those contingently produced by exposure to the sun. Even more significant than the mere fact of the illegibility of skin within Forster's humoral system is the fundamental theoretical incoherence such illegibility manifests. What the eighteenth century proliferation of global exploration, colonial and otherwise, has made apparent is that individuals' skin color does not always correlate straightforwardly with their geographical locales. The fact that one's skin color is as likely to resemble that of one's parents as it is that of the people living in the same general area suggests, in Kant's analysis, that "the fitness of human beings to their mother lands could not coexist with their dispersion over the face of the earth" (46). Why is it, Kant asks of Forster, that the same Providence whose wisdom manifested itself in locating people whose "predisposition makes them suited for this or that climate" is too "short-sighted" to anticipate the possibility of a "second transplanting"? Forster's mistake, Kant avers, is in understanding the "seeds" that announce the workings of divine intentionality to mark a fitness for only one climate. In Kant's view, the seeds are caused by God insofar as they mark a "complete original predisposition . . . still undivided for all future deviate forms," an individual "(potentially) fitted for all climates" (47).

Of course it is tempting to see Kant's quibble with Forster over the nature of divine seeds as signaling his remoteness from, rather than his engagement with, anything resembling the paradigms of modern race or medicine, his analogy elsewhere in the essay notwithstanding. But if Kant's terminology seems resolutely and definitively nontechnical, both his introduction of "seeds" here—the same term he used to name the inaccessible interiorized disease in *The Conflict of the Faculties*—and his attempt to resolve many of the questions of temporality and contingency that animate the final two essays of the *Conflict* suggest that the racial body he conceptualizes, in all its varied skin tones, in many important respects resembles the body conceptualized by anatomical medicine. For Kant, the seeds that manifest themselves in different skin tones demonstrate the lawfulness of humans inasmuch as they manifest the human potential to be various—their common "potential [to be] fitted for all climates": "The variety among human beings even from the same race was in all probability inscribed just so purposively in the original line of descent in order to establish—and, in successive generations, to develop—the greatest diversity for the sake of infinitely diverse purposes, just as the difference among races establishes fewer but more essential purposes" (47).

But while differences in skin tone announce the essential likeness of humans insofar as that standardness names the capacity of humans to direct their activities to a potentially infinite variety of ends, Kant insists that such variety can only manifest the purposiveness and singularity of intention so long as the contingency bodied forth in the activation of any particular form of the infinitely potential possibilities is confined to the past. If "the development of these predispositions [existing *in potentia* in the seeds] conforms to the places" in which subjects contingently happen to find themselves, "all this is understood . . . to have happened only in the earliest times and to have lasted long enough (for a gradual populating of the earth) in order, first and foremost, to provide a people having a permanent place to live the requisite influence of climate and land needed for the development of those predispositions fitted to this place" (47).

As we have seen, a persistent, even constitutive challenge facing Kant's critical method is how to reliably distinguish the likeness or lawfulness born of the condition of having been caused or intended from the merely descriptive contingency that identifies objects or events as having taken place, the descriptiveness that is, for Kant, mere accident. Phenomena are only recognizable as being elements of a unitary, lawbound world so long as those phenomena remain stable. Their stability demonstrates that they have been caused or intended, that their qualities serve a governing idea or purpose. Qualities that don't meet these standards are understood to be contingent, accidental. Where the pages of a book are part of its essential purpose, the wetness of a book that has fallen into a puddle is not part of that book's essential, lawful qualities and is thus a way in which it is likely to be different from other books. Where the public/private distinction Kant presents in "What Is Enlightenment?" seems to imply that the body, in its opacity to the living philosophical subject who inhabits it, offers itself as a useful alternative to republican state institutions, the capacity of such a body to organize and render discernible disinterest is predicated upon the presumption that disinterest can be measured as a future effect. This presumption effectively locates all contingency in the past: while the subject is understood as an effect of prior causes, the notion that the disinterest of this subject's ends can be measured in the future depends on the guarantee—the fundamental noncontingency—of that subject's future existence. The disinterested body's presumptive futurity is registered negatively, I have suggested, in the form of Kant's excising of the Terror, an excision that cloaks the way in which the body's vulnerability to (contingent) pain and injury in the present limits its usefulness as a foundation of disinterested lawfulness.

Viewed as a gloss on the standardized body, Kant's theory of seeds would seem to provide a solution to the fundamental tension between the diagnostic and therapeutic claims of anatomical medicine. The notion of "seeds" that Kant uses to name a universal likeness of human bodies not immediately legible correlates with the inaccessible but standard interior of the anatomical medical body. But where anatomical medicine's standardized body involves a comparison of sick and dead bodies that requires overlooking the ways in which those bodies differ from one another—the process of dying—Kant's various skin colors simultaneously make manifest the standardized universal lawfulness of the body and signal the contingent fact of a particular migration having taken place. Kant's racialized skin thus superimposes the likeness of the body to other bodies and the changeful, contingent particular history as qualities of a single seamless sign.[36] By creating such a sign, Kant's skin provides a framework for resolving the fundamental tension that haunts anatomical medicine's diagnostic authority, the tension between the standardness of bodily interiors and the changefulness of a contingent individual life span. Racialized skin makes causation—the condition of having been made with the capacity to inhabit any place and do anything—perceptible in an instant: having been endowed with the potential to do anything anywhere, this particular individual has done this here.[37] In this way, skin absorbs the threat posed to Kant's critical method by the fact—indeed, the inevitability—of his dying: the threat that lawfulness, standardization, might not render insignificant the contingency of change, the press of historicity, but instead might turn out to be inextricable from such changefulness. Where the critical philosophy has been haunted throughout by its inability to indicate particular mechanisms of causation and therefore to distinguish between the different causations that constitute lawful change, Kant's racial skin makes lawful change apprehensible by signaling particular causation—this person migrated from here—in an instant. It is this instantaneousness of perceptibility that gives this particular causation the quality of universality: this particular skin color is like everyone else's particular skin color in showing all people to have migrated from somewhere.[38] In creating this instantaneous mark of particular change—in making the lawful change apprehensible—Kant makes skin the bulwark against the threat that the freedom he understands to be the birthright of the human might diffuse itself into an irreducibly particular materiality, illegibly implacable stuff.

So where Nancy Stepan offers a conception of the Enlightenment as a fundamentally hypocritical moment in which a range of European cultures theorize universalism while actively institutionalizing the most egregious forms of inequality, and where George Frederickson presents an account in which race is theorized as an alibi for these cultures' failure to practice their professed commitments to universal equality, in the version of the Enlightenment whose contours follow the intersecting lines of Kant's critical philosophy and anatomical medicine, we discover another relation entirely in the new primacy of racialized skin. As we have seen, the subjects who come to recognize the lawfulness of the material world and in so doing provide the grounds for a polity organized around the principles of equality are both capable of a certain kind of rationality and presumed, if not always explicitly, to exercise their rationality from within bodies that are fundamentally like other people's bodies. But if it is the likeness of bodies that allows Kant to imagine that the fairness of a given political program might be measured by the possibility of assigning surrogates to enact it without violating those surrogates' own freedom and lawfulness, the bodies capable of undergirding this freedom and equality must be impervious to alteration: un-aging, invulnerable to sickness or injury, incapable of dying. Kant manages this problem of embodied subjectivity by making the universal likeness of bodies something that might be experienced instantaneously, by way of the immediately perceptible mark of skin color. But it is the demand that universalism be not simply a political aspiration but something that might be *experienced* that transmutes the idea of likeness into the experience of difference: likeness, known in a particular time and place, can only go so far. In this regard, racial difference turns out to be less a betrayal of Enlightenment universalism than a testament to its fragility, the difficulty of knowing sameness from within bodies that are themselves changing, haltingly and unpredictably, tumbling toward death.

The Instant of the Skin

My reading of Kant has explored the ways in which his category of race operates to render lawful change an object of understanding by signaling in an instant the existence of change that has occurred in and is confined to the past. I have intimated that the contemporary history of medicine might offer an account of why Kant seized upon skin color in particular as the sign that announces the particular form of changeful standardness that is race. To understand the function of skin in this period is to see how skin came to be newly legible, while the evolution of this legibility is the story of the ways in which racial perception became imbricated within systems of knowing and perceiving that seemingly have little to do with race. In this spirit, I want to conclude by examining skin's emerging status as a visible organ. This notion of a visible organ is paradoxical within an anatomical logic, since the standardized body and the structure of anatomical medical knowledge founded on that body rested upon the premise that the particular bodily organs in which diseases originated were not available to direct observation. But I want to suggest that this paradoxical status was what made the skin an especially useful site for overcoming the contradictions between medicine's diagnostic and therapeutic authority. As a visible organ, skin became a favorite structure upon which to develop and test a variety of emerging technologies of medical perception. Most of these technological instruments were designed to resolve the contradiction between anatomical medicine's diagnostic and therapeutic goals by offering methods for examining the interiors of bodies while patients were still alive.

We recall that even the staunchest proponents of autopsy were forced to acknowledge that its value for generating therapeutically useful knowledge was limited, both practically and theoretically. At best, the information about organic lesions uncovered by autopsy might be used retrospectively to test the efficacy of various treatments aimed at treating symptoms rather than disrupting the relation of cause and effect. While the practical constraints of autopsy were obvious—the conditions of patients' organs could not be known until they were dead—the history of the development of various technologies aimed at making live patients medically legible suggests that the theoretical restrictions underwriting anatomical knowledge operated to direct the nature of technological development. The physician-inventors who developed the earliest instruments for examining sick-but-not-yet-dead patients tended to focus on methods that kept the skin intact as a structuring principle of anatomical knowledge.[39] In introducing his new invention of the stethoscope to the world in 1816, Rene-Theophile Laennec did not merely produce a new instrument, but published a detailed treatise, *On Mediate Auscultation* (1819). Laennec's insistence that expert training was necessary to generate and interpret stethoscopic evidence functioned to keep intact an anatomical medical authority structure around an intact living body. Early discussions about the usefulness of the microscope and magnifying glass likewise tended to work around rather than attempt to breach the skin as a barrier to direct observation of the inner organs. This history is illuminating for our discussion because the arguments raised in opposition to the use of the microscope for diagnosing the causes of disease closely resembled the arguments mustered in opposition to autopsy. For the philosopher-physician John Locke and his physician friend Thomas Sydenham, whose unpublished 1668 manuscript "Anatomica" was initially conceived to be just one element of a comprehensive view of the state of clinical medicine, microscopy, like autopsy, represented an unwarranted effort to investigate the complex causes of disease, distracting from the need to develop treatments whose procedures could be evaluated empirically, via externally measurable trial and error:

> Now it is certaine and beyond controversy that nature performs all her operations on the body by parts so minute and insensible that I thinke noe body will ever hope or pretend, even by the assistance of glasses or any other invention, to come to a sight of them. For suppose any one shall have so sharp a knife and sight as to discover the secret and effective composure of any part could he make an occular demonstration that the pores of the parenchyma of the liver or kidneys were either round or square and that the parts of urin and gall separated in these parts were a size and fiture answerable to these pores. I ask how this would at all direct him in the cure either of the jaundice or stoppage of urin?[40]

Historians of medicine have long observed that the available microscopic technology could only find serious medical application once the emergence of an anatomical paradigm ontologized disease, turned it into a mechanism whose functioning could be localized, if not quite observed. But the fact that arguments already deployed against autopsy came to be mustered in the battle against the authorization of microscopic knowledge suggests that the usefulness of such knowledge was not fully revealed by the initial structuring insight of anatomical medicine—that the diseases plaguing patients' inaccessible interior organs might be seen in other people's autopsied organs.[41] Rather, the usefulness of microscopes and other technologies that provided access to the interiors of live patients became apparent only with the subsequent explorations of the paradox underwriting that anatomical structure—the notion that the physician's authority predicated upon a standardized body requires the exclusion of the process of dying and, with that exclusion, such authority necessarily forfeits any therapeutic claims.

While the development of technologies like the stethoscope and microscope was animated by a desire to address the theoretical and practical difficulties that follow from the inaccessibility of patients' interiors to direct observation, the power of these new instruments to extend anatomical physicians' observational ranges was typically not exercised on actual interiors. In the same spirit that led Laennec to develop the stethoscope as a means of gauging the state of health of patients' interior organs and yet restrict its use to trained physicians whose exclusive expert authority derived from the inaccessibility of those organs, the early users of the microscope and magnifying glass tended to ignore internal anatomical structures like blood and tissue in order to focus their attention on the skin. As Ann La Berge has convincingly demonstrated, the thriving microscopic medical community that emerged in Paris in the 1840s around the Hungarian émigré David Gruby was inspired largely by his efforts to employ the microscope to identify the parasites that caused common skin diseases, including thrush, ringworm, and "the itch."[42] Rather than indicating the irrelevance of the structural logic of anatomical medicine to the microscope's development, the focus on the skin indicates the particularity and intensity of its practitioners' engagement with anatomical medical authority, in all its contradictions. Early microscopy's almost exclusive focus on the skin marked the technology's attempt to solve the problem of knowing what is going on inside patients before they die, while keeping intact the anatomical physician's authority to diagnose, an authority that follows from keeping those interiors inaccessible to nonexpert observation and knowledge. As we shall see, the focus on skin makes possible this conciliation of anatomical medicine's contradictory aspects by constituting a subject that is always changing, being begun and completed, in ways not altogether legible to itself. This peculiar and complex epistemology of skin and microscopy's extension of perception provides the analytical context within which to make sense of the racial fantasy with which we began, that of dermatologist Robert Willan. By examining Willan's turn to magnification alongside his narrative of racial origins, we will be able to understand the problems of knowing subjects that get solved when skin becomes the bearer of racial meaning.

While microscopy would not be institutionalized as part of the training and practice of clinical anatomical medicine until the middle of the nineteenth century, in the 1809 *On Cutaneous Diseases*, Willan describes his use of a somewhat cruder instrument—a magnifying glass—in his efforts to discern the parasitic etiology of the skin ailments Gruby will turn his attention to in the 1840s. Willan's use of the magnifying glass to see and describe the skin ailments he so assiduously classifies barely registers, appearing less a deliberate diagnostic innovation than a discovery as accidental as his encounter with the tiny bugs he sees through its lens. But, as we shall see, the lack of deliberation with which Willan picks up the magnifying glass to examine his patient's skin turns out to be key to the technology's power to reorganize anatomical medicine's epistemological relations:

> In one case of the Prurigo senilis, I accidentally discovered, on the patient's skin and linen, a number of insects, so minute, and so quick in their motions, as not to be discernible without considerable attention. I at first took them for small Pediculi, but when viewed through a magnifier they appeared to belong to the genus Pulex, though not to any of the species described by Linnaeus. Although this patient had a wife and family, none of them were affected in a similar manner; nor could any of the insects be found upon them by the strictest examination. No general conclusion should be drawn from a solitary instance; the present case, however, tends to confirm the supposition that the Prurigo senilis, and Prurigo Formicans, may be generally owning to cutaneous insects. With a view to ascertain this point, I have since paid close attention to every case that occurred, but have not hitherto been successful in the research. (65)

The bugs and his own observational powers are equally objects of investigation here, and this is what allows Willan to imagine that his own process of observing might enfold within it a potentially infinite number of cases of bug-infested skin. The "considerable attention" he turns toward the bugs in his efforts to see them in spite of their quick movements marks out a subjective process by which a local and identifiable act of observation ("I at first took them for small Pediculi") is subsumed within an activity both agentless and decidedly less punctual ("but when viewed through a magnifier, they appeared . . ."). The multiple instances of *Prurigo senilis* he might have observed are incorporated into this impersonal process of microscopic attention, much as the temporal diffuseness that is the bugs' scurrying registers as the ongoing cause of the skin's visible irritation. Given this observational ambiguity, Willan feels simultaneously authorized and unjustified in generalizing his discovery, offering it as a standard account, the grounds of a "general conclusion." Without a pause to reconcile seemingly irreconcilable conclusions, he informs us both that "no general conclusion should be drawn from a solitary instance" and that "the present case tends to confirm the supposition that [these diseases] may be generally owing to cutaneous insects." The fact that he persists in maintaining such a conclusion even after his subsequent "close attention" fails to turn up confirmatory evidence suggests that it is as much the quality and capacity of his attention as the pathology of a disease at issue here.

In Willan's account, then, the objects being observed seem to produce the terms of their own discernibility, while the process of discernment in turn becomes the grounds upon which the observed phenomenon might or might not be generalized. The very speed of the darting insects renders them virtually indiscernible, commanding a mode of understanding so expansive that it seems to produce the rule in the single instance. Here we are presented with a version of induction in which instances accumulate so rapidly as to become as indiscernible as bugs. With the time between iterations accelerated to the speed of a scurrying insect on the skin, Willan generates a version of lawfulness in which empirical and critical ways of knowing come to seem continuous with one another. The accidental nature of Willan's discovery is crucial in this regard, as it is an inadvertent sighting of the tiny bugs that leads him to introduce into his examination the magnifier necessary to discern the tiny bugs; the bugs discover him just as surely as he sets out to discover them. In this way, Willan and the tiny insects become mutually and interchangeably subjects and objects of analysis, with the magnifier doubly mediating Willan's capacity to discern the bugs. He discovers the bugs crawling across the patient's skin and linen—and presumably causing the visible symptoms of the *Prurigo senilis*—and by the same process is led to discover the limits of his own visual acuity.

In some sense, we can read this account of magnification as an explicitation of Willan's more general taxonomical project. In this project, the division of diseases into categories does not simply extend to diseases of the skin the authority of natural history's method, but insists that the epistemology implied by the dermatological object be understood as reconfiguring a logic of natural history that would classify natural objects by placing them within unchanging categories. In the introduction to *On Cutaneous Diseases*, Willan sets out the principles of his systematizing effort, emphasizing in particular his commitment "to constitute general divisions or orders of the diseases, from *leading and peculiar circumstances in their appearance*; to arrange them into distinct genera; and to describe at large their specific forms, or varieties" (8). With this close interest in "leading . . . circumstances in their appearance," Willan would seem to be offering a principle by which to understand the practice of "considerable attention" he describes in the passage on magnification. The double valence of "appearance," thrown into relief by the diachronic "leading," bespeaks the analytical promise of a description of the way things look that is indistinguishable from the process by which this appearance comes into being—the process, that is, by which it makes its appearance. Because Willan does not simply seek to organize a set of identified, already named diseases, but instead to trace and describe the course of a disease as it moves from, say, an initial rash to suppurating tubercules to wheals, the taxonomizing process—how this disease appears different from another—often seems indistinguishable from a description of how the various stages of a single disease make their appearance. Indeed, in *On Cutaneous Diseases*, even Willan's fundamental divisions of disease types are often pressed into service as metaphors, as "scurf" becomes "scurf-like," part of the vocabulary available for rendering diseases recognizable.

The difficulty of using Willan's treatise as a diagnostic handbook lies in the fact that the moments that seem to invite categorization and diagnosis frequently turn out to be signs of a sufferer's affliction by an entirely different disease. But in the difficulty also lies the promise of the skin for resolving the tensions of anatomical medicine and Kant's critical method. Both systems of thought, we recall, are simultaneously constituted and afflicted by their incapacity to take account of lawful change. Willan's project constitutes the skin as a structure in a constant state of production, at once recognizable and constantly transmuted. In offering a narration of his discovery of cutaneous insects in which he uses a magnifying glass to know what he is already seeing and what he is not, Willan effectively relocates the structure of anatomical knowledge onto the surface of the skin. The revolutionary force of anatomical medicine lies in the notion that disease is located in a body's inaccessible interior organs made visible in other people's autopsies, and the political and philosophical promise of such a body, at least for Kant, lies in the notion that, simultaneously known and not known, it might provide material ground for a disinterested philosophical rationalism. Willan, glass in hand, at once knows and doesn't know, sees and doesn't see, the transformation of the seat of disease into tiny bugs scurrying across the skin. Inasmuch as the authority of anatomical medicine and the philosophical system constituted around this authority are compromised by the fact that they must suppress the body's changing and aging over time, Willan's technologically aided dermatology would seem to resolve the problems endemic to anatomical medicine's notion of a standardized body by making the causation of disease (bugs on skin) entirely present, discernible at every moment, even as it might be looked away from.

That Willan's narration does not actually describe a mechanism of causation, but rather infers it from the almost indiscernibly quick motion of the insects on the skin, does not in fact diminish the power of the magnified skin to accomplish the relocation of the standard. As the odd syntax of the beginning of his report attests, the body being standardized is as much the examining dermatologist's as it is—or is in complex relation to—the patient's whose skin is under diagnosis. Willan's magnifying glass constitutes the body as standard to itself by making it at once subject and object. The magnifying glass, which Willan comes to be using more by accident than by a deliberate act of will, seems to produce something resembling anatomical knowledge—in some sense, replacing the skin—by enabling those who use it to know and not know at once. But this version of partial knowledge, in pointed distinction from that of the anatomical physician, can take place within the knower's own body at a single instant because what becomes known is not simply the quality of the skin, or even the insects that disturb and make over that skin, but the limits of the knower's capacity to see.

But if this reading seems to suggest that the technology of the microscope or the magnifying glass functions by transmuting the difference between an infinitely various and changing material world into knowledge of an invariable self-difference,[43] Willan's narration offers a much more complex account. The passage we have been examining makes apparent that it is only because the surface of the skin examined through Willan's magnifying glass carries the history it does—only because, as the mediating structure of anatomical knowledge, it signals the transmutation of the unknowability of the body's interior into its standardization, its constancy—that the instrument trained upon the skin can stand in for the material world more generally. So where a historian of technology like Jonathan Crary might assume that something inherent in people's understanding of certain technologies as extensions of the natural capacities of the body allows those technologies to redefine the material world as a version of self-difference, both the generally documented importance of the skin for establishing the authority of the microscope in the 1830s and '40s and the particular details of Willan's narration make apparent that it is not simply the emergence of a set of perceptual instruments, but the use of those instruments in relation to the particular object of the skin, that imbues them with transformative force.

Willan offers a story in which the authority of the magnifying glass and the role of cutaneous insects in producing *Prurigo senilis* are established at the same time—or, more accurately, they are established in the oscillation between viewing with the aid of a magnifying glass the tiny insects scurrying across diseased skin and seeing nothing but diseased skin without such aid. One can only believe that tiny bugs are the cause of a rash on the skin when one looks through a magnifying glass and sees those bugs again and again, and one can only believe that a magnifying glass makes visible without distortion structures that actually exist and matter in the world rather than generating phantom images when one sees what one can see with the unaided eye—the surface of the skin—through a magnifying glass as well. Both these authorizings appear to necessitate repeated trials: the cutaneous insects can only be presumed to be the cause of the rash, rather than stray wanderers across the skin, when they are seen on the skin of *Prurigo senilis* suffers again and again, while the magnifying glass can only be seen to present distortion-free images when the microscopic bugs on the skin can be correlated with the skin rash that is visible to the naked eye. The necessity of the repetition would seem to mean that the two authorizations, dependent as each is on the preexisting authority of the other, cannot be established together.

But what is remarkable about Willan's narration is not only his ability to assure himself of the reliability of his magnifying glass at the same time he discovers tiny bugs to be the cause of a skin rash, but to do both things with a single trial. While he avers that "no general conclusion should be drawn from a solitary instance," he can still report that "the present case . . . tends to confirm the supposition that Prurigo senilis . . . may generally be owing to cutaneous insects." Willan is able to trust in his magnifying glass at the same time he is able to trust in his diagnosis. He is able to do both on the evidence of a single instance, I want to argue, because the skin in relation to which both the glass and the diagnosis are authorized is understood to signal, instantaneously and in itself, a condition of standardization. The magnifying glass is conceived as offering distortion-free images insofar as the skin it reveals can be understood to mark its likeness to other skin (which it does insofar as it implies that the organs that lie beneath it will doubtless operate the same way as those that might be revealed by an autopsy of someone else's organs). And Willan is able to know for certain that the tiny bugs that scurry across irritated skin are in fact the cause of that irritation because the skin announces, in that instant, its fundamental identity to itself through time.

Under the lens of the newly refined technologies of magnifying glass and microscope, then, the skin becomes in the first decades of the nineteenth century the location where likeness and causation are both perceptible in an instant and become the same thing. With a genealogy in the internal incoherences of an epistemology of the anatomical body, this standardized skin is understood to be contingent and self-identical in the same moment. A guarantor of disinterest insofar as the body whose surface is traced by skin is no longer conceivable, even in isolation, as purely individual. In this context, Willan's notably earthbound fantasy of racial origin, reiterated here, turns out in its narrow dermatological materiality to be the telling story:

> [Edward Lambert] is now forty years of age; a good-looking, well-shaped man, of a florid countenance, and when his body and hands are covered, seems nothing different from other people. But except his head and face, the palms of his hands, and bottoms of his feet, his skin is all over covered in the same manner as in the year 1731, which therefore I shall trouble you with no other description of, than what you will find in Mr. Machin's account, only begging leave to observe, that this covering seemed to me most nearly to resemble an innumerable company of warts, of a dark brown colour, and a cylindric figure, rising to a like height, and growing as close as possible to one another, but so stiff and elastic, that when the hand is drawn over them they make a rustling noise. . . .
>
> . . . But the most extraordinary circumstance of this man's story, and indeed the only reason of my giving you this trouble is, that he has had six children, all with the same rugged covering as himself. . . . It appears therefore past all doubt, that a race of people may be propagated by this man, having such rugged coats or coverings as himself: and if this should ever happen, and the accidental original be forgotten, 'tis not improbable they might be deemed a different species of mankind: a consideration, which would almost lead one to imagine, that if mankind were all produced from one and the same stock, the black skins of the negroes, and many other differences of the like kind, might possibly have been originally owing to some such accidental cause. (155, 156–57)

If we take the passage's final sentence as a summing up of all that has preceded it, then Willan's narrative of racial origins would seem to fit squarely within the critical tradition of thinking about race I earlier termed "linguistic" or constructionist: we end with a gesture of unveiling by which a seemingly natural racial sign is revealed to have originated with some entirely contingent "accidental cause." But the rhetoric that precedes that final sentence operates to frame the passage's concluding gesture in ways that offer a much more complex account. The passage begins by introducing a patient rendered particular by both the span of his life (forty years) and his location in time. But by the end of Willan's account, not only have these particularities been standardized by way of a skin surface comprehending massed likeness—"this covering seemed to me most nearly to resemble an innumerable company of warts"—but the standardized skin has itself become exemplary, less a thing to be known than a mode of knowing. As Willan moves into what is more explicitly an account of racial formation, what is striking is his insistence on setting the racial and the genealogical in opposition to one another; race is not a version of descent but rather a kind of species. For Willan, this distinction is predicated upon the forgetting of an "accidental original." With the species, as with the genealogy, elements are all related by virtue of having been caused by one another, but in the case of the species, causation has been dissociated from accident and confined entirely to the past, as was the case for Kant's racial "seeds." No longer traceable to a single accidental moment, the causation of species, like the bugs that generate rashes on skin, is ongoing, discernible entirely in the present.

Willan thus offers a narrative of race that accords with an exemplary version of pathological skin. But his description likewise makes apparent the inadequacy of a redesignation of the object alone to render the skin standard. While the "forgetting of the accidental original" is what apparently transforms race from a genealogical to a species relation, this forgetting takes place within an almost vertiginously complex temporality of knowing. In a way that seems altogether consistent with the project's more general effort to generate a natural history whose moment of organization is perpetually diffused, Willan seems strikingly unwilling to designate his racial origin narrative definitively as either speculative or historical, theoretical or empirical. "It appears therefore *past all doubt* that a race of people *may* be propagated by this man, having such rugged coats or coverings as himself: *and if this should ever happen, and the accidental original be forgotten, 'tis not improbable* that they *might* be deemed a different species of mankind." Here, with a rapidity that is at once dazzling and self-canceling, certainties are replaced with probabilities that then give way to contingent speculations, and chains of events transmute into the eventfulness of knowing.

The beginning of that key sentence is especially difficult to parse in this regard: it is, Willan informs us with no apparent confusion, "past all doubt" that a race of people "may" be propagated. The two halves of Willan's contention seem irreconcilably contradictory, inasmuch as the certainty of outcome insisted upon by the first part of the sentence appears in tension with the qualifications of the second. But the tension between the two parts is irresolvable only insofar as the epistemological condition of certainty is understood to follow as a consequence of the events themselves: in such a situation, it seems impossible that our knowledge of events might be more certain than the events themselves. The contradiction disappears once the certainty is seen not to attend the likelihood of the events' occurrence but rather to gauge the quality of our knowing. What is "past all doubt" is not that the events *will* occur but that they *may* occur, that we can know for certain only within the limits of the probable. Insofar as the sentence evokes a process by which the contingencies of the external world are circumscribed within an accounting of the limits of the subject's knowledge, we can understand it to enact the epistemological transformations of the magnifying glass, which functions as a synecdoche for the external material world in general to the extent that it marks the limits of the subject's powers of vision.

Moreover, just as Willan's use of the magnifying glass only becomes authoritative once it has been trained upon the cutaneous insects that replicate its own contingency-enveloping logic, the epistemology evoked by this undoubtable possibility is shored up by the production of a version of race that requisitions the magnifying glass's epistemological structures. Willan's next comment initially appears to split the difference between the thesis of unequivocal certainty and its antithesis of mere probability by setting a steady course of noncommittal subjunctive. But rather than simply establishing a speculative realm in which the relations of linked postulates render irrelevant the apparent contradictions of the framing conditions, the passage's grammar insists upon the dependence of its chain of hypotheses on the ambiguities that frame it: "And if this should ever happen and the accidental original be forgotten, 'tis not improbable that they might be deemed a different species of mankind." Not only do the opening conjunction and the referentially indeterminate "this" work to reinforce this dependency, but the echoing of this subordination in the sentence's second "and" suggests that the peculiar epistemology of the opening might even operate as the mechanism by which Willan understands race to be constituted. But this syntax leaves unclear whether Edward Lambert's propagation of descendants with skin like his is necessarily accompanied by the forgetting of its contingent origins (the "if" circumscribes within it both elements so as to insist upon their inextricable connection) or whether race is constituted as a result of two, independently contingent processes—the creation of like descendants *and* the forgetting of the contingency of those relations.

The familiar linguistic account of race operates by revealing the apparently inevitable meaning of the racial sign—in the terms laid out here, "the creation of like descendants"—to be a consequence of the "forgetting" of an "accidental original." Not only is the seemingly inevitable revealed to be contingent, but less obviously, the significance of the set of events that culminate in the creation of like descendants shifts from the quality and content of the events themselves to what is known about them. In Willan's description, there is no moment of revelation because the events that unfold and what is known about them have no formally predictable relationship to one another. There is no triumph to be had in knowing what "really happened" if the world that has happened continues to be transformed even as one comes to know it. In insisting that the events that occur and what is known about them remain of equal significance because neither is definitively ended, Willan effectively assimilates his description of racial knowing to the kind of knowledge he has of the bugs that dart across his patient's skin and produce, it would seem, "the itch." In this regard, Willan offers an epistemology of the skin per se, a description of an object that enfolds within it the process by which it is known. Both racial likeness and "the itch" thus turn out to be significant because they are phenomena of the skin.

Willan's turn to the subjunctive announces the elevation of a version of subject the process of whose formation is discernible in an instant because it is never quite finished. Inasmuch as this subject "of cutaneous disease" is always in the process of being constituted and is legible by virtue of that ongoing constitution, the subject is always in essence a historiography as well. The indeterminately speculative history Willan ventures here ought thus to come as no surprise, since it simply renders explicit what is already implied by Willan's cutaneous subject. The "past" events by which the "black skin of the negroes" came into being are made legible on the model of events that have yet to occur, events conceivable via a present act of imagination. He need not establish decisively whether the history of skin he offers in the form of Edward Lambert's narrative is meant to be understood as a speculative or an actual history of race, since finally what the racialization of skin announces is the elimination of the force of such a difference.

Once the general fact of causation is understood to be visible in a present and instantaneous moment of perception, the historical truth of that causation, its condition of having happened at any particular moment, becomes beside the point. With this gesture toward the historiographical, Willan returns us to the point of historiographical crisis that sent Kant in search of something like the racial subject. This crisis, the crisis of symbolic history registered by the French Revolution and the Terror, is the moment at which the political surrogacy that identifies the principles of republican disinterest with a subject's possession of a standardized anatomical body ceases to guarantee the subject's disinterest. In transmuting the body of the subject from a structure organizing the subject's self-opacity into a locus of acute and palpable vulnerability, the Terror turns the body into a thing entirely exhausted by its own presence, an importunity to interest and therefore an occasion for the subject to disappear into his own implacable condition of embodiment. By contrast, when Willan gazes through his magnifying glass and discovers in the tiny darting bugs the key to a logic of racialized skin, the skin he describes is one whose "appearance" can be seen to be caused at every instant, and one that as a consequence of this ongoingness instantly marks the body it covers as a standard body. In making its standardization immediately palpable, the skin works to rescue the anatomical body as the ground of philosophical and political disinterest by constituting a body relieved of its vulnerability to those who would harm it in the present by demonstrating that it can never be just itself. It articulates the fervent hope that a subject be entirely individualized and yet unconstrained by the conditions of particularity. At once present and elsewhere, individual and corporate, the body bounded and announced by racial skin instantiates a notion of the standard heretofore heuristic, and in so doing, it saves both philosophy and modern medicine from the specter of their own dying.

TWO

Paranoid Imagining: Wilkie Collins, the Rugeley Poisoner, and the Invisibility of Novelistic Ekphrasis

In chapter 1, I argued that the emergence of the skin as the preeminent mark of racial identity in the final decades of the eighteenth century and early decades of the nineteenth makes it possible for us to see the centrality of the category of race to a fundamental Enlightenment project: to make the universal likeness of individuals immediately palpable. In advancing the case for attending to skin as something other than an arbitrary sign of and alibi for a multitude of social relations, I insisted that race comes to be legible in the skin just as—and because—skin comes to matter for the nascent epistemology and practice of anatomical medicine, announcing a standardness of the human body that cannot be directly observed. My claim for the particular significance of skin challenged the notion that the pervasiveness of a particular cultural phenomenon and the arbitrariness of the sign used to express that phenomenon necessarily imply one another.

In short, we read skin rather than read through it. This is how we begin to make sense of one of the enduring historical paradoxes of the Enlightenment: Why is it that the era that ventured the revolutionary claim that all humans are by their very nature equal was also the era in which differences in skin color came to be understood as indelible evidence of essential differences in human capacity? The coincidence of universalism and embodied and inalterable racial difference was the consequence, I have been suggesting, not of the Enlightenment's failure to live up to its professed ideals, but rather of the conflict of two not entirely compatible sets of political and intellectual commitments. In skin, we get both the vision of likeness and the impulse to turn likeness into a vision, a (political) commitment to a universal equality that can be observed empirically rather than taken as a matter of faith. Likeness—of a subject through time, of various subjects in relation to one another—is transfigured from a political aspiration or philosophical discovery into something seen in the world in an instant and, in its transfiguration, flickering away. It thus requires hardly any shift at all, a mere conceptual cock of the head, to go from understanding racialized skin as a sign of a general if unobservable likeness of human bodies to seeing it in more familiarly racial terms as a thing that is like or different in and of itself.

In this chapter, I explore the logic of race from the perspective of this impulse to literalize, to make likeness manifest into something that can be witnessed. I do so through a close examination of a number of interrelated texts, debates, and events—most sustainedly, Wilkie Collins's 1859 novel *The Woman in White*. I take up Collins's novel not simply as an instantiation of the epistemological context I have been exploring, but as an investigation of instantiation itself, of that literalizing impulse in skin that tilts Enlightenment universalism into something like its opposite. Put another way, *The Woman in White* rewards examination, not in its exemplarity but in its genericness, not because it is a particular textual manifestation of a culturewide phenomenon but because it is a novel. To the degree that realist novels treat the unseen as if it were visible, inviting readers to pretend that verbal descriptions of people, places, and events are witnessable phenomena, they test the perils and possibilities of transforming likeness from a political commitment into a thing in the world. Where race is a structure of knowing, the novel becomes a racial technology.

As I have argued, the impulse to make likeness perceptible that is modern, skin-based race was not simply born of a generalized empiricism, but emerged as a solution to a particular Enlightenment problem: to make likeness visible instantaneously, so as to circumvent the incapacity of certain modes of Enlightenment thought to register lawful change. In this regard, *The Woman in White*, which turns the novel form's generic power to treat indiscernible likeness as if it is visible into the stuff of its own pointedly diachronic plot, can be seen both to illustrate the process by which realist description and racial knowing are brought into being and to engineer the undoing of that racial and novelistic knowing. For Collins, we shall see, the genre of the novel is especially well suited to the task of thinking through the relations of materially present likeness and a sameness that is elsewhere, dedicated as the form is to representing particular characters who can't actually be seen and whose legibility rests on readers' capacity to imagine them to be like people those readers have seen. In Collins's hands, this ordinary practice at the heart of nineteenth-century realism becomes an instrument for coming to understand why it matters that we recognize subjects *as subjects* because they occupy the same body over time, as well as what exactly it is we are thinking and seeing when we look at "individuals."

As much time as I devote in this chapter to analyzing some formal aspects of the novel, this is not, finally, a story about the nineteenth-century novel. Rather, it is a story about the nineteenth-century subject. In shifting my analysis from Collins's novel to the 1856 murder trial that inspired it, that of the so-called Rugeley Poisoner, William Palmer, a physician charged with poisoning his patients under the guise of medicating them, I mean in part to provide something like an anatomical medical context to make sense of the crisis of plausibility of the instantaneously perceptible (ekphrastic) identity enacted and analyzed novelistically by Collins. But I mean also by this redirection of attention to trace a turn in the history of the subject, to show how the challenge to the notion that we can glimpse the likeness of bodies and of subjects in the color of their skin produces in its aftermath a profound sense of the opacity of the body to the subjects who inhabit it. With this opacity comes an even more generalized cultural threat, an anxiety that the incapacity of the body to make legible its own likeness and stability—to other bodies, to itself across time—also threatens subjects' control over the functioning of their own bodies and exposes a deep vulnerability to incursion from forces outside. In the context of this new worry that the agency of individual subjects might be constrained, even undone, by the hidden operations of the body, racial knowing appears to be less a technology for identifying others than a technology by which individuals come to discover and hence to shore up their own power.

Qualifications of Character

If, in an era of Jane Eyres and David Copperfields, there is something curiously generic about "the woman in white," we might surmise this is because she is two women, not one. When Walter Hartright, the first of the novel's rotating cast of narrators, unexpectedly encounters a mysterious woman clad in filmy white on the road to his new post as a private drawing instructor, we are as surprised as he to discover another like her, when he arrives at his destination and is introduced to the young woman he is meant to teach. Collins's novel, *in nuce,* is the story of this likeness, even if the baroque complexities of plot, designed alternately to reveal and to obscure the semblance, are likely to distract us from that fundamental point. The two women's interchangeability essentially turns on the fungibility of the sick body of one woman and the dead body of another. In this regard, I will be arguing, the likeness at the heart of Collins's novel tells the story of the newly dominant anatomical medicine paradigm, a framework in which the likeness of bodies and their capacity to cause and control their own operations imply one another.[1]

But to the degree to which *The Woman in White* is a *story*—to the degree to which, that is, Collins presents the identity of these two bodies as the consequence of elaborate machinations of plot rather than simply asserting it as an analytical postulate—it stands as much as a challenge to as an affirmation of the logic of anatomical medicine.[2] In detailing the events, the temporal chain of cause and effect, by which a sick body and a dead one come to be substituted for one another, Collins's novel insists that we attend to the gap of time and state between being sick and being dead, precisely the period of transformation that anatomical medicine excludes in its positing of the standardized body as a theoretical first principle. In focusing on the temporal process by which sick bodies come to be dead, *The Woman in White* engages the contradiction between physicians' therapeutic authority (their capacity to make people well or to sicken them) and physicians' authority to diagnose by way of a standardized body. Indeed, this contradiction becomes the structuring principle of the novel's plot. Bodies can only be understood to be fundamentally identical to one another—and rendered visible by way of this imputed identity—so long as the process by which one is transformed into another is overlooked (whether, for example, a sick woman is substituted for a dead woman or a woman ages, sickens, and dies). Collins allows us to see how the novel's familiar ekphrastic practice of offering its readers detailed and particularized descriptions of bodies they cannot actually see functions as an instrument of this overlooking and thus provides the ground for examining the implications of anatomical medicine's conception that a standardized body is not quite visible. These implications fundamentally challenge the notion that individual subjects are identifiable over time by virtue of the fact that they occupy the same, essentially unchanging, body. By insisting that to be known, bodies must be known over time, *The Woman in White* complicates any hard-and-fast distinction between the particularity of individual bodies and the bodily resemblances by which groups of people come to be understood as connected to one another—between Jane Eyre and "the woman in white" or, perhaps more provocatively, between a woman in white, the novel's two women, and white women generally. As we shall see, Collins seizes upon this ambiguity not merely to undo the force of any opposition between recognizing the identities of individuals and recognizing those of groups, but also to make apparent the ways in which the direction, dispensation, and signification of happenings we tend to gather under the rubric of "individual agency" ought more properly to be understood as social and communal.

Collins begins this deindividualization of agency, not surprisingly, with an attempt to reconceive the action of fiction making, the authority of authors. When, in 1860, he appended a preface to the new, three-decker version of his previously serialized novel *The Woman in White,* he immediately placed his readers on notice that they were about to encounter something unprecedented. "An experiment is attempted in this novel, which has not (so far as I know) been hitherto tried in fiction. The story of the book is told throughout by the characters of the book. They are all placed in different positions along the chain of events; and they all take that chain up in turn, and carry it on to the end."[3] The apparent inspiration for this narrative innovation was a certain criminal trial Collins attended in 1856, a trial John Sutherland has identified as the William Palmer poisoning trial.[4]

Collins recalled the novel's genesis in a diary entry made toward the end of his life, recalling how each witness at the Palmer trial stood in turn to offer a personal fragment to the accumulating evidence:

> It came to me then . . . that a series of events in a novel would lend themselves well to an exposition like this. . . . One could impart to the reader that acceptance, that sense of belief, which was produced here by the succession of testimonies. . . . The more I thought of it, the more an effort of this kind struck me as bound to succeed. Consequently when the case was over I went home determined to make the effort.[5]

In distributing narrative responsibilities among the various characters whose actions drive the novel's plot, Collins's "experiment" invites us to admire the author's innovativeness in eliminating the position of the author. While we might be tempted to understand this subsumption of the distinctness of the author into characters' everyday activities as a kind of naturalization of narrative authority harkening back to the genre's epistolary origins, Collins instead leans upon the paradox. The author's dispensability, it appears, is essentially like the dispensability of the characters: neither can be presumed as the originating force behind the narration that follows because neither is assured of being sustained through time. The chain is initially presented as a structure that preexists and is thus capable of ordering the consequent narration: "they are all placed in different positions along the chain of events." Here, the author deploying (if not exactly inventing) the chain metaphor, assumes the authority of the originator. In the second half of the sentence, the chain is suddenly transmuted into a thing subject to being handled and deployed by the character/narrators: "they all take the chain up in turn, and carry it on to the end," offering a model of narrative origin in which neither characters nor narration preexist one another. This coevalness seems to displace even as it follows temporally the model of authorial priority laid out in the sentence's first half.

The shifting syntactical context of the specific chain figure effectively nudges the model of fictionality from one of creation or generation to one of readerly reception: the figure means differently as it is read, and thus reading, rather than the fact of the fiction's having been made, becomes the site for the generation of meaning. As we shall see, Collins occupies himself over the course of the novel with trying to invent a strategy to rid himself of the burden of invention, to imagine a model of generation that will allow his imaginative creations to break free of the particularizing links to their inventor. For now, Collins's efforts fall back into paradox: the relocation of authority from creation to reception remains circumscribed by the fact that it is engineered by way of a figure produced by an author; the privileging of reading remains the privilege of the author.

Thus brought up short by the constraint of his own authority, Collins casts his story yet again, finding in serialization a means of introducing not only the idea or figure of a reader, but also the actual contingency of the novel's reception as an element of the novel's unfolding authority:

> By frankly acknowledging the recognition that I have obtained thus far, I provide for myself an opportunity of thanking many correspondents (to whom I am personally unknown) for the hearty encouragement I received from them while my work was in progress. Now, while the visionary men and women, among whom I have been living so long, are all leaving me, I remember very gratefully that "Marian" and "Laura" made such warm friends in many quarters, that I was peremptorily cautioned at a serious crisis in the story, to be careful how I treated them—that Mr. Fairlie found sympathetic fellow-sufferers, who remonstrated with me for not making Christian allowance for the state of his nerves—that Sir Percival's "secret" became sufficiently exasperating, in course of time, to be made the subject of bets (all of which I hereby declare to be "off")—and that Count Fosco suggested metaphysical considerations to the learned in such matters (which I don't quite understand to this day), besides provoking numerous inquires as to the living model, from which he had really been taken. (3–4)

Collins here insists on the multiplicity of audiences, and it is in the nature of this multiplicity that we can see registered a fundamental change in the social logic of novelistic fictionality. Such authorial shout-outs to readers of course have a historical pedigree nearly as long as the novel form itself: Samuel Richardson famously complained of readers' efforts to intervene to redirect Clarissa's fate. My interest here is not only the ways in which Collins revives this rhetoric previously associated with epistolary novels to frame his just-invented multinarrator form, but also how he adopts it so as to draw out a temporal diffuseness within narrative authority. Less important than determining the success or failure of any given readerly intervention is the way in which the impulse to intervene indicates an understanding of novelistic fictionality as something that has been produced in the past but need not necessarily or predictably extend into the future. Readers seized with the impulse to write letters to an author in hopes of "saving" the characters they favor do not mistake fictional characters for real people. If they did, they would logically call doctors or police officers, not novelists, to rescue their imperiled "friends." But the letter writing of Collins's readers does suggest that an understanding of characters and the events that have already befallen those characters as an author's created fictional effects need not imply the continued authority of that author into the future. The attempt to intervene pays only to the degree to which neither the general fact of that authority nor the specific consequences of its exercise are presumable in advance, extrapolatable from the present condition of the authored fiction. The readers who implore Collins to act on behalf of their favorite characters understand him to be a part of the social network those readers themselves inhabit. They understand the action that brings such characters and narratives into being to be only one of the various sorts of actions he might perform.

In essence, Collins is here pulling apart the author's identity from the acts of authorship, of fiction making, that the author performs. He need not continue to create the characters in the future that he has created in the past because doing so is not who he is but what he does, and what he does he may simply stop doing. While this emphasis upon the dependence of characters' existences on authorial whim might seem in some tension with Collins's decision to reassign storytelling responsibilities from an author-like narrator to a variety of characters, within the logic of the novel it is entirely consistent with that reassignment, insofar as both gestures similarly represent storytelling as just one of the many sorts of activities narrators do. If the first paragraphs of his preface can be seen as a series of provocations by and about change—don't assume that the figures you read will mean the same thing that they did a minute ago, or that authors will keep on doing what they have been doing, or that the reader who identifies with one part of a narrative will identify with another part, or even that characters will keep being only characters—Collins closes by offering a framework for organizing these provocations into something like a theory of fiction or authorship.

Having offered a laundry list of readerly demands that he was contented to relate without feeling compelled to respond, Collins presents his theory of representation as a sudden acceding to readers' imprecations.[6] To the serial readers' demand that he name the "living model" from which the character of Count Fosco "had really been taken," Collins insists "that many models, some living, and some dead, have 'sat' for him." He goes on: "The Count would not have been as true to nature as I have tried to make him, if the range of my search for materials had not extended, in his case as well as in others, beyond the narrow human limit which is represented by one man" (4). In our initial encounter with it, this observation is likely to seem entirely familiar and thus entirely unremarkable: the superior truth of fictions based on the genericness—that is to say, the universality—of their qualities represents Collins's most explicit nod to the theoretical tradition first articulated by Aristotle. But insofar as he suggests that his characters escape the inevitable distortions of particularity not merely by way of their fictionality but also by virtue of their status as a synthesis of many models, "some living and some dead," and places that synthesis at the center of his novel's plot, Collins offers a version of fictionality that is innovative and historically particular to the degree that it draws out the resemblances between Aristotelian fictionality and anatomical medicine's standardized body, that not-quite-empirical synthesis of the living and the dead. In this regard, the doubled, generic referent of *The Woman in White*, signaling as it does the novel's commitment to narrating the process by which two women become interchangeable and then cease to be, is the story of the possibility and reach of novelistic fictionality in the very same measure as it is the story of what anatomical medicine can know.

Aristotle's Fictive Community

Collins was certainly not alone at midcentury in turning to Aristotle as a touchstone for thinking about the relations of agency and likeness or about the role of the fictional in organizing these relations. In his posthumously published *Autobiography*, John Stuart Mill notes the pride of place granted to Aristotle's *Rhetoric* within his childhood's seemingly endless list of compulsory readings: "As the first expressly scientific treatise on any moral or psychological subject which I had read, and containing many of the best observations of the ancients on human nature and life, my father made me study with special care." Several years later, as part of a course on logic, Mill was to encounter Aristotle's *Organon,* a text he engaged more fully in his own *System of Logic.*[7] William Whewell, Mill's antagonist in a series of debates over the nature of philosophical induction, likewise made Aristotle the subject of an 1850 lecture before the Cambridge Philosophical Society entitled "Criticism of Aristotle's Account of Induction."[8]

The context of Aristotle's own composition is well known. Impelled to mount a defense of fictionality per se so as to refute Plato's effort to equate poetry with lying and thus to banish it from his Republic, Aristotle articulates a theory of fictionality that understands social communities to be constituted around the effort to assign actions to agents, to make legible the relation between causation—the events of a plot (*muthos*)—and the agents who set such relations into motion. At the core of Aristotle's defense of fictionality lies his startling contention that poetry—by which he means tragedy specifically, plotted fictions more generally—is superior to history because it speaks of universals. It speaks of what *can* happen, as opposed to the particulars of what actually *does* happen: "Poetry is a more philosophical and more serious thing than history; poetry tends to speak of universals, history of particulars. A universal is the sort of thing that a certain kind of person may well say or do in accordance with probability or necessity—this is what poetry aims at, although it assigns names [to the people]. A particular is what Alcibiades did or what he suffered."[9] If truth is stranger than fiction, such strangeness is for Aristotle sufficient grounds for rejecting historical truths out of hand. The improbable turn of events that actually have taken place has less to teach us about the nature of human capacity and freedom than the probable, though fictional, chain of events that has not occurred and never will.

Aristotle's privileging of dramatic plots has everything to do with his conviction that the specific task of fiction is to make knowable what is universally human. For him, humans become human by virtue of their capacity to act freely, to make events happen, one following consequentially upon another. But the unfolding of events always runs the risk of appearing merely particular, the consequence of the idiosyncratic qualities and behavior of an idiosyncratic individual rather than the expression of an individual's universally human aspect. Here, then, is the animating theoretical difficulty of Aristotle's notion that human universality lies in the capacity to make things happen. The sequence of cause and effect is expressive of humanness to the degree that it stands as evidence of human agency, yet the more closely any specific sequence of events is aligned with the particular acts of a particular individual, the more that sequence runs the risk of seeming merely the consequence of that individual's actions, idiosyncratic and historical rather than universal.

It is this difficulty of reconciling the imperatives of agency and universality that generates both the formal logic of fictionality and its usefulness. Insofar as the plot of a fiction can seem at once both the consequence of the actions of the characters within the narrative and the effects of the actions of an author (the made-up quality of the fiction), a plotted sequence of events need not be unambiguously assigned to either character or author. A causal chain can plausibly lay claim to universality to the extent to which it escapes such specific assignment. What is crucial to note for the purposes of this argument is that fictionality can only perform this ambiguating function so long as making fictions—the way that authors express their agency—is understood to be an action that is similar in kind to the sorts of actions performed by characters within the fiction and capable, at least theoretically, of being performed by the kinds of people those characters represent. Fictionality can only perform the task for which it is generated, that is, so long as there is no special realm of language and no particular thing as professional authorship.

But even as Aristotle offers fiction making potentially performed by anyone as the structure through which agency and causation are demonstrated to be the foundation of universal humanness, he develops his account of tragedy in the *Poetics* in such a way as to allow the foundational power to cause effects to be recognizable even *within* fictions. We are most attuned to the universality of causation, he explains, at the moment a causal chain of events takes the form of a reversal. Only under these circumstances, only when events unfold in ways their agents did not quite envision or intend (think of Oedipus), do such events appear as things that could be done by or could happen to anyone, rather than as the effects of an actor's particularity. This emphasis on reversal seems, at least initially, simply to recapitulate the original paradox of universal agency. Events turn out to be evidence of the universal human capacity to cause effects only to the degree to which they appear not fully under the control of the actors most immediately associated with them, as a proliferation of unintended consequences.

Aristotle quickly rushes to shore up the foundational status of causation, however, by insisting that the sorts of tragedy characterized by unexpected reversals are most illuminating when they take place within established communities among people who know one another:

> Let us consider, then, what sorts of occurrence arouse dread or compassion in us. These sorts of action against each another necessarily take place between friends, enemies or people who are neither. If it is one enemy [who does the action] to another, there is nothing pitiable, whether he does it or is [only] about to do it, except in the suffering itself. Nor [is it pitiable] if the people are neither [friends nor enemies]. But when sufferings happen within friendly relationships, e.g. brother against brother, son against father, mother against son or son against mother, when someone kills someone else, is about to, or does something else of the same sort—these are what must be sought after. (18)

The difficulty of finding a grammar to describe such reversals at once bespeaks the threat they pose to the notion of the efficacy of human agency and the solution to that threat: if the dynamics of reversal make it hard to differentiate between events that happen to one and events one makes happen, Aristotle makes the distinction unnecessary with his insistence that already existing communities are the most appropriate context for such reversals to indicate the events' significance. Although reversals present causal chains of events that appear to make the actors who set the events into motion more the victims or objects than the agents of unfolding universal effects, the communal context collapses the condition of being an object and the condition of being an agent. The force of this context is particularly apparent in Aristotle's progression of examples, where he moves from simply listing the clashing actors to describing the reversibility of the relations of conflict ("mother against son or son against mother"), a reversibility that seems to pave the way for the rearticulation of the sort of universality ("someone kills someone else") that might otherwise seem in tension with the privileging of preexisting (and implicitly circumscribed) communities. Indeed, in Aristotle's view, it is this very indistinguishability of object and agent—what I do hurts me if it hurts you—that constitutes communities as such.

Aristotle's notion of community is thus a notion of a public without specialists, a social organization in which individuals are drawn into relation with one another by their common capabilities and common vulnerabilities. Community constituted around the mutual and reversible relations of agency and vulnerability operates as a structure for resolving the paradoxes of the act-based universal humanism that haunt the *Poetics* throughout. The alienability of effects from actors demonstrated by fictionality and standing as evidence of the universality of causation avoids demonstrating tenuousness of individual agents' control over the effects of their actions only so long as those actions and agents are located within existing communities—that is, only where the unintended consequences of my individual actions hurt me to the degree to which they harm my friend or fellow citizen. While the bounds of Aristotle's public are congruent with the bounds of the relations of people who can hurt and be hurt by one another, what might appear a measure turns out to be a tautology: the people who are judged to be vulnerable to and capable of acting upon one another are those who have already been determined to be members of the same public or community. Thus the Aristotelian conception of fictionality as a kind of significance grounded on the comparability of fiction making to other forms of action is one that must presume a closed and legible community within which such fiction making takes place.

In its commitment to a notion of universalism grounded in subjects' capacity to cause and be caused, Aristotle's *Poetics* can usefully be understood as a precursor text to Kant's critical philosophy. A quick comparison is illuminating: for Aristotle, the straightforwardly diachronic nature of narrative fictionality allows narrative causation to appear universal by not seeming at any given moment to be fully attributable to a particularized author or any specific character. Kant likewise understands his analytical task to be the reconciliation of two grounds of the universalism of the human: first, the likeness or lawfulness that is a manifestation of the condition of having been caused and, second, human agency—one's capacity to cause effects oneself. Aristotle renders these grounds noncontradictory by splitting causing and being caused between author and character while avoiding, by way of the diachronicity of the plot, associating these capacities wholly with either. Kant enlists the concept of disinterestedness to a similar end: subjects' particular acts do not particularize them or violate their universal condition of having been intended or caused, so long as those acts could just as well have been performed by surrogates. In this sense, Kant can be understood to transcendentalize what can retrospectively be recognized as the literalism of Aristotle's fictionality. Where Aristotle insists that both authors' capacities to create characters and characters' capacities to act within their own (fictional) worlds be seen as fundamentally alike despite the ontological differences between real and fictional subjects, Kant eliminates this ontological distinction and simply distributes doing and (the benefits of) being done arbitrarily among various subject-citizens.

I suggested in chapter 1, in my discussion of the second essay in the *Conflict of the Faculties*, that Kant's notion of disinterestedness is finally limited by the fact that subjects inhabit particular bodies. In the same way that anatomical medicine's standardized body is predicated upon an essential likeness and interchangeability of "living and dead bodies" that can only be sustained conceptually so long as the actual process of dying is ignored, the interchangeability of bodies mandated as the test of Kantian disinterestedness only works so long as the ends or effects of surrogate subjects' acts are measured at some indeterminate point in the future, rather than in the present at the moment of someone's choice between, say, the injuring or killing of one body and not another. It is this unstable relation, we recall, between the promise of the interchangeability of abstract bodies, redeemable only at some unspecified moment in the future, and the implacable particularity and distinctness of actual bodies in the present, that produces the oscillation between a notion of the skin as a mark of human likeness that is elsewhere and a conception of the skin as something that ought to be understood as like or unlike other skins in and of themselves. In this regard, the literalism structured into Aristotle's fictionality in the form of ontological bodily difference offers a way around the impasse of embodied subjectivity within Kantian disinterestedness: authors make; characters are made; everyone is an agent. Inasmuch as the body of the author who creates is ontologically different from the (imaginary) bodies of the characters created, the particularity of these very different real and fictional bodies need not contradict the shared capacity for agency that undergirds their likeness, since universalism and particularity exist within discontinuous and noncompeting registers. But while the likeness or interchangeability of author and character need not be compromised by the worry that some revolutionary might choose to hurt one of them rather than the other, the very condition of embodiment that frees the author from the fates of his characters also finally excludes him from that character's universe. The existing community within which, for Aristotle, the most profound tragedies take place—the sort of community in which the acts by which one character hurts her neighbor ultimately redound upon that character as well—is not one that can include the embodied author within its bounds.

I hope this brief comparison of Kant and Aristotle helps make apparent that when Collins introduces the innovation by which characters assume the duties of authors by telling their own stories in turn, he does not simply return us to the register of Kantian disinterestedness in which there are no ontological differences among embodied subjects. Keyed to a variety of different characters acting within the novel, the fictional authority of *The Woman in White* potentially will function differently in the future that it has in the past or does in the present, and consequently it neither presumes nor can be expected to produce the kind of social likeness Aristotle understands the fictional to announce. Thus the multiplicity of Collins's audiences and their fictional investments in his novel are inextricable from one another as well as from these audiences' overlapping, if nonidentical, views of Collins the author as someone not quite professional, someone whose fictions matter because they are only one of a variety of sorts of things he makes and does.

In insisting on a contingent relation between past audiences and future ones, between an author's creation of a fictional world and characters in the past and the author's capacity to create them in the future, Collins offers a vision of the novel as the conduit by means of which a nonempirical notion of historicity might be extended to the world outside the novel. The notion of fictionality that would allow readers to intervene to make things come out differently in the future is a notion of fictionality whose unfolding has the potential, if hardly the inevitable or predictable power, to transform those multiple audiences so that they are unlike one another and unlike past or present versions of themselves. This is the case because the condition of the author's addressability—the future fiction is not presumable, and the author's creation of fiction is just one of the many social acts he undertakes—renders the social world into which such fiction emerges capable of being transformed by that fiction's contingent emerging. Because his concept of seriality is not simply a narrowly conceived publication history but instead describes the mechanism by which fictions can help create publics who understand themselves as able to change the state of their world by virtue of the historicity of their own emergence, the complex dynamics of seriality implied by Collins's ruminations need not be confined to actual serial novels.

The contingency of narrative authority is further underscored by *The Woman in White*'s notoriously confusing opening. The movement from the serialized version that ran from November 1859 until August 1860 in *All the Year Round* in England and *Harper's Weekly* in the United States, through eight three-volume editions in 1860 to what is now considered the definitive edition—the 1861 three-decker—reshuffled the elements of the opening without resolving its confusions, suggesting Collins's investment in maintaining its ambiguities. Just under the title, we are presented with a heading "The Story Begun by WALTER HARTRIGHT, of Clement's Inn, Teacher of Drawing." The presence of this subheading seems to speak both to Collins's professed design of distributing narrative responsibilities among various characters and to the design's status as an unprecedented "experiment" derived from the testimonial structure of the legal trial. But what is peculiar is that the paragraphs dedicated to describing the narrative form that is to follow refer to Walter Hartright in the third person: "No circumstance of importance, from the beginning to the end of the disclosure, shall be related on hearsay evidence. When the writer of these introductory lines (Walter Hartright by name) happens to be more closely connected than others with the incidents to be recorded, he will describe them in his own person. When his experience fails, he will retire from the position of narrator; and his task will be continued, from the point at which he has left it off, by other persons who can speak to the circumstances under notice from their own knowledge, just as clearly and positively as he has spoken before them" (9). While the principle announced here—a narratorial rotation organized by proximity to the events, suggests a set of happenings that preexists their narration, the further splitting of the narrative voice that occurs implies Walter's autonomy and preexistence: describing his narrative plan, Walter refers to himself in the third person; narrating the events to which he is most proximate, he refers to himself in the first person. The strangeness of the use of the third-person self-reference is exacerbated—and arguably, made even less tonally convincing—with a shift to the (self-) imperative in the final line of the opening section: "Let Walter Hartright, teacher of drawing, aged twenty-eight, be heard first." In the serialized version of the opening, the heading "Begun by Walter Hartright, etc." comes only after the opening section, and therefore its conclusive imperative eliminates the syntactical oddness of the third-person self-reference. But it does so only at the cost of leaving the narrative authority of the opening section—and with it, the occasion of the entire narrative—thoroughly unaccounted for. In that version, we know who is narrating at any given moment, but we have no idea who has pulled the discrete narratives together and for what purpose. By locating the ambiguities of point of view within the text in the three-decker version and outside the text of the serialized version, Collins moves beyond the suggestiveness of the 1861 preface and turns the publication history of *The Woman in White* into an actual mechanism for rendering continuous the dynamics of authority within serialization and the historical effects of his novel in the world.

Collins's account of serialization insists that the authority (or authorities) that undergird fiction's power to make meaning are multiple, overlapping, and unpredictable, resting with an author and with readers potentially as varied as they are numerous. This multiplicity and unpredictability mean, as we shall see, that the authority of fictions cannot be confined simply to the authors who write them or the various readers who read, identify with, argue about, and discard them. It is because we cannot know precisely where and with whom the authority of fiction named by the dynamics of serialization lies that such serialization can be understood to describe the actions of more than novels, their authors, and their readers.

My account of Collins to this point sees his reenvisioning of agency accomplished within fairly familiar categories of narrative authorship, where the relations of individual subjects, actions, and communities are understood to be alterable by the reshuffling of the interactions of narrators and characters, acts of storytelling, and events of plot. I have suggested that we ought to recognize his description in his preface of Count Fosco as a synthesis of many models "some living and some dead" as at once invoking and revising Aristotle's conception of narrative fictionality. By distributing the measures of universality across the fictional apparatus, divided between authors and characters in ways that render them noncontradictory, this fictionality defuses the tension between likeness and agency that Kant attempts to resolve by way of racialized skin in quite a different way. Aristotle implicitly makes immanent this fictional solution by redefining the condition of being intended or acted upon. It is no longer glossed as the state of being authored; instead it is figured as the condition of being recognized as part of a community and hence instantly legible as having acted and been acted upon by other members of that community.

Seeing Is Imagining

While Collins may be a canny reader of Aristotle, he is not, to his credit, an entirely faithful one. Synthesizing not just the real and the fictional but also "the living and the dead," Collins excavates the tension between legible likeness and agency from the anatomical medical "standardized" body that theorizes and hides such incoherences. In relocating this tension within the anatomical body, Collins does not simply return us from Aristotle's fictionality to Kant's race. Rather, as we shall see, *The Woman in White* invites its readers to understand the problem of agency and the legibility of likeness experienced by those who would observe anatomical bodies from the outside and those who inhabit those bodies as one and the same problem. In preparing the way for this conflation, the novel transforms the conundrum from an exclusively aesthetic problem to a cultural one as well. Aristotle thus gives way to William Palmer, his trail of victims, and a host of horrified onlookers of various professional stripes. But as I will make evident, Collins's novel registers this shift not as a movement from the textual to the real, but from the body as a mechanism for making happen the events the narrator would narrate—the bodies of characters as agents of the narrator—to the body as a thing whose own changes count as the novel's most salient action.

And so, in this spirit, a turn from narration to description, but one that masks its deviation by beginning as if with business as usual, with what initially appears a perfectly conventional narratorial lament decrying the vagaries of memory. Walter Hartright recalls his initial encounter with Laura Fairlie, before she marries the older man to whom she is promised and becomes Laura Glyde:

> How can I describe her? How can I separate her from my own sensations, and from all that has happened in the later time? How can I see her again as she looked when my eyes first rested on her—as she should look, now, to the eyes that are about to see her in these pages?
>
> The water-colour drawing that I made of Laura Fairlie, at an after period, in the place and attitude in which I first saw her, lies on my desk while I write. I look at it, and there dawns on me brightly, from the dark greenish-brown background of the summer-house, a light, youthful figure, clothed in a simple muslin dress, the pattern of it formed by broad alternate stripes of delicate blue and white. A scarf of the same material sits crisply and closely round her shoulders, and a little straw hat of the natural colour, plainly and sparingly trimmed with ribbon to match the gown, covers her head, and throws its soft pearly shadow over the upper part of her face. Her hair is of so faint and pale a brown—not flaxen, and yet almost as light; not golden, and yet almost as glossy—that it nearly melts, here and there, into the shadow of the hat. (51)

The narration here invites us to weigh an equivalence between a problem of representation—"How can I describe her?"—and the complexity of subjective knowing over time, the not-easily-parsed relations of sensation and memory: "How can I separate her from my own sensations, and from all that has happened in the later time?" In asking "How can I see her again as she looked when my eyes first rested on her?" Walter effectively renders indistinguishable the relations of subject and object.[10] The ambiguation turns on an "as" that can be seen in equal parts to indicate a representational (= like) and a temporal difference (= at the same time as). This "as" functions as the hinge by which the squarely subjective, if imperfectly delineable, relations of knowledge, representation, and memory slide, via a more forcefully temporalized "when" that may or may not gloss the same difference as the "as," into the relation of Laura's body as it was first encountered and the more aged body it has since become.[11] While this initial series of clauses privileges neither the subjective description nor the objective account, it does suggest that the problems of knowing gestured toward in the first part of the sentence can be encapsulated in the legibility of the aging body, a claim that is bolstered by the sentence's concluding "rearticulation": "as she should look now to the eyes that are about to see her." In this final segment, the undecidability of the earlier part of the sentence is picked up and carried over by the repetition of the "as," but by locating that "as" in relation to an object that exists prior to being observed—it is an element of how Laura appears to the eyes that are *about* to see her—Collins affirms this relocation of knowability from subject to object: the qualities exist in the object even before they are seen.

While Walter can no longer see Laura's body "as she looked when [his] eyes first rested upon her" because that body has aged, the aging of the body is likewise something that cannot be seen, at least as it is taking place. Think of how difficult it is to notice the aging of someone with whom one is in continuous contact. By contrast, the shock one is likely to feel on seeing someone one hasn't seen in some years is in its essence the shock of coming to know what one hasn't seen, what has eluded one's observation: How grown-up (or old) she looks! How distinguished (or fat, or bald, or grey) he has become![12] In this undermining of ekphrastic logic, moreover, Collins radically expands the scope within which the human body is opaque to observation. If this opening paragraph is likely to lead us to ask in frustration, "At what moment exactly *can* we actually see Laura?" we might productively generalize the question by asking, "Of what use is it to see at one moment exactly?" Very little, it seems, if what we are asking such observations to do is to buttress the identity of the person inhabiting the body—to see *Laura*—to reassure us that, however various the behavior, opinions, interests, or fears may be from one moment to the next, the person behaving those ways, possessing those attitudes or fears, remains the same person, which is to say, a person at all. Having suggested how inadequate the aging body is, in and of itself, to the task for which it has been enlisted—Walter can neither recognize the Laura of first sighting in the present Laura nor see how she changed from one to the other—Collins invites us to look elsewhere, to consider the possibility that the body might become legible to the degree to which it is anchored in the particularities of its immediate environment. In the paragraph immediately following his opening lament, Walter describes a body that similarly eludes direct observation but that nonetheless gains a quality of presence, thanks to its relation to details of clothing that are at once particularizing and ephemeral:

> I look at [the drawing], and there dawns upon me brightly, from the dark greenish-brown background of the summer-house, a light, youthful figure clothed in a simple muslin dress, the pattern of it formed by broad alternate stripes of delicate blue and white. A scarf of the same material sits crisply and closely round her shoulders, and a little straw hat of the natural colour, plainly and sparingly trimmed with ribbon to match the gown covers her head, and throws its soft pearly shadow over the upper part of her face.

What matters about Collins's description is both how little we see of the body and how little we notice what we are not seeing. The portrait renders legible Laura's aging body not by picturing it—we are initially presented with virtually no description of the body itself—but by laying out a broad spatial framework whose component elements converge to produce a knowable body as something composed of its limits: a torso is implied by the coming together of dress, hat, and scarf; a face becomes legible by way of the shadow of a hat cast upon it. There is nothing particularly foundational about this body, and we discover it by noting the relations of the objects it organizes.[13] Once he has created a sense of the particularity of the body by tracing the contours of its opacity, Collins goes on to extend this bodily iconography to the structure of description more generally. When Walter the narrator remarks that Laura's "hair is of so faint and pale a brown—not flaxen, and yet almost as light; not golden, yet almost as glossy"—we are invited to understand this description by way of negation as simply a variation on the logic by which we discover shoulders by way of the patterned scarf that enfolds them. Collins does not contradict himself when he insists both that the qualities of Laura's aging body exist prior to their being seen and, by the same token, that we can only perceive the texture of her hair by knowing how it is not, since such claims are only contradictory so long as we presume that the relations among present things are understood to impel a different order of knowing from that impelled by the relations of what is and is not present.

What Walter as narrator needs to know about Laura is not how she appears or what she can be observed to do at any given moment but how she exists over time and what are the ways of knowing that might make such an existence legible. How, for example, can Walter know for certain that the Laura whom he tutors in drawing in her home is the same person he looks up to find standing on a hill by her own gravestone? Such questions lie at the heart of *The Woman in White* and are revealed in this passage as indistinguishable from the question of what we can know of significance about a person from the fact that we can observe her at a particular instant.

The contemporaneous presence of anatomical medicine goes a long way toward making sense of how the particular composite of the living and the dead might have become available to Collins. But what is most noticeable about his treatment of identity in the *Woman in White* is the rigor with which, by transforming the process by which identity is discerned into the central events of the novel's plot, Collins insists upon the indistinguishability of identity and the process by which it is known. In making a case for the resemblance of the blurring of memory and sensation produced across time and the blurring of subject and object—"How can I separate her from my own sensations, and from all that has happened in the later time"—Collins blocks his readers from considering the difficulty of figuring out who Laura is as simply a problem of being out of position. All identity suddenly appears in Collins's version of midcentury England as if it might simply be the product of someone's imagination: the reader's, the author's, or Walter the narrator's. The force of the novel lies in its capacity to make palpable the ontological fragility of identity, to produce the experience of a selfhood that seems as likely to slip free from one as the errant effects of one's own actions.

For Collins, the formal structure of novelistic ekphrasis offers particular access to this sense of fragility, and it provides an instrument for generalizing and communicating the mutability implied by such fragility. Consider the conclusion of Walter's description of his efforts to think about his first encounter with Laura:

> Lovely eyes in colour, lovely eyes in form—large and tender and quietly thoughtful—but beautiful above all things in the clear truthfulness of look that dwells in their inmost depths, and shines through all their changes of expression with the light of a purer and a better world. The charm—most gently and yet most distinctly expressed—which they shed over the whole face, so covers and transforms its little natural human blemishes elsewhere, that it is difficult to estimate the relative merits and defects of the other features. It is hard to see that the lower part of the face is too delicately refined away towards the chin to be in full and fair proportion with the upper part; that the nose, in escaping the aquiline bend (always hard and cruel in a woman, no matter how abstractly perfect it may be); has erred a little in the other extreme, and has missed the ideal straightness of line; and that

> the sweet, sensitive lips are subject to a slight nervous contraction, when she smiles, which draws them upward a little at one corner, towards the cheek. It might be possible to note these blemishes in another woman's face, but it is not easy to dwell on them in hers, so subtly are they connected with all that is individual and characteristic in her expression, and so closely does the expression depend for its full play and life, in every other feature, on the moving impulse of the eyes. (52)

What is striking about this passage is the way in which the narrator manages to describe precisely what he announces cannot easily be seen: "It is hard to see that the lower part of the face is too delicately refined away toward the chin to be in full and fair proportion with the upper part." For Collins, fictional description does not so much sharpen perception as it refuses to privilege it. Though it remains difficult to see Laura's faults, we have no difficulty knowing of their existence, because the passage describes what precisely it is that we can't see. At long last, we get the sort of detailed description of bodily detail that was pointedly withheld in the earlier passages. Indeed, we are likely to assemble the particular details with which we are presented—the slightly off-center nose, the tightened lips—into an image in our minds, discounting the fact that what is being detailed is what we aren't "seeing." But then, suddenly, the structure of negation that existed *within* the description of the body—we know the body by the folds of clothing that bisect it, by the hair color that is not quite the color it is compared to—is revealed to organize the relation of description to what is *without*, to the readers who construct imaginative worlds they cannot see out of authored details they don't perceive. The description we get is no less detailed and precise in its account of what we can't see than it would be if we could see it. Because the descriptions we get in novels represent perceptions by transforming them into knowledge, such knowledge stands in for what is not perceived as effectively as it stands in for what is.

Novelistic fictionality thus operates for Collins as a privileged mode of understanding because it invites readers to experience perceiving and knowing as distinct yet interchangeable modes of apprehension. That is, readers don't actually themselves perceive the objects that are described as present and immediate within the novel, but still they come to have knowledge of them via the description. We are likely to go on imagining Laura's face without registering that we are being provided with details of what we cannot see because imagining things we cannot see is what we almost always do when we read fiction. Suddenly, we realize what it is we have been doing all along when we read descriptions in novels—we have been laying claim to knowledge of people and places we don't actually see. That what we do seems far less strenuous and contested than my own rhetoric of "laying claim" would suggest is precisely the point, since as Collins would have it, it is the imperceptibility of the objects of description that makes knowledge of them feel like something as easy and beyond contestation as mere familiarity. In case we have missed the point, overlooking our reading as usual by reading as usual, Walter tells us what in fact we have done by telling us what to do: "Think of her as you thought of the first woman who quickened the pulse in you that the rest of her sex had no art to stir" (52). How else to discern Laura's ineffability, the quality that makes Laura *Laura*, but by imaging it to be precisely like the ineffability of someone else entirely, someone likewise unpictured and unseen? In offering up the peculiar case of a description of what can't quite be perceived, Collins at once enacts the general operation of such fictional description and explains how such description works.

With this double gesture, Collins seems to invite another question: If we regularly behave as if a person who is vivacious, healthy, wealthy, and confident and a person who is tentative, distracted, and sickly are the same person by virtue of the fact that these people inhabit the "same" body at different moments (a body that is itself constantly aging and changing), what is the difference between doing that and acting as if we actually see characters we only read about? Put this way, the particularity of individual identity suddenly appears to be anything but, becoming instead a kind of inductive exercise in which we gather the fragments of our encounters into generalities we love so far as we can recognize them. Individuals are individuals, it seems, to the very degree that they are generalized, generalizations of their various particular instantiations over time. By this account, the body functions as an epiphenomenal sign of the more fundamental problems surrounding the legibility of identity, whereby the turn to the evidence of the not-quite-visible aspect of a fictional body operates simply as an illustration of the difficulty of tracing an individual's identity from one moment to the next.

In the extended passage I have been analyzing, Collins stages both the logic of fictional ekphrasis and its undoing. Bodily descriptions only function to identify fictional characters through time, from one narrative moment to the next, so long as those descriptions aren't actually visible—so long, that is, as they can as fully evoke for us that particular unseen person who has made our own pulses race as an author's imaginative vision. In drawing our attention to the fact we are not actually seeing the bodily aspects being described but are instead "knowing" some standardized composite, Collins allows us to recognize that we have no empirical evidentiary grounds for tracking that body through time and, consequently, no grounds for understanding such a body to offer a foundation for identifying characters or individual subjects. In the span of time between the moment when Walter's "eyes first rested on her" and the moment at which he narrates, Laura has been interchanged, at least temporarily, with Anne Catherick, the mysterious "woman in white," and one of the two of them has died. In this regard, the ekphrastic challenges are not confined to a realm of representation generally conceived, but are pegged specifically to bodies—aging and perhaps dying bodies. Collins's account here is remarkable not merely for his suggestion that the changefulness of bodies inhibits their being known either through time or at any given moment: that claim could be made equally plausibly of any changing object. But Collins's account also allows us to understand that our normally untroubled assurance that the passage of time need not disturb our capacity to recognize the bodies before us rests upon our conviction that we have adequate grounds for knowing about what we can't actually see. So while we may be tempted to assume that Collins is making a point about the processes by which we recognize (or fail to recognize) the surfaces of bodies over time, the fact that he chooses to explore the problem of the legibility of changing objects by investigating the dynamics of fictional ekphrasis means that the issue is not the appearance of things but the correlation between what we understand ourselves to be capable of seeing and what remains beyond our capacity to observe. In this regard, I want to argue, Collins's exploration of the problems of recognizing bodies over time operates squarely within the paradigm of anatomical medicine analyzed in chapter 1 and is animated by that paradigm's tensions. We are able to assume the likeness of bodies—which is to say, the correlation between the sick body whose interior workings we cannot directly observe and the visible organs of the dead body revealed by way of the autopsy, or the likeness between the Laura Glyde, née Fairlie, who eludes our direct observation and that woman who has "the power to quicken the pulse"—only so long as we ignore the fact that bodies change over time, sicken, and die. We come to realize that we as readers, like Walter, cannot be entirely certain that the person we are seeing is Laura because we are not able to see her body over time, and seeing it in an instant—is not adequate to the task of grounding her identity. In aligning the elusiveness of Laura's aging body with our own readerly incapacity to see the fictional characters described to us, Collins's novel invites us to recognize the novelistic realism's capacity to function as a technology for thwarting the instantaneity of racial sight.

Collins further underscores the idea that his interests go beyond the legibility of observable surfaces by shifting his attention from the question of how and to what extent his readers, along with Walter, their narratorial stand-in, can identify Laura over time to the question of whether and in what ways Laura can know herself. In making the interchange of Laura's sick body and Anne Catherick's dead one the center around which the novel's plot is structured, Collins, I have already suggested, transforms the relation undergirding the legibility of anatomical bodies from a set of presumptions governing the legibility of characters to a process undergone by those characters, an aspect of their experience. But one of the hallmarks of anatomical medicine, we recall, is the notion that the interiors of bodies are both the site of disease—the locus of significant bodily activity—and are opaque to the subjects inhabiting those bodies. In making the likeness or interchangeability of bodies a plot element, something that happens rather than a founding presumption, Collins dramatizes Laura's lack of access to the "events" of her own body. The novel makes explicit that the woman who escapes from the asylum with the help of Walter and his co-investigator Marian Halcombe (Laura's stepsister and fierce advocate) can offer no testimony as to what has taken place up until that point. Once we admit the possibility that subjects might not be positioned to know themselves, the individuals inside and outside fictional worlds suddenly seem less like people and more like characters: which is to say, they have histories and identities only so long as they are recognized as having them by other people.

In inviting us to consider the legibility of bodies not simply from the perspective of those who would observe bodies but also from the perspective of those who inhabit them, *The Woman in White* joins the problem of identity and recognition—How do we know Laura?—to a cluster of problems of self-knowledge: How does Laura know herself? What sorts of things might be happening inside her body she knows nothing about? But in engineering this shift, Collins's novel does something else as well. While the anatomical body's opacity to the subject who inhabits it is predicated upon its autonomy as a system—only because its internal organs are understood to operate independently of the environment in which it finds itself is such a body opaque to its inhabitant—that very opacity makes such autonomy impossible to experience. So not only do midcentury subjects suddenly find themselves confronting the possibility that things might be going on inside their bodies they know nothing about, but this historically new sense of their bodies' opacity introduces the related, if not entirely coherent, anxiety that one's body is vulnerable to others as well. If one cannot know enough about what is going on inside one's body to know what that body is doing to itself, how can one be certain one knows enough to know what others are doing to it? And what is to assure that the circumscription of agency signaled by an opaque body need be limited to events within it? In externalizing the inner workings of the body in the form of the events of the novel's plot—in making the process by which Laura's sick body comes to be interchanged with Anne's dead one the novel's mystery—Collins articulates and enacts this paradoxical expansiveness of an autonomous system opaque to itself.

The Woman in White thus not only traces the diffusion of the instantaneously perceptible identity that is race but discovers, in the wake of this diffusion, new worries for the embodied subject, a new sense of being vulnerable to outside forces and limited in the power to recognize, ward off, or respond to such forces. Anatomical medicine posits the likeness of sick and autopsied bodies, we recall, not simply because (or in spite of the fact that) bodies age and change, but because the causal mechanisms driving the body's functioning, both healthy and pathological, escape the observation and the control of patient and physician alike. To inhabit an anatomical body is to experience oneself at the mercy of forces beyond one's knowledge or control: the autonomous operation of one's own internal organs. But just as the theoretically synchronic, theoretically self-contained operation of the body is revealed to depend upon the forceful overlooking of both the diachronic relations of cause and effect by which one's organs may make one sick and the medical interventions by which such sickness can be mitigated or intensified, the revelation of this willed opacity through the plotting of bodily causal process effectively extends the embodied subjects' sense of their tenuous control over the forces that buffet them beyond the bounds of their own bodies. Turning the formal structure of anatomical medicine into a diachronic plot, Collins startles his readers into recognizing that we aren't actually seeing the (fictional) bodies we think we are seeing. He then invites us to see the condition of fiction's unboundedness as the ground of his creation's broadened scope. In this regard, we would do well to understand the murder trial of the notorious poisoning physician William Palmer and its aftermath as not merely the historical inspiration for or enabling condition of Collins's novel, but also as its formal double, a doubling that matters inasmuch as it accomplishes, rather than presumes, the elimination of any clear distinction between Collins's fictional creation and what is beyond it.

In order to make both the terms and the force of this doubling clear, I want to take a few moments to review briefly the tense logic undergirding anatomical medicine's particular organization of the body. Anatomical medicine and physicians' claims to expert and exclusive knowledge come into being in a single stroke: anatomical medicine distinguishes itself from the humoral science that precedes it insofar as it posits a standard and self-enclosed body, legible in the comparability of the patient's sick body and the exposed organs of the anatomized corpse as its diagnostic ground. Inasmuch as such a comparison is necessarily unavailable either to the sick patient (who cannot see her own internal organs) or to the autopsied corpse (who is already dead), the very fact of comparability, as well as the notion of a standard body named and constituted by such comparability, is predicated upon the exclusivity of the physician's point of view and knowledge. But if the anatomical physician's capacity to diagnose illness rests upon an exclusive access to this idea of a body, that authority is nonetheless not quite as stable as it might seem. As I detailed in the first chapter, the logic of standardness turns out to be a diagnostic logic only, since the comparability of the sick and dead body depends upon excluding analytically the progression of the disease; the process by which the sick patient comes to be dead. To the degree to which a disease's progression must be excluded, so too must the possibility of intervening to bring about a cure, that is, of affecting the body from the outside. In this regard, anatomical physicians' authority to diagnose what ails a given patient stands in significant tension with their therapeutic claims. Doctors assert the exclusive authority of their knowledge to figure out what is wrong with a patient only at the price of losing the ground from which they might claim to be able to do something about it.

This fundamental contradiction between anatomical physicians' diagnostic and therapeutic authorities can be seen to structure much of the history by which the institutions of professional medicine emerged and developed in Great Britain over the course of the nineteenth century. But this structural tension at the heart of anatomical medicine also provides a framework within which we might understand the ways in which the trial of physician William Palmer was so deeply troubling to England's urban, literate, rapidly professionalizing middle class, in terms of its sense of its capacity to recognize itself and to act upon its own interests.

The Trial of the Poisoning Physician

At the time thirty-four-year-old William Palmer first came to the attention of the legal authorities in 1855, he had already spent nearly ten years as a licensed general practitioner in the town of Rugeley, in Staffordshire, earning himself a reputation as an inveterate gambler and racetrack devotee as well as a doctor. Beginning in the fall of 1854, Palmer entered a sustained period of what was either extraordinarily bad luck or chillingly systematic malignity. First, his wife Anne, upon whom he had taken out three life insurance policies totaling £13,000, sickened and died following an illness whose symptoms appeared consistent with cholera. The following August, Palmer's brother Walter, whose life William had also insured as sole beneficiary, died in a fit of apoplexy while William himself was the only medical practitioner in attendance. William's efforts to collect on Walter's policy prompted an investigation by an insurance company agent, resulting in a delay of payment that was especially burdensome for the young doctor, who by that time had embroiled himself within a complicated network of creditors. One of those creditors was Palmer's gambling associate John Parsons Cook, whom Palmer accompanied to the racetrack on 13 November 1855, where Cook won a substantial sum betting on his own horse. Cook collected only a portion of his winnings that day, with the remainder to be paid within the week. In the meantime, however, Cook fell ill while out celebrating his victory with Palmer and others. Cook recovered his health, and he and Palmer returned to Rugeley, where on 16 November, Cook again fell sick after lunching with Palmer. Cook died on 20 November, with Palmer again serving as the sole attending physician, "following an erratic pattern of physical distress that appeared to coincide with Dr. Palmer's ministrations."[14]

The suspicious circumstances surrounding Cook's death led local authorities to order a group of four doctors to perform an autopsy of Cook's body. Working under decidedly adverse conditions—Palmer repeatedly attempted to disrupt the proceedings, twice going so far as to attempt to cause investigators to spill the viscera—the medical examiners were nonetheless able to complete the postmortem. They then sent the extracted matter to London for analysis by the eminent forensic physician Alfred Swaine Taylor, already well known as the author of the 1848 *On Poisons*, the massive tome that effectively established toxicology as a distinct area of specialization. Taylor's findings were not, at least immediately, definitive. Nothing in the appearance of Cook's internal organs would account for death from natural causes; at the same time, tests for poisons revealed only trace amounts of antimony, a chemical that sometimes occurred naturally in the body but which could also be fatal when given in repeated doses. Despite the absence of definitive postmortem findings, Taylor eventually ruled decisively, basing his ruling of death by strychnine not upon any evidence revealed by way of the autopsy, but rather on the testimony regarding Cook's behavior in the final hours of his life given by a chambermaid at the inn who had been attending to the patient along with Palmer. In Taylor's view, the kind of convulsive movements described by the maid could only be the result of tetanus. Given the absence of any kind of external lacerations, the symptoms of tetanus must have been caused by the administration of strychnine, the only substance capable of producing such effects, despite the fact that no evidence of strychnine had been discovered in Cook's autopsied corpse.

Less significant than a betrayal of some implied trust between doctor and patient was the way in which the case highlighted the impossibility of distinguishing in any hard-and-fast way between ministrations designed to cure and those meant to harm, between medicine and poison. What the Palmer case did was make palpable and immediately comprehensible to the public the essential theoretical tension plaguing anatomical medicine: the incongruence, that is, between its diagnostic and therapeutic claims. It did so by presenting this tension within the structure of anatomical medical authority as a real and present threat to the well-being of the public at large. Within an epistemological system in which patients' sick bodies are taken to be fundamentally like the dead, autopsied corpses by which such bodies' otherwise inaccessible inner workings are revealed, the temporally extended process by which sick bodies turn into dead bodies (dying, poisoning) or become well again (medicating) must be made analytically irrelevant: to admit the significance of the process by which sick bodies change into dead ones is to acknowledge that the two bodily states are not always already identical to one another. Physicians fall back upon pragmatic, trial-and-error evidence—evidence gleaned *after* a particular treatment has succeeded or failed to ameliorate a given set of symptoms—because they are unable to see what is taking place in the body at the moment a given treatment is taking effect. Insofar as the process by which medicine acts upon the body remains opaque to both patient and physician, there can be no grounds for distinguishing between medicating and poisoning. Both are beyond the purview of an anatomical medicine structured around the likeness of the sick body and the dead body. In this sense, the problem of distinguishing between medicating and poisoning that follows from the standardized body's opacity is linked to the ever-changing particular body's limitation as a ground for identity. In essence, the danger made imminent by the trial of the Rugeley Poisoner was as much the danger posed by those doctors who followed anatomical medicine to the letter as by those who deviated from normal science.

One of the most explicit and straightforward responses to this newly exposed menace came from someone closely linked to both the emerging institutions of anatomical medicine and the Palmer trial itself: Alfred Swaine Taylor. The chief medical expert in the Palmer trial, whose institutional credentials had allowed him to make the largely incoherent case for medical evidence of strychnine poisoning even in the absence of any chemical traces,[15] Taylor would publish a second edition of *On Poisons* in 1859 that gave voice to many of the ambivalences and qualifications of anatomical medical knowledge he had been reluctant to express in court three years earlier. (Collins kept a copy of this edition of *On Poisons* in his private library.)[16] The preface to this revised edition engages the poison/medicine conundrum head on: "No one can draw a definite boundary between a poison and a medicine. The greater number of poisons are useful medicines when properly employed, and nearly every substance in the catalogue of medicines may be converted into an instrument of death if improperly administered. For this reason it must not be supposed that a substance is not a poison because it does not find a place in this second edition of my work."[17] The indistinguishability of poisons and medicines within anatomical medicine means that "poison" cannot function as a term of medical analysis: "Whether a particular substance is, or is not, a poison, is a question of fact left for the decision of a jury from the medical evidence given in a case." He goes on:

> It would seem that the proof of the crime of poisoning should rest upon the *intention* with which the substance is administered and on the effects produced, or on satisfactory evidence that it is capable either of destroying life or of causing injuring to health. A man may administer a substance such as tartar emetic in *medicinal doses* with good or evil intention. His intention, which is a question for a jury, may be not to remove disease, but to destroy life. He may administer it secretly under circumstances in which its lawful use would certainly not be required; he may continue to use it at intervals, in *medicinal doses*, even when its dangerous effects are clearly manifested by symptoms, and when any medical man, dealing bone fide with a patient, would immediately withdraw it as a medicine. Is such an act as this to be covered by that thin cloak of medical sophistry which was spread over it in the case of William Palmer?[18]

Here the opacity of bodies as a ground for subjects that inhabit them—an opacity that allows organs to function independently of any will, medicine, or poison to cause unobservable effects—suddenly spreads as well to subjects who would act upon bodies, as intentions become unknowable, both to themselves and to others. By this account, the threat to the public articulated by the Palmer trial is not limited to the practice of anatomical medicine, a practice whose menace William Palmer's fatal ministrations pointed up by revealing the impossibility of establishing any clear material distinction between medicating and poisoning. Instead, the threat seems to lie in the power the case has to reveal the tenuousness with which people who inhabit bodies with internal organs that can act and be acted upon without anyone's knowledge or control can be reliably linked to their actions. Here intentions and effects, each insufficient in itself, are alternately invoked as supplements to one another. If poisoning reveals an incoherence at the heart of anatomical medicine that undermines the force of its expert claims—that is, anatomical physicians may lay claim to exclusive knowledge only at the cost of being able to do anything with that knowledge, or alternately, anatomical physicians may treat their patients only so long as they and their patients accept the risk that they may be unwittingly or deliberately causing harm—Taylor seems bent on saving medicine by showing its knowledge and its efficacy to be no less reliable or efficacious than those of anyone else: intention, after all, is "a question for a jury."

But while the rhetoric of Taylor's revisions to *On Poison* suggest, at least initially, that he understands his strategy to be one of saving medical knowledge by evacuating it of much of its epistemological particularity, for most of the writers of the periodical press, both medical and general, who weighed in on the Palmer case, what mattered about Palmer—both what rendered the case threatening and what made its lessons and effects potentially generalizable—had everything to do with its medical specificity. Taking up the topic of the approaching trial in a March 1856 article in the *Lancet*, Britain's leading medical journal, one writer opined:

> The importance of the point at issue will be at once seen if we reflect upon the logical consequences of such a conclusion as that arrived at by Dr. Taylor. Antimony is found in a dead body; therefore, antimony must have been taken within a short period of death. Now, if we assume it to be proved that no antimony was prescribed by a medical practitioner during the last illness of the person whose death is the subject of inquiry, there arises immediately a *prima facie* proof that it was administered for a nefarious purpose, and someone connected with the deceased might be placed in custody upon a charge of murder.[19]

Bracketing the issue of the legibility of the Palmer postmortem evidence, which was decidedly more ambiguous than this writer allows, what is striking about this formulation is the way in which the writer is able to use the very indistinguishability of poison and medicine that was so troubling to Taylor in order to make the case for the efficacy and transparency of anatomical physicians' therapeutic efforts. (This case, we recall, could not be made from within the epistemological framework of anatomical medicine itself.) We know that medical practitioners act in the proper spirit because those who administer antimony "for a nefarious purpose" are not medical practitioners. But this isolation of intention, as well as the distinction of the acts of poisoning and treating that follow directly from such isolation, actually depends upon the material and structural identity of medicine and poison. That is, only because administering poison and administering medicine might otherwise resemble one another entirely does the isolation of intention become necessary, and only because these sorts of actions might otherwise appear identical does this isolation of intention operate to ground these identities as mutually exclusive from one another. Medical practitioners can't poison and those who poison can't be medical practitioners because, if either condition were to be true, there would be nothing to distinguish poisoning and administering medicine.

Only because the structure of anatomical bodies renders illegible the intentions of the physicians who act upon them does the category "physician" become a professional identity—the sort of thing that might be authorized by educational or licensing institutions in advance of any particular acts rather than by the performance of a set of practices or the possession of a body of knowledge. Strangely, then, while we might have expected the Palmer case to offer a staggering blow to the authority of anatomical medicine, for the *Lancet* writer, the trial offers the occasion for the reformulation of such authority. It presents a set of circumstances, rather than a description of professional knowledge or activities, by which a medical practitioner can happily and persuasively possess the sort of identity ascribed to doctors by an outside observer—here, a lay writer for a general medical journal, but also presumably the same institutional authorities set up for the purpose of educating, licensing, and regulating doctors.

While the *Lancet* author's implicit evocation of a kind of professional identity conceived in terms distinct from what professional physicians actually know or do would seem to respond to the threat posed to expert medical knowledge by the Palmer trial, it does not speak in any way to the more general vulnerability made apparent by the case of the physician-poisoner—the vulnerability posed by the sense that people's bodies act and can be acted upon without their knowledge. Indeed, the generalizability of this vulnerability is part and parcel of its threat, since the fact that everyone's bodies are opaque to themselves means that there is no position outside the dynamic from which the opacity might be countered.

For the author of "Poisoning in England," writing in the 22 December 1855 edition of the *Saturday Review* with a more general audience in mind, the possibility that one might find oneself poisoned by anyone, even the physician one went to in order to find out what was going on inside one's own body, represented a threat to the notions of publicness and national identity: "Since the beginning of the present month, public feeling has been shocked and the national character disgraced, by no fewer than three most fearful cases of poisoning. . . . People are beginning to ask, are these cases typical? Do they reveal a state of things in England which recalls the ominous names of Mrs. Turner, Brinvilliers, and Laffarge? Is the art of poisoning—above all, of secret and slow poisoning—revived?"[20]

The term "secret poisoning" seems here to have two senses: both the poisoning some deceptively innocent person might undertake in secret and the slow process of death by poison so gradual that one might be dying and not even know it. The threat posed to the public here goes beyond the danger of more deaths to encompass the difficulty of pulling apart the two meanings of "secret poisoning." The possibility of a revival of the once-pervasive epidemic of poisoning has left "public feeling . . . shocked and the national character disgraced," but the animating anxiety seems less a product of either of those affective responses individually than a consequence of the possibility of both being operative at once. The passage, which opens the article and establishes its pervasive tone, seems haunted by the implications of the possibility that "public feeling," presumably existing in some overlapping if nonidentical relation with "national character," might be at one and the same time "shocked" and "disgraced." In part, this not entirely predictable relationship between "national character" and "public feeling" seems an acknowledgment of the fact that of the three poisoners whose history haunts and helps to characterize the contemporary "state of things in England," two are French, not English.[21] The *Saturday Review* writer conceives of a notion of publicness that need not coincide with the bounds of a national community, and whose boundaries are consequently unpredictable.

From a strictly grammatical standpoint, the problem seems one of slightly wobbly point of view. How can one be disgraced, a condition that bespeaks the responsibility born of deliberate action, by a set of events whose occurrence comes as great a shock to one as it was likely to have been to its unwitting victims? But here the grammatical confusion appears to manifest anxiety rather than simply contain it, since it suggests an epistemology of the body politic that forcefully resembles that of the anatomical body: there may be things going on in one's body one knows nothing about. The very assertion of national identity thus seems to carry with it a paranoiac cast, as the possibility of conceiving of oneself as like one's compatriots introduces the notion that one cannot possibly know them (or oneself) well enough to know for certain that one will not be hurt by them. And with this threat, the writer suggests, publicness becomes not simply expressive, a matter of feeling, but ought to be understood as epistemological as well, a charge of responsibility for a certain kind of vigilance. As varied as these solutions are—Taylor's careful scientific explanation, the *Lancet*'s professional defense, the *Saturday Review*'s call for vigilant self-examination—what is perhaps more remarkable than the differences is the extent to which all of the writers, each working independently, understand the Palmer trial to be posing essentially the same challenge to the legibility of agency. The trial raises the possibility that we would do well to worry not just about what our doctors are doing but also about what our neighbors and relatives—indeed, what we ourselves—are doing, and it is therefore unclear to which external authority or institutional body we might turn to help us distinguish those who might hurt us from those who will not. This is the case not only because the social phenomenon of poisoning is culturally pervasive in midcentury England, but also because what *is* pervasive is a sense of individuals' unfitness for the task of recognizing what about or among them is pervasive at all. In this regard, the Palmer case stands as both an occasion of paranoia and the revelation of its formal structure. There is nothing to fear but fear itself, and that is precisely the problem.

Taylor is arguably the most unflinching of the three writers in his diagnosis of anatomical medicine's incapacity to sort out the relations between subjects and their actions. But if we return to his preface and look more closely at his language, we can see the beginnings of an alternative epistemology of action:

> A man may administer a substance such as tartar emetic in *medicinal doses* with good or evil intention. His intention, which is a question for a jury, may not be to remove disease, but to destroy life. He may administer it secretly under circumstances in which its lawful use would certainly not be required; he may continue to use it at intervals, in medicinal doses, even when its dangerous effects are clearly manifested by symptoms.

Taylor's insistence that the dosage at which tartar emetic is administered not be taken in and of itself to indicate poisoning is partly an insistence that causation cannot be determined objectively from the outside, independent of the gauge of the intentionality of the person dispensing the medicine. But his discrediting of dosage as an indicator also seems to occasion a rethinking of the nature of intentionality, a rethinking of the temporality by which intentions are to be discerned. The more easily assimilable implication of Taylor's testimony is that intention becomes discernible only retrospectively. By this account, intention exists, and it can be seen to initiate and direct action. It just can't be discovered by other people until after it has already done its initiating and directing.

But Taylor's ruminations circle around a more radical conception of intentionality as well. Once the defining qualities of poisoning are reconceived from being a specific dose of poison administered at a particular time into being understood as a process of administering dosages over time in response, or with studied obliviousness, to the effects of the already administered substance, the intention to poison is something that must be expressed and reexpressed over and over. At any given moment, Taylor's testimony would have it, Palmer might have chosen to stop giving Cook more strychnine—realizing in horror, on observing Cook's uncontrollable seizures, that he had given his friend too much or, alternatively, watching his friend in agony and being struck with guilt and remorse for having planned to do away with him. Stopping short of killing Cook, deciding not to give just one more dose, Palmer would cast off the opprobrium of having intended to poison his friend, whatever he himself might have originally understood his own plans to be. By this second, more disruptive account, intention not only becomes discernible to others once it has produced externally measurable effects, but it only comes into being *for the intending subject* as he comes to discover what he has done. In this account, intentionality is recursive, a temporally diffuse, ongoing causing, continually modified and readjusted in response to a reading of its effects. Within this recursive model, not only is intention not to be understood as a delimited state of consciousness that precedes and sets into motion a causal chain of events, but knowledge, interpretation, and the chain of cause and effect cannot be fully pulled apart from one another. Agents form intentions and direct their actions with an eye toward what is likely to happen—one can't *intend* to poison someone without at least some understanding of what will have to occur for such an outcome to take place. But inasmuch as intentions are constantly being modified and readjusted, an agent's "reading" of a set of circumstances or an event in a causal chain can be understood to create the intention to direct that set of events to a particular end.

If anatomical medicine turns us all into novelistic characters, the Palmer poisoning case allows us to become readers as well.

Moreover, not only does Taylor's conception of intentionality imagine that people's intentions might to some degree be formed by the events they set into motion, but in offering a model of intentionality unconfined to any single moment and uncircumscribed by the consciousness of a single mind, the effort to sort out who meant to do what in the Palmer case also effectively lays out a model of intentionality that is fundamentally social. If a subject cannot quite be said to have meant to do something until she actually knows what it is she has done, then the intentionality formed out of that process is almost necessarily the product of the history, experience, desires, and aspirations not only of that particular subject but also of those who effect and are affected by the actions set into motion and read.

In this series of responses to the Palmer trial, it is thus possible to trace the case's widening circles of significance, as the unit of analysis moves from the motives and behavior of the individual poisoner to the professional identity of medical practitioners to the public or body politic. But this account of Palmer's historical resonance suggests that cultural "events" produce effects that matter more as time passes, extending over a broader and broader swath of the world. If we have ended not with the *Saturday Review*'s writer giving witness to the ways in which the Palmer trial has "shocked and disgraced" the English public but with a detour back to the toxicologist Alfred Swaine Taylor, this is not least because Taylor's recursive intentionality suggests a far more complex trajectory of cultural cause and effect. Taylor's account certainly suggests that recursive intentionality might structure the acts of even those who are not in the business of secretly poisoning others. More to the point, Taylor's recursive intentionality challenges the authority of the event's origin—the self-conscious intentions of its agent or agents—as well as the cultural conditions or social organization from which such an event might be thought to "emerge" to structure its meaning or significance. In part, this recursivity registers the historiographically incontrovertible fact that things sometimes go awry, events unfolding in ways not intended or even anticipated by those who set them into motion. Less obviously, Taylor's recursivity implies that the relation of a given actor to the social unit within which the event takes place and toward which it is directed is not simply the relation in place at the moment the intention is conceived or carried out. Neither the boundaries and membership of a culture nor its attitudes and practices are so fixed or pervasive that individual actions might not change both what counts as what the culture "does" as well as who counts as part of that culture. For Taylor, grappling with the opacities of the Palmer poisoning trial, the fact that contemporary subjects' bodies are capable of doing things without their knowledge or will means that these bodies are vulnerable, not impervious, to actions directed from the outside. By this understanding, cultures cannot identify, direct, or imply what happens to the citizen-subjects who exist proximate to them because neither the beliefs nor the behaviors of subjects and cultures, nor the precise ways in which they press and influence one another, are fully legible at any given moment.

Within this model of subjectivity and the historiography it implies, novelistic fiction stands as more than simply one of an array of possible genres for representing the dynamic relations of subjects and cultures. It stands as the privileged mode. What the Palmer case and the various responses to it make palpable is the tenuousness of any claim for the priority and fixity of cultures, in either their determinative or their heuristic functions—that is, in either their capacity to make people believe certain ways or in their reliability as indexes of how those people will and do behave. In questioning the relation between the reproduction of a culture and the creative acts of individual author-subjects, novelistic fictions undermine the default presumption of the priority of culture, the idea that cultures exist as distinct, legible entities, and that in preexisting the particular actions that occur within them, they largely determine what those actions will be. I want to make clear that while such a recursive notion of culture seems an effect of the formal qualities of novels that preexist Palmer's own machinations, the availability of fictions to be put to such uses only becomes recognizable at the moment people come to understand that they have little access to what their bodies are doing and having done to them.

The Disappearance of the Author

I want to suggest that Collins himself, mindful of the lessons of the Palmer case, tries to imagine a way of slipping the shackles of his own authorial priority—that is, of his own, fully past, imaginative authority—so as to make it possible to conceive of a version of *The Woman in White* that does not originate with him. By working in two directions at once— by creating a novel whose unfolding plot seems only partly traceable back to its author's act of imagining, while at the same time inviting his readers to grapple with something other than the sum total of the narrative presented in his novel—Collins is able to liberate the process of knowing his novel from reference to his creation of it. If bodies can function independently of the subjects who inhabit them, and if such bodies thus become capable of (and vulnerable to) actions only tenuously linked to a specific agent's local intentions, then the products or effects of such actions themselves hardly get to count as being "done." By withdrawing the novel from functioning as a completed object in the world, Collins clears the space for the operation of an audience of interpreting readers the scope of whose membership is not implied by his own authorship, by his acts of fictional making.

The most explicit signal that writerly authority is being reconceived by way of a loosening of the relations among agents, the (aesthetic) effects they produce, and the publics that frame and apprehend those effects, comes in the novel's final Epoch, as Walter assembles an audience at Limmeridge in order to present them with the results of his investigation—that is, to tell them what has happened on the evidence of the various narratives we have ourselves just finished reading. (Walter has launched his investigation in order to determine whether the ailing Laura came to be interchanged with the already dead Anne Catherick, or, alternatively, to discover the process by which Laura herself has come to be dead.) The notion that Walter can stand before the assembled public and offer them a narrative account of the causal chain by which Laura Glyde and the woman rescued from the asylum and now standing before them can be understood to be identical to one another is predicated upon the assumption that the disclosure of the conspiracy would involve the piecing together of the novel's disparate narrations into a single coherent narrative, a kind of paraphrase. According to both Walter's public summary and the novel's own overlapping narratives, the uncovering of the conspiracy turns upon the discovery and proof of a discrepancy between the date "Laura" is supposed to have died as it is designated on the death certificate and the gravestone and the date on which Sir Percival Glyde's wife travels by coach from Hampshire to London. That the journey evidently took place after the person supposedly embarking upon it had died should, in Walter's view, be understood as positive proof that the traveler and the dead woman are not the same person, and more to the point, that the body buried under Laura Glyde's gravestone is not in fact that of Laura Glyde.

What the account elides, however, is the process by which determining the events' chronology has come to be understood as the definitive piece of evidence. In a world in which a poisoner only turns out to have poisoned when he and others see what he has done, we cannot simply piece together events into a single seamless narrative, but must make the conditions by which we come to apprehend these relations of cause and effect—including our conditions of not knowing—part of what it is we have discovered. In our reading of the novel itself, we only discover that the precise moment at which Laura leaves Limmeridge might be crucial to tracing her fate because it takes place at the moment that Marian Halcombe fails to know—during the period of time, that is, when she is unable to assume her usual role of Laura's ever-vigilant protector. Marian is unable to guard Laura from those who would do her ill, and she is unable even to function as narrator/witness of Laura's travails because Marian herself has been laid unconscious by what she understands to be typhoid fever. By redacting Marian's narrative of her experience into a chronology of events, Walter's account erases the extent to which the knowledge of the novel's mystery is produced as a reading of the complex relations between what is and is not known. Like the chain of events that make up the conspiracy, coming to know is, for him, a series of discoveries that, once they have taken place, can be transferred to or appropriated by anybody. According to this model, once something is known, it ceases to matter how, when, or by whom it came to be known.

But in *The Woman in White*, chronology *does* matter when events that happen become not just the form in which happening and knowing take place but things to be known in themselves. This highlighting and abstracting of chronology allows us to see the order of events as one possible structure of knowing, rather than the form all knowledge inevitably takes. By rendering contingent this model that would conceive of knowledge as a kind of cumulative chronology, the novel invites us to recognize the structuring significance of Marian's moments of *not* knowing.

Not only does the novel make the unraveling of the mystery of Laura's identity contingent upon tracing what Marian knows and fails to know and when she does both, but it also insinuates that we would do well to be cautious about presuming we can know for certain what precisely happens to Marian herself.[22] Up until now, I have been pointing out how the resistance of the body to being seen racially, in an instant—its aging, the developmental course of its sicknesses and diseases, its medicating, its poisoning—offers a structure through which to make sense of the ways characters act, are acted upon, and are made legible. In this final section, I want to examine how *The Woman in White* turns this bodily capacity into the stuff of its plot, rather than simply its formal structure and, in so doing, wrests the questions concerning the capacity of bodies to organize subjectivity and makes it recognizable from the confines of the structure of individual characters.

Marian Halcombe ventures onto the eaves of the family mansion one dark and foggy night in an attempt to overhear the details of a conspiracy she suspects is afoot between the mysterious Count Fosco and Sir Percival

Glyde to deprive Laura of her inheritance. Balancing herself on the narrow balcony just outside the library window, Marian hears Fosco plan: "I must wait a little, yet, to let circumstances guide me; and I must know, in every possible way, what those circumstances are likely to be" (325). A storm breaks out suddenly, and Marian is forced to return to her room. Soaked to the bone, she becomes feverish, and then falls into unconsciousness. We readers trace this trajectory by way of the growing incoherence of her diary entries, which trail off into illegible blottings until, to our horror, we find them punctuated by the "Postscript by a Sincere Friend," Fosco, who announces with one and the same gesture Marian's illness and his presence within our ranks as readers of her diary. With Marian so dispatched, Laura is transported to the lunatic asylum, where she either dies or is made to assume the identity of an already-dead lookalike, Anne Catherick.

It would be tempting to say that the success of the conspirators' plot rests upon Marian's illness, but for the fact that such a formulation underplays the degree of the dependence of Fosco and Percival's plot on Collins: the novel offers us little ground for imagining there could even be a conspiracy, much less one that unfolds successfully, without this apparently unanticipatable turn of events. So dependent does the characters' plotting appear upon the author's that we might be forgiven for seeing Collins as simply a coconspirator in the plan to relieve Laura of her fortune, opting to tip his hand toward Fosco and Percival at the cost of his authority to produce a fully imagined and seemingly autonomous fictional world, a world in relation to which the author, having finished creating it, has no local or particular interests. But if Fosco seems, on the one hand, privy to knowledge of the likelihood that authorial aid will be forthcoming, urging caution as circumstances array themselves to his advantage—"I must wait a little, yet, to let circumstances guide me"—he is at the same time loathe to cede the power to make things happen to any external author of circumstance: "I must know, in every possible way, what those circumstances are likely to be."

We are thus equally likely to speculate that if Marian has gotten sick in ways that allow the conspiracy to go forward, it is because her sickness is one of the consequences of the conspiracy—that is, she has been poisoned—rather than merely its condition of possibility. Such speculation is only heightened in Fosco's postscript to Marian's diary, when, having elbowed Collins aside as the diary's conduit to the reader, he praises Marian for the "accuracy of her report of the whole conversation [between himself and Percival] from the beginning to the end," and announces his plan to offer the physician now attending her the resources of his "vast knowledge of chemistry, and [his] luminous experience of the more subtle resources which medical and magnetic science have placed at the disposal of mankind" (337).[23] Nor are the grounds for such a reading limited to the events surrounding Marian's "illness." Immediately following Fosco's abrupt supplantation of Marian's narrative in her diary, we are informed by the new narrator, Laura's hypochondriacal uncle Frederick Fairlie, that Fanny, Marian's maid, "has fainted dead away, for the first time in her life . . . after drinking a cup of tea with the Countess [Fosco]." The countess has painstakingly prepared the tea herself, "a proceeding," Mr. Fairlie informs us, "which might have interested [him], if [he] had been her medical man; but being nothing of the sort, [he] felt bored by hearing of it" (342–43). As a consequence of her drugging, Fanny is unable to receive the messages from Marian whose delivery was the pretext of Countess Fosco's visit. In his final narrative, Count Fosco confesses to having had a hand in Fanny's poisoning: "On two occasions only . . . did I summon to myself the assistance of chemical knowledge. . . . I availed myself of the services of my invaluable wife, to copy one and to intercept the other of two letters which my adored enemy [Marian] had entrusted to a discarded maid. In this case, the letters being in the bosom of the girl's dress, Madame Fosco could only open them, read them, perform her instructions, seal them and put them back again by scientific assistance—which assistance I rendered in a half-ounce bottle" (603). While Fosco confesses to poisoning Fanny in order to rebut the assumptions—"Odious insinuations both!—"that [he] used [his] vast chemical resources against Anne Catherick; and that [he] would have used them, if [he] could, against the magnificent Marian herself" (602), he is nonetheless keen to insist upon his pharmacological expertise:

> The best years of my life have been passed in the ardent study of medical and chemical science. Chemistry, especially, has always had irresistible attractions for me, from the enormous, the illimitable power which the knowledge of it confers. Chemists, I assert emphatically, might sway, if they pleased, the destinies of humanity. Let me explain this before I go further.
>
> Mind, they say, rules the world. But what rules the mind? The body. The body (follow me closely here) lies at the mercy of the most omnipotent of all potentates—the Chemist. Give me—Fosco—chemistry; and when Shakespeare has conceived Hamlet, and sits down to execute the conception—with a few grains of power dropped into his daily food, I will reduce his mind, by the action of his body, till his pen pours out the most abject drivel that has ever degraded paper. (601–2)

In linking the question of the author's capacity to interfere within an already established and seemingly autonomous fictional world to the kind of intervention in the theoretically autonomous operations of an anatomical body that poisoning and medicating represent, Collins registers the degree to which the realist novel's notion of representational authority follows the contours of the anatomical body's legibilities and opacities, even when bodies are not the objects being represented. But we would be rash simply to conclude that the novel offers itself as a kind of historical allegory. We are not allowed definitively to rule out that Marian has been sickened by being soaked in the rain.[24]

Rather than announcing a concatenation of causes, an author in secret league with his characters to make a certain outcome inevitable and, in that inevitability, to demonstrate the existence of a kind of hypertrophied agency, the excess of possible causes can be seen to signal the absence of any certain ones, the difficulty of definitively linking subjects, actions, and effects. Marian writes: "The plan which had now occurred to me was to get out, at my sitting-room window, on to this roof; to creep along noiselessly, till I reached that part of it which was immediately over the library window; and to crouch down between the flower-pots, with my ear against the outer railing" (319). As Marian elaborates her plan, we are likely to find it increasingly difficult to remember that it is in fact merely a plan. The extraordinary detail with which she renders the journey from here to just over there has the effect of tipping us from the subjunctive to the strange temporality of novelistic description, a thick account of the here and now written at some time and place that isn't quite. Marian's plan, of course, is evident: she means to eavesdrop.[25] But what makes the plan remarkable is its literalism: she means to eavesdrop from beneath the eaves. It is this literalism that makes sense of the peculiar, already-in-progress quality of a supposedly prospective plan. The distance between the conception of a series of events and their unfolding narrows to nothing, inasmuch as the word's meaning, the ways in which it has been used, rather than any individual agent, generate the happening. Suddenly, it appears a dramatization of the recursive logic Taylor felt his way toward in his effort to make Palmer's action morally legible: once intentions are understood to be legible upon the evidence of their effects, in what sense can those actions be understood to be done by a particular agent?[26]

And if the novel's literalism culminates with Marian's ascension to the eaves to eavesdrop, it does not begin there. She is moved to describe her plan after observing suspicious activities in the yard below:

> Just as I was turning away wearily from the window, to go back to the bedroom, and make a second attempt to complete the unfinished entry in my journal. I smelt the odour of tobacco-smoke, stealing toward me on the heavy night air. The next moment I saw a tiny red spark advancing from the farther end of the house in the pitch darkness. I heard no footsteps, and I could see nothing but the spark. . . . The spark remained stationary for a moment, then moved back again in the direction from which it had advanced. As I followed its progress, I saw a second red spark, larger than the first, approaching from the distance. The two met together in the darkness. Remembering who smoked cigarettes, and who cigars, I inferred, immediately, that the Count had come out first to look and listen, under my window, and that Sir Percival had afterwards joined him. (317)

Here the inaccessibility of the characters' bodies to direct observation is manifested as a fracturing of the scene of encounter into a series of discrete sensory fragments. Not only does the presentation of the scene in the form of a list of smells, sights, and sounds make it impossible to distinguish the figures encountering one another from the ground they inhabit, but the inclusion of the absence of sounds—no footsteps, sounds themselves characterized by their organization of absence into a series—makes it difficult to distinguish the present scene from what is not happening now, but which might have happened in the past or which may yet happen. This evocation of the not-quite-present is immediately generalized as a narrative mode—Marian must remember who smokes cigarettes and who cigars in order to make sense of the activity taking place beneath her window—and so crucial is this knowledge gleaned from past experience that we readers are not in fact offered it as a distinct set of facts but are simply presented it in the form of the conclusions she is able to draw by way of this synthesis.

Marian thus finds herself tracing the progress and halting convergence of the two red sparks, with Sir Percival and Fosco, one a cigarette smoker and one a smoker of cigars, having been turned into subjects whose legibility is predicated upon their inhaling and exhaling together. Within a world in which eavesdropping of necessity takes place beneath the eaves, these two con-spire—breathe together—no matter what it is they finally talk about. Insofar as it is Marian's observation of the two sparks that sends her toward the roof for further investigation, we can say she is sickened by conspiracy, whether it is poisoning by Fosco and Percival or Collins's narratively improbable downpour that does her in. In offering a moment in which literalization is continuous with the agency of characters and authors, *The Woman in White* suggests that the language of a culture—the ways in which people use a word collectively to make it mean—is as capable of generating narratives, of making things happen, as characters or authors would be.[27] The possibility of such collective agency would seem predicated upon the sort of opaque relation between agents and events that the Palmer case makes evident, the opacity associated with the inhabitation of an anatomical body, whose functions are driven by causal mechanisms that escape the subject's observation or control. Here, by way of the framework of the Palmer trial, the novel's point becomes clear: inhabiting a world in which they may at any moment discover themselves to have been poisoned, slowly, secretly, by someone who may not know what he is doing, individual subjects participate in a collective agency not because they choose to but because they cannot choose to. By making discernible the experience of one's body through time and the degree to which the functions and acts of such a diachronic body can neither be seen in an instant, nor known, nor controlled, the threat of poisoning reveals the fact of collective agency to be a consequence of the impossibility of individual agency, the incapacity of subjects to make their aging, changing, dying bodies act.

By displacing the author's agency as the cause of its made-up events, *The Woman in White* allows its readers to experience a culture as culture, as a particular and contingent set of practices and habits of making that seem to exist independently, rather than as a consequence, of the actors who understand themselves to move and be moved by its patterns. In this independence, the novel offers a vision of sociability in which social relatedness can no longer be presumed, brought into being as it is by each act cast against the future horizon of not-yet-performed or known actions.

THREE

Picturing Utilitarianism: John Stuart Mill and the Invention of a Photographic Public

There is a John Stuart Mill we know, and this John Stuart Mill would not be an unexpected presence in a history of thinking about race. Mill opens his best-known work, *On Liberty*, with a genealogy of tyranny that culminates in what is arguably his most widely quoted formulation. As Mill tells it, in distant times—specifically in the earliest familiar histories of Greece, Rome, and England—"subjects, or some classes of subjects" were locked in conflict with "the Government," and "by liberty, was meant protection against the tyranny of the political rulers."[1] More recently, Mill goes on, as representative governments have come to replace the authoritarian governments of hereditary monarchies, a new form of democratic tyranny has emerged, in which "society itself is the tyrant, society collectively, over the separate individuals who compose it" (8). It is this Mill—a Mill who not only theorizes and elaborates upon the evils of the "tyranny of the majority" (a phrase he borrows from Tocqueville's *Democracy in America*) but who also articulates a framework for protecting the rights of the minority against such modern tyrannizing—who has come to command attention in contemporary conversations about the political representation of (racial) minorities.

In entitling her 1994 essay collection *The Tyranny of the Majority: Fundamental Fairness in Representative Democracy*, Lani Guinier clearly means to locate herself within this account of Millian liberalism. Guinier assembled the collection in the wake of her failed 1993 nomination to serve as assistant attorney general in charge of the Civil Rights Division during Bill Clinton's first term, in a concerted effort to respond to charges that she was a "quota queen" and reverse racist, "consistently hostile to the principle of one person, one vote."[2] I want to spend a few moments examining the terms of Guinier's self-defense, not as my framing thus far might suggest in the name of genealogy, but rather in the name of anachronism. That is, my goal in this opening is not to draw a line of influence from Mill to Guinier that will lend the conventional wisdom a scholarly heft, but rather the opposite: to suggest that we attend to the line of influence running from Guinier to Mill, to notice the ways in which the intellectual and political contexts animating Guinier's writing have shaped (distorted?) a prevailing sense of Mill's project. Guinier's rebuttal to her critics rests upon her insistence that the politics of race are properly subsumable within the politics of representation. She is arguing not for altering the ways in which raced subjects register politically, but for altering the ways in which minority positions register politically—minority positions that are only contingently racialized, positions that are only contingently minority. In this regard, both Guinier's position and the reading of Mill that would locate him as a intellectual forebear rest firmly within an analytical framework that conceives of race as a kind of sign, a framework I have been arguing comes into prominence only toward the end of the nineteenth century, with Darwin's late-career work.

Guinier focuses on remedies for what she calls "third-generation" tyranny, a version of domination that persists even after minority voters have gained the formal, legal right to vote as well as reliable access to polls. In this version of tyranny, minority voters are disempowered by the permanence of their minority status: they are not simply outnumbered on a particular issue, but they are permanently and persistently outnumbered. "When majorities are fixed," Guinier explains, "the minority lacks any mechanism for holding the majority to account or even to listen" (9). Guinier's remedy is proceduralist, a political democratic variation on the tried-and-true childhood practice of "taking turns." Under the procedure of "cumulative voting," voters get the same number of votes as there are options to vote for. Thus, while black students representing a mere 10 percent of a senior class might have their choices for senior prom song consistently overlooked, if all voting students are allowed ten votes so as to produce a ten-song program, an individual student may choose to assign all of her votes to a single song, thus increasing the likelihood of that song's selection, or she might choose to ally herself with a variety of other groups of fans and distribute her votes among a variety of preferences.

Guinier's solution is noteworthy in a number of aspects. Undergirding its conception of "taking turns" is the notion that the essence of democracy lies in its production of certain outcomes: to take turns is to multiply endpoints. This multiplication of endpoints counts as a solution to the problem of a democratic process that has failed, in Guinier's view, insofar as its outcomes are insufficiently contingent: the same side wins all the time. By multiplying the iteration of outcomes, Guinier's "cumulative voting" reduces the certainty that any particular voter will get her way any particular time and, in that regard, loosens the association between being a particular kind of voter and being assured of a certain kind of outcome. Individual voters' identities are fragmented by being split into a variety of different preferences. Inasmuch as a given person does not merely represent herself by voting but expresses a desire for a variety of different outcomes, multiplying endpoints makes it both less certain that a particular position will win (or lose) and less certain that that individual voter can be understood to be the kind of person whose positions are realized. Guinier stands accused of advocating a distribution of voting power according to racial identity, but a more just account would be that her system distributes voting power to undo stable political identities, identities that in their rigidity come to function like races. Or one might put it this way: Guinier borrows a mode of racial critique—the revelation that qualities that might seem sufficiently stable and self-evident to constitute an identity turn out to be contingent and changeable—in order to demonstrate the contingency of political identities, while in the same gesture invoking the resemblance of racial and political identities to insist that it is politics, and not race, she is talking about.

In highlighting the ways in which Guinier's democratic solution to the problem of tyrannical majorities borrows from the rhetorical arsenal of racial critique, I mean not only to suggest the ways in which her political intervention presumes and participates in a particularly twentieth-century notion of race, but also to make discernible a second, less familiar Mill—which is to say, a nineteenth-century Mill. Mill and Guinier do not merely offer different solutions to the problem of tyrannical majorities: they conceive of the nature of the threat posed in crucially different ways. Furthermore, these different conceptions of the ways in which majority power can come to keep democracies from doing what they ought to be doing serve to point up the two thinkers' fundamentally different understandings of what it is democracies ought to be doing. Guinier argues that democracy is best served when various groups of citizens take turns winning. Such a solution designates winners as only contingently winners, and particular races as only contingently minorities, but it also implies that the value of democracy lies in the outcomes it produces, in the moment of turning citizens into winners. For Guinier, democracy's central function is to determine who ends up with the power to realize their vision of the way things ought to be. In this regard, her model of democracy is fundamentally identitarian, even as it demonstrates the identities of democratic winners to be changeable.

For the new-old Mill, by contrast, democracy is valuable not as a mechanism for producing or distributing holders of power but rather as a framework for a certain kind of civic practice, the discipline of deciding for oneself how the world of which one is a part ought to be and of discovering in oneself the capacity to make such determinations. I am certainly not the first to see in Mill's protection of the individual from the pressure of tyrannical majorities a valuing of what Kwame Anthony Appiah has termed, also in reference to Mill, "the enterprise of self-creation," a "capacity for autonomy."[3] But I contend further that Mill's valuing of a process that insists upon the impossibility of recognizing civic commonness in an instant (say, in the decisive outcome of a democratic election), turning recognition into a ongoing process of self-creation, can be seen as animated by his fundamental rejection of the instantaneously visible likeness of the nineteenth-century understanding of race. In pointing out the ways in which the most familiar understanding of Mill's particular relevance to race—here represented by Guinier—is structured around a model of race that to some degree postdates him, I mean to prepare the way for a particular historicization of Mill's writing, one that reads his work in terms of its engagement with the earlier "epistemological' conception of race I have described in previous chapters. I have argued that Kant's privileging of skin as the primary mark of racial difference ought to be seen as a manifestation of his commitment to making human likeness immediately perceptible. In this chapter, I will be making the case that Mill's suspicion of a public consensus that comes into being or can be perceived in a single instant—the outcome of an election, the conclusion of a debate—ought to be understood as a reaction to and rejection of the fundamentally racial logic articulated, if not fully endorsed, by Kant. In place of the implicitly racial model of public opinion, Mill attempts to imagine the possibility of a common vision of the world that comes into being at no particular moment of agreement, a commonness brought into being by the mutual engagement of citizens who are nonetheless not fully defined by it.

While Mill's project shares with Guinier's a notion of the public that is fundamentally political, the mechanisms he turns to in order to bring about this public commonness are not limited to modes of representation or statecraft. Mill's interest in identifying a commonness without a moment of agreement is discernible across the length of his career, not only in his overtly political writing but in his early work on poetry as well. And insofar as he does not presume that commonness is simply the outcome of the proper sorts of democratic or legislative processes but might be created by the aesthetic deployment and management of feeling as well, Mill is attentive to shifts in the technology available for transmitting a sense of the state of the world and hence rendering it common. Consequently, the historicization of Mill I undertake here involves more than reading his writing in relation to eighteenth- and early-nineteenth-, rather than late-twentieth-century, models of race. It also involves examining the ways in which Mill's understanding of the possibilities for the existence of a commonness that comes into being at no particular instant depends upon the invention of alternatives to writing and print as modes of transmission. For this reason, I read the movement of Mill's career in relation to writings detailing the midcentury development and proliferation of photographic reproduction. As its earliest proponents would have it, the technology whose methods of storage and reproduction developed over the middle decades of the century allowed people to perceive in a photographic image what they had not yet witnessed. I will be arguing that this mode of photographic generalization functioned as the condition of possibility for a reorganization of the terms of political and cultural commonness that Mill struggles toward in his earliest writing but is unable to realize fully. The development and popularization of methods of photographic storage allows Mill to envision the creation of publics whose commonness does not rest on the (real or imagined) existence of the sorts of discrete moments of political agreement—outcomes—posited by either twentieth-century theorists of democracy like Guinier or early modern social contractarians like Locke and Hobbes, but rather upon the creation of a realm of overlapping but nonidentical perceptions. I will trace the emergence of this alternative, perception-without-event model of publicness by way of a punctuated examination of Mill's career, as he moves from a poetically produced, but ultimately circumscribed, affective commonness through the debate-honed consensus of *On Liberty*'s marketplace of ideas to, finally, *The Subjection of Women*'s cultivation of multiple capacities for perception—a version of Mill, I hope, with which Mill himself, at least momentarily, might rest easy, discerned at no single moment of his career but in the testing and revision of ideas across the space of his oeuvre, the project of a lifetime.

Reproducing the Photographic Moment

When, in 1844, William Henry Fox Talbot published his collection of essays and photographs entitled *The Pencil of Nature* and so officially staked his claim to the mantle of inventor of photography, the question of who made photography first hung upon the answer to another question altogether: What exactly makes photography photography? Is it the combination of undistorted images and portability that allowed the prism-based camera lucida to displace the lens-cast shadows of the darkened room that was the camera obscura? Louis Daguerre's technique for fixing images on metal plates? For Talbot, the plausibility of his claim to priority rested, I want to suggest, on his locating his invention of a technology for both fixing images and rendering them endlessly reproducible within a history other than the one we might retrospectively assume, a history other than that connecting one light-casting technology to the next.[4]

To illuminate this alternative history, which will eventually lead us to John Stuart Mill, I begin by considering a reflection by Talbot. On an early October day in 1833, by the shores of Lake Como, the erstwhile inventor, whose photographic experimentations drew on his training as a mathematician, chemist, and linguist, suddenly halted in frustration his efforts to take sketches using Wollaston's camera lucida. "When the eye was removed from the prism—in which all looked beautiful—I found that the faithless pencil had only left traces on the paper melancholy to behold," Talbot recalls in his essay "A Brief Historical Sketch of the Invention of the Art."[5] In 1839, six years after the failure of the Lake Como sketches set him casting about for an alternative method for storing images of light, he announced the success of his experiments before the Royal Society, having hit upon a mixture of silver and iodine that produced negative images that could be printed repeatedly before they faded. By the time he finally published "A Brief Historical Sketch" along with a quarto of his own prints as *The Pencil of Nature* in 1844, Talbot no longer understood himself to be presenting the wholly unfamiliar: "The term 'Photography' is now so well known, that an explanation of it is perhaps superfluous; yet as some persons may still be unacquainted with the art, even by name, its discovery being of very recent date, a few words may be looked for of general explanation." For Talbot, photography was not simply a new technology. It had become a discourse as well. Any "explanation" he might offer of photography's meaning needed to take account of the term's public proliferation and reception as well as its technical details. Discursive and technological histories join here. Nestling his "Brief Historical Sketch" within his *Pencil*, Talbot redoubles his title's metaphor and so infuses it with a new descriptive instability in what was the world's first volume to bring together photos and text. His pencil both traces images of light and details the chemical experiments leading to the technology of photographic storage. Talbot thus creates an expansive rubric that brings together drawing and writing as a unified representational medium born of a common technological history.

To appreciate Talbot's claim to innovation and, more significantly, to understand the social and political possibilities made available by his new technology, we need to examine the contours of the history constituted by this expansive rubric: we need to consider photography, as I am arguing Talbot himself does, as an innovation within a history of writing.[6] (The relevance of the relation of photography to writing will become apparent below, as I trace the consequences of Mill's association of writing and print with historical locatedness.) By figuring nature wielding its own pencil so as to represent what it sees of itself, Talbot presents us with what has become the most familiar account of photography's revolutionariness: the collapse of seeing and storing that seems to allow, as if by magic, the representation of perception without the mediation of a human agent.[7] Yet as he extends and elaborates this initial writing metaphor in the form of the written history that is his "Brief Historical Sketch," the version of photography Talbot offers at once highlights the technology's contingency—but for the precise combination of silver and iodide, it might never have come into being—and implicitly anatomizes the writing it revolutionizes. If nature "writes itself," everyone sees the same image, the logic goes, because photography circumvents mediating perceptual agency. Seeing and storing are conflated. In this regard, photography appears both to escape the kind of historical locatedness associated with a specific agent of representation as well as to vault all those who view photographic images from their own historical locations. You no longer have to be there. But because Talbot presents this conflation as the outcome of a specific technological development,[8] the relation between seeing and storing—as well as the common vision that supposedly follows from such a relation—appears to be something less than absolutely necessary or inextricable. Instead this alignment of seeing and storing seems a produced effect that depends upon a pointedly contingent, historically local process of experimentation and invention whose outcome might never have occurred and that might be marshaled for not yet determined ends. In Talbot's words: "They are impressed by Nature's hand; and what they want as yet of delicacy and finish of execution arises chiefly from our want of sufficient knowledge of her laws. When we have learnt more, by experience, respecting the formation of such pictures, they will doubtless be brought much nearer to perfection; and though we may not be able to conjecture with any certainty what rank they may hereafter attain to as pictorial productions, they will surely find their own sphere of utility." Naturalness and transparency here bespeak not the absence of a process of experimentation, but the achievement of such experimentation's goals. And it is in this regard that the emergent technology of photography at once evokes and announces its departure from a history of writing. In writing, as Friedrich Kittler reminds us, the representation of perceptions and the storage of that said representation are one and the same. Where we can easily imagine, not least because Talbot narrates such scenes for us, the casting of an image of light that does not outlast the instant at which it is produced and perceived, whether falling victim to an inept sketcher or a faulty combination of chemicals, in the case of writing, the act of representing an event or perception and the storage of that representation are thoroughly inextricable from one another.[9] One cannot represent a "chair" in writing, for example, without storing it as well. This inextricability of perception and storage is what for Kittler makes impossible the circumvention of mediating agent and act of writing.

Contextualized in this way, Talbot's "history" presents a photography in which the relation between seeing and storing is both contingent and conflated and thus frames a technology that is capable of abstracting perception from particular and localizable "events" of seeing and experiencing. Crucial to photographic technology, at least in Talbot's account of it, is that it brings together and renders noncontradictory a material world that is the consequence of human actions and interventions—the combination of silver and iodide that might not have been—and a realm of perception that makes such distinct actions and interventions beside the point, a realm of perception in which perceivers need not be, or do, anything at a particular place or time.

What we can begin to see is that photography's capacity to yoke together such seemingly contradictory accounts of the necessity of human action allows it to function as a framework for organizing forms of social community or commonness in the absence of the moments of self-creation, polity building, legislation, or shared historical experience that are usually understood to undergird modern conceptions of community. No longer tied inextricably to clearly delineable acts or moments of seeing, visual perception—indeed, sensory perception more generally construed—emerges as the foundation of a new sort of publicness, one in which commonness need not presuppose a moment of agreement.[10]

Although Talbot's immersion in a process of experimental invention allows him to glimpse both the possibility and the tenuousness of such a perceptual notion of publicness, Talbot cannot quite be said to invent the concept. Nor is it confined to his technological innovation. The emergence of a perception-based publicness also, as I have suggested, helps us to make sense of certain movements over the course of John Stuart Mill's career as one of nineteenth-century Britain's foremost theorists of the concept of the public. This framework makes it possible to see connections among various elements of Mill's oeuvre that might otherwise seem distant from one another. My argument is in part historical and chronological: we can discern the contours of such a public in Mill's thinking as early as his 1833 essay "What Is Poetry?" (written the same year Talbot produced his imperfect Lake Como sketches and consequently launched his project of photographic storage). But Mill is unable to imagine this new public's establishment so long as he understands writing to be the primary medium for conveying feelings to large numbers of people. As we shall see, Mill's most well-known and influential writing on publicness, his 1859 *On Liberty*, is dogged by the difficulties surrounding the sort of writing-based public he first identifies in the poetry essay, and his famous discussion of public debate can be understood as his effort—ultimately an unsuccessful one—to circumvent the coercive effects of this notion of publicness. Only in his final work, *The Subjection of Women* (1869)—published after the 1867 Reform Act fundamentally altered prevailing notions of electoral representation and the development and popularization of photographic technology made it possible to abstract and separate seeing and hearing, as well as to detach visual perception from delimited "acts" of seeing—was Mill able to realize the concept of the perceptually generated, rather than written, agreement-based public he gestures toward in "What Is Poetry?"[11]

I am hardly the first to claim the central importance of the 1833 poetry essay and of poetry more generally to the shape of the development of Mill's career. Indeed, Mill himself famously in his *Autobiography* identified Wordsworth's poetry as the antidote to what he termed the "Crisis in My Mental Condition":

> I was in a dull state of nerves, such as everybody is occasionally liable to; unsusceptible to enjoyment of pleasurable excitement. . . . In this frame of mind, it occurred to me to put the question directly to myself, "Suppose that all your objectives in life were realized; that all the changes in institutions and opinions which you are looking forward to, could be completely effected at this very instant: would this be a great joy and happiness to you?" And an irrepressible self-consciousness distinctly answered, "No!" At this my heart sank within me: the whole foundation on which my life was constituted fell down.[12]

Mill's story is by now familiar, as is its interpretive gloss. Together, the flatness, the savorlessness of the imagined satisfaction of his life's goals, and the remarkable efficacy of the poetic remedy he comes up with can only signal one thing: Mill's recognition of utilitarianism's failure to value complex feelings adequately. Certainly there is plenty of evidence in the *Autobiography* to support such a reading: "What made Wordsworth's poems a medicine for my state of mind was that they expressed, not outward beauty, but states of feelings and of thought colored by feeling, under the excitement of beauty." From this time on, Mill observes, "the cultivation of the feelings became one of the cardinal points in my ethical and philosophical creed" (89). That the goals of utilitarianism might be attained, and that the value of this attainment might be taken measure of "at the very instant" of the goals' framing and their accomplishment, might be seen to testify to their exiguousness; a more expansive and complex vision of human needs and aspirations would resist both instantaneous implementation and instantaneous measure.

I will discuss in detail below the ways in which Mill's conception of poetic production and reception work to dissolve the possibility of such local "events" of institutionalization and valuation. But in resisting what philosopher of science William Whewell elsewhere called utilitarianism's "Downwards Mode," Mill effectively affiliated himself with a set of positions with a great deal of contemporary currency, perhaps the most famous articulation of which being Thomas Babington Macaulay's 1829 denunciation of James Mill's "deductionism." In his reading of James Mill's *On Government*, Macaulay roundly criticized the elder Mill for his reasoning by way of logical syllogism, arguing that Mill's pious eschewal of metaphor and his disregard for the existence of actual governments with real and varied practices of ruling were part and parcel of one another.

"It is one of the principle tenets of the Utilitarians," Macaulay writes,

> that sentiment and eloquence serve only to impede the pursuit of truth. They therefore affect a quakerly plainness, or rather a cynical negligence and impurity of style. The strongest arguments, when clothed in brilliant language, seem to them so much wordy nonsense. . . . They do not seem to know that logic has its illusions as well as rhetoric—that a fallacy may lurk in a syllogism as well as in a metaphor.[13]

Clearly, part of what is at issue for Macaulay is a misguided, though consistent, utilitarian commitment to asceticism. Only a political philosophy that could reduce human motivation to the pursuit of pleasure and the avoidance of pain and the role of government to the management of these minimalist motivations would see virtue in a disdain for expressive forms. Only such an ascetic philosophy would aspire to the communication of pure argumentative content by way of logical syllogism or mathematical equation. But in Macaulay's view, Mill's commitment to principle *follows from* the utilitarians' contempt for metaphor. In pointed contrast to the "quakerly plainness" of utilitarian deduction, "the inductive method not only endured but required a greater freedom of diction. It was impossible to reason from phenomena to principles, to mark slight shades of difference in quality, or to estimate the comparative effect of two opposite considerations between which there was no common measure, by means of the muted and meagre jargon of the Scholastics. Of these schoolmen, Mr. Mill has inherited both the spirit and the style" (273). Arguing inductively, from facts to principles, requires metaphor to bridge the various kinds of differences among the iterations of objects deemed to be, when all is said and done, fundamentally alike. In this regard, metaphor can be seen to register the fact that induction takes time: to the extent to which it involves the comparison of a series of phenomena—events, facts, objects, effects—that share only certain, not entirely self-evident, qualities in common, such an empirical mode of necessity takes place over time, and in that sense can be understood to take place at no particular instant.

Macaulay's suggestion that James Mill's utilitarianism might have a characteristic temporality thus seems to offer us an alternative framework for understanding the younger Mill's crisis: utilitarianism is as disheartening for the possibility it offers of instantaneous realization as for its indifference toward "feeling." But given that the younger Mill began his intellectual life as a committed utilitarian means we should hardly be surprised to discover that the process by which he marks his distance from utilitarian premises and methodologies was more fraught than it was for Macaulay. Mill explicitly announces his abandonment of a deductionist "syllogistic method" in his essay "On the Definition of Political Economy, and on the Method of Investigation Proper to It," written in 1833 (the same year as "What is Poetry?) and published in 1836 in the *London and Westminster Review*, a shift in position he later attributed to his reading of Macaulay's critique of his father.[14] As Laura Snyder has recently argued, the younger Mill's interest in induction, which culminated in the 1843 publication of *A System of Logic, Ratiocinative and Inductive*, was fueled less by an interest in epistemology per se than by his desire to extend his insights regarding the knowability of the natural world to the moral and political realms. Specifically, Mill hoped that offering an account of the process by which individual thinkers transformed their experiences of the material world into ideas would work to undermine the "intuitionism" he understood to be pervasive in both scientific and moral-political realms—the notion that what is most true is what individual thinkers have the greatest feeling of certainty about.[15] In a similar vein, I will be arguing that Mill's focus on the temporality of knowing—in particular, his investment in coming up with a version of knowing that takes place at no specific, isolated instant—has everything to do with his vision, articulated most explicitly in *On Liberty*, of a world that is fundamentally political, one whose elements have come into being by way of the acts and agreements of members of a given societas. (It is worth noting that such a position, which effectively disarticulates political association—the commonness of citizenship—from ways of knowing the world that citizens share, is a marked departure from that theorized by Kant, for whom not only political association, but the very possibility of comprehensibility, was predicated upon the possibility of recognizing the lawfulness of one's fellow subjects.) For Mill, poetry's—and implicitly, photography's—inductive capacities to produce an apprehension of the material world that takes place at no particular moment allows it to become the grounds of social commonality, a salutary supplement to the limits of a political-material world where presence implies the existence of prior agreement.[16] This interest in temporal diffusion as an instrument for creating political and social commonness helps make sense of one of Mill's differences from Macaulay. Macaulay aligns poetry, metaphor, and eloquence with one another against the "quakerly" asceticism of James Mill's utilitarianism as overlapping tools for registering the irreducible particularity of the material world. Macaulay's interest, that is, is in the object world itself, a world whose realness and truth is best registered by figures that signal its particularity through time. By contrast, John Stuart Mill's interest is less in the material world than in the ways in which experience of that world does or does not function as the grounds of commonness among the various people who might experience it. Mill's complex and not altogether stable delineation of the distinctions between poetry and eloquence serves to frame his investment in the temporal diffusion of knowing within a more general investment in distribution (of knowledge, feeling, perception) as a means of producing social commonness.

In suggesting that we might discern the ways in which new photographic logics of perception and reproduction help direct the evolution of John Stuart Mill's notion of the public by seeing them as part of Mill's more general attempt to think his way outside of utilitarianism's deductive premises, I mean to do more than simply offer a reminder of the truism that particularity mattered to the Victorians. By following Macaulay's lead in routing his engagement with particulars through lyric poetry rather than the realism of the novel and thereby associating it with the complex structure of poetic address, Mill makes the legibility of particularity inextricable from the issue of its transmissibility. As we shall see, Mill's adoption of the unstable relation between poetry and eloquence enables him to link the process of how we come to know what other people know with how we come to feel and see the way they do as well. He is willing, that is, to contemplate the possibility that knowing, or feeling, or seeing something transparently and instantaneously might be the consequence of a complex (technological) process of rendering common rather than the mark of the absence of such a process. His willingness to admit complexity allows him to understand the public-generating power of poetry to be the ground, rather than the consequence of, a more capacious, "feeling" utilitarianism.

The perception-based notion of public culture that Mill theorizes also provides the framework within which I understand the linking of Mill and the photographer Talbot to be meaningful. In juxtaposing the two, I am suggesting that Talbot distills a general cultural transformation represented by Mill as well, but I am also making an argument about the ways in which discursive and technological histories might be understood to interact with one another. Mill can glimpse how thinking about culture as a set of endlessly reorganizable perceptions rather than a series of acts or events might offer new possibilities for thinking about what it means for people to inhabit a common culture. But he is unable to elaborate any detailed logic of such a culture, much less to realize it, until photography, with its infinitely reproducible negatives, is invented and popularized. In this sense, the history I am offering is one enabled by technological invention, although it is hardly determined by it. Talbot and Mill both frame the desire to be able to separate visual perception from local acts of seeing well before they are able to realize that desire. By contrast, we shall see, Macaulay, who likens the poetic image created in the reader's imagination to the ephemeral images of the proto-photographic "magic lantern," confines his aspirations for poetic perception to the limits of extant technologies.

In framing his invention of photography as an innovation in the history of writing, Talbot both makes a case for his rightful place in an evolving common culture and presents a model of technological invention that alters the ways cultural commonness might be conceived. In this way, it actually matters to my argument that the influence of a given technology upon the intellectual topography of a given thinker might be registered even if that thinker does not identify the technology by name in his writing. Given the ways in which Talbot's version of photography complicates the experience of bounded historical events, we might also anticipate that when an author (Mill) engages with a predecessor (Macaulay) who uses a historically delimited technological metaphor (the poetic imagination functions like a magic lantern) in order to make a certain set of conceptual claims, it is possible that he might be influenced by both the technological framework he inherits and by subsequent innovations to that technology even if he does not (as Mill does not) employ the technological metaphor in his own writing.

Agreements without End: *On Liberty* and "What Is Poetry?"

While, chronologically, the story I tell about Mill commences in or around 1833 with "What Is Poetry?" I want to begin first elsewhere, with *On Liberty* (1859)—the canonical heart of Mill—because I mean for the alternative concept of the public I excavate to cast in new light even the most familiar contours of Mill's thinking. Mill offers *On Liberty* as a description of a crisis. The liberal subject constituted by ownership of property and related freedom of agency is, by the middle of the nineteenth century, under duress on at least two fronts: from the actions of other subjects whose exercise of their own freedoms constrains not only what the individual subject can do but also what the individual subject understands to be possible or desirable to do, and from the authority of historical precedent, whose weight joins the rigidities of civil institutions to circumscribe the horizon of the world still open to manipulation.[17] It is a critical commonplace that Mill's most extended meditation on the topic of publicness evinces his most pointed suspicion. Democratic public opinion has recently gained new force, but it has brought with it a new and unprecedented threat: the tyranny of the majority, where the most populous segment of the public lays claim to representing the public as a whole, impressing its opinion generally without regard either to its wisdom or to the existence of countervailing minority opinions.[18] The perniciousness of this new tyranny manifests itself in temporal terms, as a tendency to assert the existence of public agreement prematurely so that political action appears to be something that has already taken place. Mill's formulation implies a conception of time that is at once common and historical: common, because all sorts of acts and events—from the formulation of arguments and their expression to the passing of legislation, the waging of war, the offhanded habituation to custom—take place within a unitary realm of activity and affect one another; historical, because insofar as such a common time is presumed, what has taken place in the past both enables and circumscribes what is possible in the present and future.

For Mill tyranny is less expressly a matter of other people thinking differently from you than it is a matter of their thinking before you:

> The peculiar evil of silencing the expression of an opinion is that it is robbing the human race; posterity as well as the existing generation; those who dissent from the opinion, still more than those who hold it. If the opinion is right, they are deprived of the opportunity of exchanging error for truth: if wrong, they lose, what is almost as great a benefit, the clearer perception and livelier impression of truth, produced by its collision with error. (21)

What this passage makes apparent is that both common time and historicism follow as a consequence of the centrality of politics and debate to communal life. Rigorous argumentation by individuals produces benefits for all, benefits that extend beyond the realm of ratiocination per se. While free expression is fundamentally and unambiguously an individual freedom, the benefits of its exercise accrue to society at large. For Mill the ethical force of free expression lies in this coincidence of individual and public interests, but we would do well to notice that the benefits of such debate are here only discernible negatively, as Mill invites us to contemplate the condition of its absence.

Even more crucially, argumentation possesses its own characteristic temporality. As *On Liberty* proceeds, what becomes apparent is that Mill's historicism follows from his commitment to argumentation, with its characteristic diachronicity. The benefits to the societas of the sharp thinking of individuals engaged in rational political debate accrue (and in that sense become common, shared) when, in the aftermath of debate, its wise conclusions are made the basis of state policies that benefit all. But the link between argumentation and diachronicity—and from that, historicism—is even more fundamental. Because arguments are developed point by point, because agreements are forged, and because the wisest conclusions are generated when thinkers respond to one another in time, adjusting their positions accordingly, a world with argumentation at its core is one in which prior acts, events, ideas, and opinions generate, shape, and constrain what follows.

But for Mill the historicism associated with a community built around argument carries with it serious liabilities as well. It is telling that the sort of agreement that results from sustained debate is here never quite represented. The problem is, as the language of the passage above makes apparent, that Mill cannot explain how—or, more significantly, at precisely what moment—this conciliation comes about. The "they" to whom the passage repeatedly refers seems alternately to signify the "existing generation" of the human race, "their posterity," "those who hold the opinion," and "those who dissent from it"—in short, everyone. Thus, rhetorically for Mill, the mere positing of the existence of free debate has the effect of guaranteeing the wise agreement that is the ideal outcome, the process by which this state of agreement is brought about at once signaled and erased in the slide of "they" from present to future, from advocate to dissenter. The reason Mill cannot give an account of the process by which ideas are agreed upon and subsequently, presumably, institutionalized is because agreement and institutionalization in and of themselves constrain freedom of conscience. As Mill argues later in *On Liberty*, "He who does anything because it is the custom, makes no choice. He gains no practice either in discerning or in desiring what is best" (65). Any agreement or institutionalization that produces a sense of "the way things are" thus constrains subsequent freedom of conscience by allowing people to act without thinking twice. For Mill, debate must go on endlessly in order to keep citizens from being consigned to a stultifying and unreflective habit simply by virtue of inhabiting cultures and participating in institutions.

Mill's deep ambivalence regarding the institutionalization of those wise opinions he understands rational public debate to generate becomes most apparent in "Applications," the final section of *On Liberty*. He suggests there by way of example that the state employ its centralized civil institutions to authorize and enforce the *principle* of universal education, rather than adjudicating among the various curricula vying to be established as the national standard. In essence, Mill envisions institutions that operate in order to disrupt institutionalization, to prevent the consolidation of opinion except in the most limited, local communities by occupying the position of national authority, such that no set of ideas might gain that position. In this way, he seeks to evacuate institutions of any specific content.

In grounding his historicism ideologically in the importance of argumentation for the healthy operation of (political) communities, Mill effectively conflates realization and agreement. In *On Liberty*, such a conflation means that the existing organization of the world, its institutions and social relations, must be understood to have been agreed upon. The authority of historical events rests on the fact that they have been generated as a consequence of agreements. In this regard, agreement reveals itself to be not simply a political principle but a historiographical one as well, an account of how things came into being.

But however much the Mill of *On Liberty* presents this notion that the world that is ought to be seen as evidence of past agreements as a kind of logical postulate, he did not always do so. The differences between Mill's early position on the issue and that of his midcareer—the moment, that is, when Mill feels impelled to delineate the dangers posed to individual liberty by the potential tyrannies of the democratic process—are most salient if we compare his accounts during these two periods of the origin and significance of terminological variety. In addressing the question "What is poetry?" in 1833, Mill is scornful of the "half-philosophy" that would "disdain the classifications and distinctions indicated by popular language." He elaborates: "The distinction between poetry and not-poetry, whether explained or not, is felt to be fundamental, and where everyone feels a difference, difference there must be. Appearances, too, like everything, must have a cause, and that which can cause anything, even an illusion, must be a reality." Here, historicism and commonness need not go hand in hand. Meanings—all meanings—matter because they have been caused, because they have been brought into being at some point in the past. The fact that there is no agreement or consensus about such meanings, or that many of them flatly contradict one another, ought not, in Mill's view, bar any of them from consideration: "Philosophy carried to its highest point frames new [meanings,] but rarely sets aside the old, content with correcting and regularizing them."[19]

Compare this openness with Mill's dismay in *On Liberty* at the proliferation of meanings surrounding the language of publicness:

> It was now perceived that such phrases as "self-government" and "the power of the people over themselves," do not express the true state of the case. The "people" who exercise power are not always the same people over whom it is exercised, and the "self-government" spoken of is not the government of each by himself, but of each by all the rest. The will of the people, moreover, practically means the will of the most numerous, or the most active *part* of the people, the majority, or those who succeed in making themselves accepted as the majority; the people, consequently, may desire to oppress a part of their numbers. (8)

In marked contrast to his nominalistic analysis of the term "poetry," which rejects that "half-philosophy that disdains the classifications and distinctions indicated by popular language," Mill here sees the failure of the language of politics to refer reliably—"to express the true state of the case"—not only to indicate a historical shift in the meaning of self-government, but to evince a situation in dire need of correction, a state of tyranny. The neutrality of the historicism implicit in the nominalism of "What Is Poetry?"—the existing world matters because it has happened, because it is the consequence of some "cause"—cannot easily be adapted to the task of defining a public, since the collectivity of the notion of publicness implies that its very existence would be undermined by a proliferation of meanings caused by multiple agents.

The collapse into incoherence of collective abstract nouns like "public," announcing the end of the sort of terminological catholicity Mill celebrates in "What Is Poetry?," is a manifestation of the dynamics of precisely the democratic tyranny he is attempting to name: "When society is itself the tyrant—society collectively, over the separate individuals who comprise it—its means of tyrannizing are not restricted to the acts which it may do by the hands of its functionaries" (8). Where once the meaning of "tyranny" was restricted to the acts of governmental agents carrying out the business of state institutions, it has now come to include as well the power of the majority of society to impose its will over the minority. The lifting of restrictions upon the meaning of tyranny is thus twofold: tyranny is no longer limited to government functionaries, and it is no longer limited to "acts." That Mill's account of public debate offers a version of agreement constituted rhetorically by way of the floating referent of the pronoun "they" (rather than chronologically or by way of illustration with any specific examples of the process by which public agreement comes about) suggests that the agreement that is the desired outcome of public debate is so thoroughly identified with the operation of government institutions generally as to turn debate and agreement into a process implied by the very existence of government institutions rather than actually or contingently performed by them. What is comes to seem to be what has been agreed upon. To the degree that a public is understood to be constituted by way of agreement, then, everything turns out to be subject to agreement, and the specific sphere of politics, conceived as a realm marked off by its provisionality (one might be included or kept out), expands into nonexistence.

But it is also within this context of a broadened—indeed, we might say limitless—notion of agreement that modes of perception, rather than qualities of belief, emerge as instruments by which the consensus that is the present state of things might conceivably be disrupted. I have suggested that Mill's willingness to entertain multiple, even contradictory, meanings of "poetry" in the 1833 "What Is Poetry?" bespeaks the existence of an early historiographical model that Mill has largely abandoned by the time he writes *On Liberty* in 1859. I want now to explore the ways in which this earlier analysis of the meaningfulness of historical events provides the framework within which Mill could come to see poetry as an invaluable practice for producing the sort of social cohesion that political institutions inevitably fail to provide. Though Mill's historicism would seem to follow from his commitment to politics, the fact that he forges the connection between the two by insisting upon their shared relation to time allows him to imagine that new sorts of social relations might be created by constituting new sorts of temporalities (including those brought into being by the new technology of photography) and foregoing the political realm altogether. Poetry can be seen to function for Mill as the perfection of an imperfectible process of public debate, generating commonness (of feeling) without a moment of agreement, conciliation without the danger of institutionalization.

Although Mill is emphatic about the need to account for the various definitions of poetry, including "the wretched mockery of a definition" that would "confound poetry with metrical composition," the movement of his own argument nonetheless effectively elevates one definition, which opposes poetry to prose. Prose derives its "interest," Mill explains, from "incident," that is, from precisely the delimited sorts of events that Mill brings under pressure by way of his shifting position on the genealogy and desirability of multiple definitions. But it is not simply that the *concept* of poetry is discernible only to those theorists who recognize that there can be no isolatable moment at which "poetry" is known. Poetry's reach is much further and more fundamental: for Mill, poetry operates to dissolve the event as the structure around which subjects' sensations, emotions—indeed, their very selfhood—are experienced and ordered. The rhetorical echoes of this early passage of "What Is Poetry?" with *On Liberty* are striking: "Poetry, which is the delineation of the deeper and more secret workings of human emotion, is interesting only to those to whom it recalls what they have felt, or whose imagination it stirs up to conceive what they could feel, or what they might have been able to feel, had their outward circumstances been different" (8). Here, poetry's link to feeling has become ambiguous to the point of circularity: emotion is at once the source, the content, and the consequence of poetry, with the delimitable "interest" of fictional incident diffusing into a generalized state of the "interesting," a state that seems equally to apply to poem, poet, and reader. This cancellation of poetic occasion not only creates a state in which an actual poet and reader become indistinguishable from one another, but one in which all possible poets and readers—those whose feelings might conceivably be imagined, those whose feelings could only be imagined given different outward circumstances—become indistinguishable.

For Mill, then, poetry matters because it is able to free the poetic subject not merely from the incidental or occasional quality of the poetic event, but from eventfulness more generally construed. But if the perpetually generative quality of poetry would seem to recommend it as a superior alternative to the implacably temporal process of political debate, this is because Mill understands its capacity to produce commonness without agreement and therefore without the threat of coercion to be the consequence of its nonmediated operation. Poetry, we are told famously, is "feeling confessing itself to itself in moments of solitude"; here the poem, imbued with poetic consciousness and the sort of self-reflexivity that seems to follow from such consciousness, offers a figure through which poet, aesthetic form, and audience all become identical to one another.[20]

> Poetry and eloquence are both alike the expression or utterance of feeling: but, if we may be excused the antithesis, we should say that eloquence is *heard*; poetry is *over*heard. Eloquence supposes an audience. The peculiarity of poetry appears to us to lie in the poet's utter unconsciousness of a listener. Poetry is feeling confessing itself to itself in moments of solitude, and embodying itself in symbols which are the nearest possible representations of the feeling in the exact shape in which it exists in the poet's mind. Eloquence is feeling pouring itself out to other minds, courting their sympathy, or endeavoring to influence their belief, or move them to passion or to action. (12)

Mill goes on to gloss this circular ideal in which the feeling that is poetry is simultaneously cause, effect, and medium in language that strikingly recalls Talbot's fantasy of self-impressing images. Where Mill's poetic feeling "embodi[ies] itself in symbols which are the nearest possible representations of the feeling in the exact shape in which it exists in the poet's mind, Talbot speculates "how charming it would be if it were possible to cause these natural images to imprint themselves durably." Poetry's circularity thus evokes the photographic logic of the self-imprinting image in order to escape the problems of mediation: mediation is here figured as the poet's consciousness of being positioned between subject matter and audience and responsible for presenting one to the other.[21] In rejecting the theatricality of attempting to please or persuade by deliberately—even theatrically—choosing to remain oblivious to an audience, the poet can escape the distorting pressure of public opinion on poetic creation and preserve the poem as the expression of feeling that is at once common and uncoerced precisely by virtue of never quite having been agreed upon.[22]

That Mill's poetic solution to the problem of generating commonness is also photographic becomes more apparent when we examine Macaulay's alignment of the two and the conceptual impasse this alignment eventually encounters. Macaulay's linking of poetry and the proto-photographic technology of the magic lantern occurs not in his 1823 critique of James Mill, but several years later, in an essay entitled, simply, "Milton" that appeared in August 1825 in the *Edinburgh Review*. The essay, which was occasioned by the 1823 discovery of some previously unknown religious writings by John Milton, ostensibly takes up the question of Milton's genius, but it soon evolves into something much broader in scope, a comparison of the relative progressiveness of poetic practice and experimental science. Macaulay, like Mill, conceives of a model of poetic practice that is not fully historical and that thus, in distinction from the realms to which it is opposed—for Mill, it is politics, for Macaulay, science—promises to free individuals from the coerciveness of general cultural acceptance. Where many people are quick to dismiss Milton's accomplishments as a poet, understanding them to be largely an accident of his historical location, Macaulay contends that such an account inappropriately applies a scientific model of progress to the realm of the imitative arts. In this scientific model, cultures become, over the course of time, increasingly determinative of the kinds of ideas generated by individual minds. "Milton, it is said, inherited what his predecessors created" and "received a finished education," in marked contrast with those writers "born at the infancy of civilization," who were forced to "suppl[y], by their own powers, the want of instruction" and who, "though destitute of models themselves, bequeathed to posterity models which defy imitation."[23] This account is unwittingly scientific inasmuch as it presumes that knowledge is cumulative, formed gradually by the "collecting," "separating," and "combining" of materials.

But such a progressive account of cultural production is inadequate as a description of what Macaulay terms "the imitative arts" to the degree that it fails to attend to imitation's particular relation to particularity. Macaulay explains in the "Milton" essay, "As civilization advances, poetry almost necessarily declines. . . . Generalisation is necessary to the advancement of knowledge; but particularity is indispensable to the realm of the imagination. In proportion as men know more and think more, they look less at individuals and more at classes. They therefore make better theories and worse poems" (4, 5). Here poetry and experimental science are mutually exclusive with regard both to their developmental trajectories and to the cultural conditions likely to support their flourishing. But this opposition is immediately complicated by Macaulay's efforts to describe the transmissibility of poetic particularity, since poetry can be seen both to function as a kind of transmission of the material particulars that animate it and also to require transmission itself. It is this tense relationship between a poetics of particularity and the generalizing pressures of transmission that generates a proliferation of technovisual metaphors whose complex overlappings will come to set the terms of Mill's discussion as well.

Macaulay's initial metaphor is premechanical, in keeping with his insistence that poetry's alignment with particularity necessarily consigns it to the rude ages: "By poetry we mean the art of employing words in such a manner as to produce an illusion on the imagination, the art of doing by means of words what the painter does by means of color" (6). Here Macaulay's governing premise—that the imitative arts are characterized above all by their shared commitment to the particular—undergirds the alignment of poetry and painting in ways that are likely to distract us from what is arguably most remarkable about the description: the fact that the imagination upon which the poetic-painterly image is produced is not that of the imaginative agent actually employing the words or engaging the particulars. The "art of employing words" is itself, it seems, strangely unparticularized. Poetry's refusal to abandon the particular for the generalizings of experimental science produces an odd "frenzying" relation of object and representation: "Truth is essential to poetry; but it is the truth of madness. . . . Every image which is strongly presented to their mental eye produces on them the effect of reality" (6). The "madness" that is this conflation of illusion and reality literally dissolves to nothing the problem of transmission signaled by Macaulay's grammar in the poetry-as-painting passage. To the degree that we are unable to distinguish an illusion of the thing from the thing itself any difficulties surrounding the movement from object-perceiving mind to representation-impressed mind become inconceivable. And it is in the context of this useful transparency that Macaulay turns to photography, or something like it: "Poetry produces an illusion on the eye of the mind, as a magic lantern produces an illusion on the eye of the body" (7). With the introduction of a magic lantern able to produce images without the intervention of any perceiving agent, the syntactical gymnastics of the painting passage ("the art of employing words . . . to produce an illusion on the imagination") relax into the not-quite-poetic abstractions of the bodily and mental "eye," made equally the possession of poet and audience by belonging literally to neither.

But if Macaulay's magic lantern eliminates the perplexities of conveying an image from the particular mind of its perceiving poet to that of its receiving audience by abstracting both into the transparency of its own figuration, the fact that the magic lantern itself lacks a mechanism for storing the projected images it generates means that it, along with the conception of poetry it embodies, only manages to escape the problem of transmission so long as the images in question are generated and perceived simultaneously, yet at no moment in particular. The illusion on the eye of the mind is like that on the eye of the body only to the degree that neither exists in or through time, and once we notice this, we will begin to notice as well ways in which Macaulay's opposition between poetic immanence and the generalizations of experimental science, an opposition at once historical and developmental, is not quite as neat as it first appears. We recall that in his critique of James Mill, Macaulay aligned metaphor and experimental science rather than opposing them: the sort of departure from the top-down pronouncements of James Mill's utilitarian deductionism demanded the heterogeneity of metaphor to make perceptible the likeness of nonidentical particulars. In the "Milton" essay, the experimental sciences (and, offhandedly, "philosophy') come to be associated with induction, but here it is less clear whether these disciplines employ induction as their methodology or ought rather to be understood as induction's consequence: "Nations, like individuals, first perceive, then abstract. They advance from particular images to general terms. Hence, the vocabulary of an enlightened society is philosophical, that of a half-civilized people is poetical" (5). National development thus follows the trajectory of inductive thought itself, a movement from particular to general. In this conception, poetry and experimental science turn out to be complementary modes, distinct but mutually necessary elements of a single process.

What such a reading leaves crucially ambiguous is the precise relation between "nations" and "individuals" at any given moment. Nations may be like individuals in moving from engaging particulars to making abstractions, but nations and individuals cannot quite be like one another at the same time. Inasmuch as a nation has moved (inductively) from engaging particulars by way of poetry to trafficking in science and philosophy's generalizations, it is unclear how any given individual would be thinking at any given time—creating poetic images or doing science?—but what any individual would be doing would apparently *not* be induction. Conversely, were we to begin by presuming an individual inductive thinker, repeatedly scrutinizing clusters of her experiences in an effort to discern their general qualities, we would need also to posit a nation that refuses to commit itself to the exclusive production of either poetry of science, but that instead allows both to flourish as the material upon which its inductively inclined citizens do their work.

This ambiguity concerning the relation between national and individual induction does make evident that the magic lantern's transparent transmission of particulars succeeds in constituting the collective abstraction of the mind's eye (a subject neither individual nor national) only so long as we don't know whether or how that process of transmission takes place. Macaulay's poetical magic lantern, like Mill's poetry, offers a figure through which poet, aesthetic form, and audience all become identical to one another, and in so doing, that figure dissolves the possibility of any tense or coercive relation between individuals and the members of a public. But both the magic lantern and poetry succeed in doing so only insofar as the mechanism and moment of transmission and conciliation are left undefined.

It is precisely this impasse that Mill finds himself engaging in "What Is Poetry?" Having conceived a version of poetry that magically (which is to say, circularly) unites poet, poem, and audience and thus recommends itself as the means of generating a public by virtue of its capacity to navigate the twin shoals of a coercive public opinion and a necessarily unceasing and therefore uninstitutionalizable public debate, Mill is nonetheless faced with the task of explaining how poetry's instantaneously generalizable feeling actually comes to be conveyed to its audience. How is he to square the poet's impulse to publish with the supposed inwardness of the poetic utterance? "All poetry is of the nature of a soliloquy," Mill announces, by way of solution. The complexly reflexive "feeling confessing itself to itself" is hardened into "soliloquy," with "poetry which is printed on hot-pressed paper" turning out to be "a soliloquy in full dress and on the stage." If such a costumed soliloquy seems a far cry from poetic speech that finds an audience only by happenstance, Mill moves immediately to shore up the distinction between hearing and overhearing even in the face of the publication that would seem to render the difference beside the point: "What we have said to ourselves we may tell to others afterward; what we have said or done in solitude we may voluntarily reproduce when we know that other eyes are upon us. But no trace of consciousness that any eyes are upon us must be visible in the work itself. The actor knows that there is an audience present: but if he act as though he know it, he acts ill" (12). Mill's revised argument for the fundamental self-enclosure of poetic expression seems implicitly to turn on the distinction between writing and print, the writing that is the mark of unconscious poetic expression retrospectively called into being by its contrast with the "hot-pressed paper." In evoking print as a technology for institutionalizing writing (or in the terms generated by our discussion of Talbot, storing writing), Mill attempts to transform writing from a medium that *inevitably* identifies seeing and storing. He thus transforms the moment and agent of perception from an inextricable element of the expression produced into something that is far more contingent and ephemeral, like Talbot's precise mixture of silver and iodide. This contingent perceptual agent nonetheless succeeds in its essentially paradoxical task of conveying expressions of feeling to those who already feel the same way. But the insufficiency of the writing/printing distinction to the task for which it is conscripted becomes apparent as quickly as it is made, as printing must at least covertly reinvoke the very public of readers the distinction was meant to banish. This dynamic occurs in the sentence that follows, as the "eyes" whose expulsion from the first half of the sentence is meant to guarantee the sincerity of the utterance's return in the second half to testify to the invisibility of any defacing consciousness. An audience is necessary, it seems, to witness and testify to the poet's unconsciousness of an audience.

Rather than offering a solution, then, this passage articulates an impasse and, in articulating that impasse, provides the outlines of a solution that can only be imagined negatively. Poetry produces commonness without coercion insofar as it generates and expresses common feeling rather than producing subjects who habitually accede to the agreement implied by the fact of the (common) material and institutional world. But the inescapably written medium of dissemination necessarily reintroduces a process by which such feeling is conveyed and hence a moment at which commonness comes about—a moment of agreement that vaults the poetic back into the realm of public opinion it was conceived to be circumventing.

It is within the context of this impasse that Mill's distinction of "overheard" poetry and "heard" eloquence becomes most provocative. Mill's distinction actually seems to differentiate aural perception from visual and to imagine that the two forms of perception might not necessarily coincide. The orator and the audience are aware of one another, while the poet appears unaware of an audience: "That song has always seemed to us like the lament of a prisoner in a solitary cell, ourselves *listening, unseen* in the next" (14, emphasis added).[24] Not only does this passage insist upon the separability of seeing and hearing, but the very fact of their bifurcation is itself seemingly sufficient, if the unremarked-upon shift from earlier singular "listener" to a plural but undifferentiated audience here is any indication, to constitute the audience as a unit, consciousness unified into consensus.

The poet's perspective presumes an alignment of hearing and seeing and thus concludes that because no audience can be seen, there is no audience at all. For the poet's audience, by contrast, seeing and hearing need not go hand in hand; an audience can hear and thus function as audience, whether or not it sees or is seen. The distinction between hearing and overhearing only seems as if it is a distinction between a poetic commonness that is created as a particular communicative act, as an event, and one that comes into being eventlessly, and it only seems to be the case to the poetic speaker.[25] In inviting us to attend not simply to the perspective of the poet, but also to the divided perceptions of the poetic audience, then, Mill brings together two different forms of abstraction—of seeing from hearing and of poetic feeling from the poetic event.[26] In splitting seeing from hearing and insisting that they need not occur at the same moment, Mill creates a category of perception that seems to be linked to the subject doing the perceiving rather than to the object world that subject is formed by or perceives. In this way, Mill, without the benefit of actual photographic technology, manages to synthesize imaginatively what Talbot understands to be the essential elements of his own photographic invention—the storing of images that print themselves in ways that allow such images to be viewed apart from the moment they are first generated and seen. And this possibility of abstracting perceptions is the condition at once particular and necessary to the production of a community whose commonness rests upon a shared feeling it can never be understood not to have had.[27]

Over the course of the passage, we can thus see, Mill evokes the possibility of abstract vision and links such abstraction to an entirely unmediated—and hence "eventless"—identity of poet, poem, and audience only then to fall back into an inescapably temporal logic of writing and reading. This movement suggests that his capacity to sustain and realize the implications of such vision is ultimately constrained by his inability to conceive of its operation outside an economy of writing and print. In this regard, Mill's investment in argumentation turns out to presume not only a specific temporality but a specific medium of diffusion as well. The notion that the world one inhabits is a world made up of prior agreements and that subjects act upon, recognize, and influence one another according to the sequence of the actions is predicated upon a mode of transmission—writing—in which the specific moment of recording or imagining remains inextricably tied to any subsequent apprehendings of it. That Mill is able to think it both possible and useful that one might see (and hear) without being seen—that seeing might take place apart from the actual perceptual event or context—without being able to know exactly how such abstract seeing might be carried out testifies to the delicate particularity of his historical position. He writes during the very earliest years of photographic experimentation, a moment in which magic lanterns and camera lucidas exist, but reproducible negatives do not—a moment, that is, when the abstractability of perception from event is conceivable but not yet realizable. And although Mill's early and inchoate insight that the possibility of separating seeing from hearing and thus abstracting vision from the event of seeing might produce a form of social commonness that need not be traceable back to a distinct moment of agreement falls by the wayside for want of the technological wherewithal to bring it about, Talbot's impulse to locate his new invention of photography within a history of writing allows us to see the ways in which questions of technology continue to structure Mill's oeuvre.

As I hope has become apparent, Mill's notions regarding the social and institutional relations of agreement and perception are, for most of his career, structured deeply and fundamentally around a logic of writing that seems to render any form of institutionalization a kind of bullying. I have been arguing that the notion that the world we inhabit is meaningful and significant because it is the consequence of prior public debate and agreement—at once the condition Mill describes in *On Liberty* and the reason he cannot help but see the establishment of institutions as a form of constraint—is predicated upon a particular understanding of the organization of sensory perception. In this account, the perceptual stands as the first and foundational realm of agreement: the visual and the auditory are distinguishable from one another, but even in their distinction they come together to reveal and establish the consistency of the object world. In presenting photographic storage as, first and foremost, a revolution in the history of writing, Talbot acknowledges the force of this logic of perceptual agreement. At the same time, he makes the case for understanding such a logic as a technologically contingent state of affairs, predicated upon the existence of a world in which perceptions are communicated to others—made common—by means of writing, a technology in which the moment of perception or representation and the moment of storage are thoroughly and inextricably identical with one another. The fact that the notion of the world as agreement turns out to presume that citizens can and will receive the same knowledge from each of their senses means that demonstrating that sensory agreement is *not necessary* opens up what counts as politics to admit relations of perception to a political realm usually considered to be composed of ideas, decisions, and acts.

The reframing of politics as perception works to invest perception, its instruments, and its representations with the promise of a new kind of social efficacy. Mill's idea that the world he inhabits is a world brought into being by prior public agreement serves at once to endow public debate—at least in theory—with tremendous transformative force and to constrain radically the range of transformative action available to individual citizens. That this world of materialized consensus is a world of mutually reinforcing, aligned sensory perceptions means that the reorganization of perceptions suddenly offers itself to him as a means for escaping the impasse of public opinion.

Overhearing *The Subjection of Women*

Read within the conceptual trajectory of Mill's major writings, *The Subjection of Women* appears a sudden shifting of gears, as Mill does not so much surmount the logical impasse of *On Liberty* as he swerves around it. Mill opens *Subjection* by teasing apart the alignment of historical materialization and political agreement he had argued for in *On Liberty*, an alignment he now sees to be belied most forcefully by the peculiar capacity of "the legal subordination of one sex to the other" to withstand rational refutation.[28] While "the generality of a practice is in some cases a strong presumption that it is, or at all events once was, conducive to laudable ends" (474)—the conclusion that follows from the presumption that realization is the final step of a process of argumentation and agreement—this is not always the case. With regard to the subordination of women, the "practice" or realization that comprises the happenings of history turns out to be not opposed to "theory" but identical to it, an example of the kind of Benthamite deduction from which Mill deliberately sought to distance himself:[29]

> The opinion in favour of the present system, which entirely subordinates the weaker sex to the stronger rests upon theory only; for there never has been trial made of any other: so that experience, in the sense in which it is vulgarly opposed to theory, cannot be pretended to have pronounced any verdict. . . . *The adoption of this system of inequality never was the result of deliberation, or forethought, or any social ideas,* conduced to the benefit of humanity or the good order of society. It arose simply from the fact that from the very earliest twilight of human society, every woman (owing to the value attached to her by men, combined with her inferiority in muscular strength) was found in a state of bondage to some man. (475, emphasis added)

Whereas *On Liberty* presents the events of history as consequences of prior discussion and consensus, by the opening of *The Subjection of Women*, the authority of historical fact is revealed to be thoroughly and uselessly tautological. In *On Liberty*, the fact of a condition's existence is understood to serve as evidence that actual debate has taken place and that consensus has prevailed. In *Subjection*, happening is charged with carrying the authority of agreement without the process, absent a relation of cause and effect. That minimal ground is at least partly to blame for the condition's illegitimacy.

But if one effect of Mill's redescription of institutions is to challenge the capacity of pastness to stand as the sign of agreement—suddenly institutions are authoritative simply because they are continuous with the past, not because they have been agreed upon—another effect is to offer a model for imagining individual agency and bodily capacity to be separable from one another. While *Subjection* presents historical authority as largely tautological, it is not entirely so. We recall that, while "the adoption of this system of inequality never was the result of deliberation," it is not merely the consequence of an endorsement of the status quo, but is partly the outcome of women's "inferiority in muscular strength." For all its immediate political interest, the system of gender inequality is analytically crucial to Mill's larger project of thinking his way around the impasse of public opinion because it presents a case of historical continuity as the combined effect of a circular causality *and* a certain quality of embodiment. For Mill, institutions would seem to be part of the machinery authorizing history by virtue of their power to make the simple fact of continuity appear self-authorizing, to create common time. But viewed in relation to the historical ongoingness of gendered bodies, institutionality suddenly becomes available as a tool to be marshaled for his critique of historicism. We are not merely told that a given set of historical or institutional conditions that we have understood to be the outcome of social agreement actually are the results of the exercise of physical force. The fact that women's bodies tend to be weaker than men's as a *class* prevents physical force and the various forms collectivity might take—agreement/institutionality/law—from being strictly opposed to one another. By insisting that the historically ongoing system of gender inequality is at least in part the consequence of women's weaker bodies, Mill effectively blocks the ongoingness of a situation from being understood as the realization of an agency that marks and is underwritten by agreement. The ongoingness of particular historical conditions turns out to be neither the mark of collective agreement nor the overriding of that agreement by coercive bodily force. Rather, the persistence of a set of circumstances from past to present is revealed to be precisely what exceeds the power of agents, either individually or collectively, to realize. Embodiment likewise turns out to be extraindividual.

Kant's presumption of a standardized body of the sort theorized by anatomical medicine compels him to posit racialized skin—a structure that superimposes lawful knowledge and perception—so as to make the standardness of the body legible even as it sickens, recovers, ages, dies. In contrast, Mill's interest in politics, broadly conceived as a kind of disposition of time, leads him to set forth a nonstandard gendered body and a version of perception distinguished from knowledge as mutual entailments of one another. To the degree that *Subjection of Women* offers a critique of the vision of politics Mill ambivalently embraces in *On Liberty* and "What Is Poetry?," it does so in part by uncovering the ways in which such politics organizes bodies as well as debates over time. Insofar as subjects are constrained by the acts and ideas that precede them, they are tied to bodies that are never entirely their own. Their freedom of action circumscribed by the past actions of others and cultural conventions alike, such bodies are handicapped as surely as if they were blind or lame. In Mill's vision, then, bodies that are like one another are diminished by antecedence: to possess a body capable of acting and perceiving as those before one have acted and perceived is to be unable to realize such a capacity. Bodies conceived as fundamentally alike are distinguishable, in Mill's account, only by differences in power. At once hemmed in by the force of historical precedent and by their own bodily weakness, women are significant for their exemplarity rather than their exceptionality, since when all is said and done for Mill, belatedness and bodily weakness cannot be distinguished from one another.

But while the overlapping effects of conventionalism and bodily weakness render women a useful example of the power the political relations of argument and agreement possess to structure bodily relations as well, Mill goes on to elaborate ways in which a social history of the gendered body functions as a framework within which capacity or force become conceivable as something irreducible to the agency of individual subjects. That is, he begins to reformulate the modes of temporality ticked off by individual acts. Although much of the frisson of the essay's contemporary reception stemmed from Mill's analogizing of women's and slaves' conditions, he scrupulously maintains an eye toward the differences of the two situations. Those differences turn out to concern, among other things, their respective constructions of temporality:

> I am far from pretending that wives are in general no better treated than slaves; but no slave is a slave to the same lengths, and in so full a sense of the word, as a wife is. Hardly any slave, except one immediately attached to

> the master's person, is a slave *at all hours and all minutes*; in general, he has, like a soldier, his fixed task, and when it is done, or when he is off duty, he disposes, within certain limits, *of his own time*. . . . Not so the wife. (504, emphasis added)

> She vows a lifelong obedience to him at the altar, and is held to it all through her life by law. Casuists may say that the obligation of obedience stops short of participation in crime, but it certainly extends to everything else. (503)

Women, in this view, are oppressed not because they are forced to labor against their wills (like slaves) but because they are prohibited from acting within common time, the time both constituted and presumed when subjects' acts are registered in the effects or things they produce, things understood to be interchangeable with one another. Where slaves are required to labor, to perform certain tasks—their obedience is measured around the logic of their agency, even as such agency fails to subtend their autonomy—women give over their time in its fullness. Set against an economy of agency, this time is valuable not for its capacity to be abstracted, via labor, and registered in the laborer's production, but instead matters in its marked *non*fungibility, by virtue of the fact that it is a specific woman's. This nonabstract time that results from the imperative to give over "all hours and all minutes" is time that is meaningful because it is lived by a specific woman without its significance resting on the effects or events that are the consequence of that living. Such particularized time offers a challenge to the self-evidence of the historical event, a departure from both the abstract temporality underwriting the labor theory of value that here describes slavery, as well as *On Liberty*'s logic of the event as agreement. Once institutionality and historical ongoingness are reframed by the logic of the gendered body, a category of time emerges that is neither quite public nor simply the measurement of a realized agency, of agreement. To the degree that an individual's capacity to dispense her time is itself particularized, that subject's defining engagement with a particular set of material conditions need not begin with a local act nor be discernible by way of a local event. We might say that such a model of time registers subjects' specificity in their potential acts rather than in their realized acts. This conception of time thus offers a framework within which capacities—modes of perception—can serve as the index of both the specificity of subjects and of the world those subjects inhabit.

I suggest that we understand Mill's turn toward perception, and his insistence upon the particularity of women's perceptual habits and capacities, as offering a rhetoric for grounding women's independence from within this emergent domestic logic of particular and nonfungible time. In this context, we can begin to see the way in which *The Subjection of Women* is engaged not merely in articulating the limits of the paradigms underwriting his earlier work like *On Liberty* but also in developing an alternative conception of publicness:

> The law of servitude in marriage is a monstrous contradiction to all the principles of the modern world, and to all the experience through which those principles have been slowly and painfully worked out. It is the sole case, now that negro slavery has been abolished, in which a human being *in the plenitude of every faculty* is delivered up to the tender mercies of another human being, in the hope forsooth that this other will use the power solely for the good of the person subjected to it. Marriage is the only actual bondage known to our law. (557–58, emphasis added)

As we have seen, the temporality that becomes conceivable as a consequence of this prying apart of capacity and agency is valuable in its particularity, rather than its fungibility or publicness, but here, this fullness of particularized time is anatomized as "the plenitude of every faculty." Mill's gloss introduces the possibility that agreement and common time signaled by the fungible effects of labor might give way to a plenitude of incompletely assimilable forces. Once acts and events performed in common time by individualized bodies are no longer available as the mechanism by which citizens come to understand themselves to be inhabiting a common world, such citizen-subjects become particularized not by the acts they perform but by the ways they perceive, while the world they inhabit, no longer a thing fixed into being by the commonness of the acts that made it, becomes available to be endlessly reperceived.

What is finally most striking about the structure of *The Subjection of Women* is the swerve that occurs between diagnosis and treatment, a swerve broadly characterizable as the movement from a logic of rights to one of capacity. While the first half of the essay largely devotes itself to analyzing the ways in which the civil status of women both departs from and distorts a discourse of public citizenship, *Subjection*'s final section spends relatively little time actually discussing legal or institutional remedies for these departures. Instead, Mill turns his attention to describing the sorts of benefits that will accrue to society as a whole by the release of women from their condition of marital inequality. The benefits he enumerates, however, apparently have little to do with a rights-based conception of citizenship. Addressing the assertion that exclusion from most realms of public and intellectual life has been the result of characterological unfitness rather than legal prohibition, Mill admits the possibility of gendered differences, while refusing a verdict of unfitness:

> Supposing it . . . to be true that women's minds are by nature more mobile than those of men, less capable of persisting long in the same continuous effort, more fitted for *dividing their faculties among various things than for traveling in any one path to the highest point which can be reached by it*: this may be true of women as they now are (though not without great and numerous exceptions), and may account for their having remained behind the highest order of men in precisely the things in which this absorption of the whole mind in one set of ideas and occupations may seem to be the most requisite. Still this difference is one which can only affect the kind of excellence, not the excellence itself, or its practical worth. . . . I believe that what is gained in special development by this concentration, is lost in the capacity of the mind for the other purposes of life; and even in abstract thought, it is my decided opinion that the mind does more by frequently returning to a difficult problem than by sticking to it without interruption. (539–40, emphasis added)

Implicit in Mill's largely unacknowledged shift in emphasis from rights to capacities is a shift in his understanding of how subjects matter within a society. As the essay slides from considering women as rights-bearing actors to considering them as thinkers, Mill's understanding of how thought and perception matter changes as well, from forms of action to forms of influence. In suggesting that women's contributions to the function of the polity will lie at least in part in the ways, with their capacity to divide their faculties among different objects, they can prevent male thinkers from flying off into abstraction, Mill uses the contrast to characterize a realm of mental activity that is expressly distinct from any particular conclusions to which such mental operations might lead. Mill's abrupt movement into formalism—subjects are defined not by what they think, their opinions, but by how they think—likewise marks out this new distinction. But rather than establishing this realm as entirely autonomous, such formalism insists upon the contingency and unpredictability of the effects produced by this mental activity. Because any particular habit of thought functions as much in relation to other habits of thought as in relation to their outcomes (the sort of outcomes emphasized by Guinier in her distributive voting solution), the effects of the introduction of women's mental eclecticism into the public realm are not predictable in advance, the oblique pressures of influence registering as something short of cause.

If the social organization that compels women to "deliver over" their time—and hence "the plenitude of every faculty"—rather than labor to complete certain tasks means that subjects can no longer plausibly be defined by their possession of a single, monolithic force or agency, or even a standard body, the fragmentation of agency into multiple faculties introduces the possibility of conceiving of those faculties as divisible from one another (the seeing and hearing that need not coincide) and among objects ("dividing their faculties among various things").[30] The passage makes it impossible to know for certain what the precise relation of these two sorts of division to one another is. And this impossibility is, of course, precisely the point. In his critical philosophy, Kant details a system in which the subjects' fundamental likeness and the stability of the world those subjects inhabit stand as evidence of one another, and in his late works, he theorizes a notion of race centered on the skin that makes that fundamental likeness legible in an instant, notwithstanding the ravages of age or illness, or the reversals of revolution. For Mill, the idea that the likeness of citizen-subjects might be constituted or discerned in a moment poses a threat to political freedom, rather than its condition of possibility. The moment a debate concludes, the political agreement manifested in the organization of the world this way and not that—these are instantaneously legible registrations of likeness that, Mill worries, function to coerce the citizens who act in their aftermath.

For Mill, then, the divisibility of faculties made realizable by Talbot's photographic storage implicitly creates perception as a behavior that defines and differentiates subjects, as a mode of cultivation or self-creation. This kind of individual and individualizable perception—pointedly non-standard—registers a world that need not be seen only one way, and therefore one whose mere existence can no longer bear weight as evidence of a prior public agreement. The opportunity afforded subjects to abstract their perceptions of the world from the causal circumstances that have generated them offers the possibility of experiencing a commonness caused at no moment in particular, and hence equally available to everyone. The world is no longer one of ordered sets of objects and ideas but instead of objects and ideas that can be abandoned, rearranged, returned to. Time is no longer a largely inert uninterruptable medium within which a linear concentration is marked and measured but instead becomes itself a resource to be parceled out, reversed, interrupted, canceled.[31] Within this new perceptual regime, a temporality that is no longer fungible or homogeneous is one in which past historical events do not exclude or limit the sorts of events that might take place in the future, because such events are never fully and definitively past. In this way, the subject endowed with the capacity to divide her perceptual faculties provides Mill with a way of conceiving a world—and a notion of history—that is no longer constrained by the fact of its having been caused or agreed upon. Instead, that world becomes endlessly reperceivable and thus capable of being endlessly revised.

FOUR

Observing Selection: Charles Darwin and the Emergence of the Racial Sign

My project to this point has been essentially revisionary. My goal throughout the three preceding chapters has been to show how what is arguably the fundamental presumption undergirding contemporary critical discussions about race—that race is constructed, organized on the model of the arbitrary relation between signifier and signified—conceals a far more complex history, one in which race constitutes ways of knowing designed to address and resolve some basic difficulties of knowing and perceiving: What is gained, and what is lost, by our commitment to the belief that individuals are essentially like one another—by our commitment, that is, to the category of the human? Can that commitment to the fundamental likeness of human beings ever be anything more than a belief? Can it rest on grounds that can themselves be known or experienced? What sorts of dangers might be entailed by the effort to do so? How can a commitment to the essential likeness of human beings be reconciled with an equally pressing commitment to human freedom? To what degree can our sense of the human—its pervasiveness, its legibility—depend upon the fact that humans have bodies, bodies that change and age? And how, and to what degree, can we know about things we cannot perceive or experience?

The notion that race is constructed has produced, with the force of the inevitable, a methodology of critique: proliferating histories of racial meaning. If the central premise of the racial construction thesis is that the signs of racial difference need not carry the associations they do, then it stands to reason that the political force of racial difference might be blunted by genealogies that reveal how those constructed racial signs came to have those meanings. In arguing that racial constructedness subtends less, rather than more, of the history of race, one of my objectives has been to consider possible limitations of the usefulness of historicist modes of critique. Here my task is different. Rather than challenging the methodology that would identify the arbitrariness of racial meaning, in this chapter I hope to account for it. In the work of Charles Darwin, I will be arguing, we discover at once the origins of racial construction and the context of its usefulness. But where the notion of the arbitrariness of racial meaning can be seen to have cleared the way for a variety of histories of racial meaning, what I offer here is a history of the arbitrary racial sign itself. It is to this history I now turn.

In 1798, Thomas Malthus published *An Essay on the Principle of Population*. I begin this chapter with a statement of fact sufficiently incontrovertible as to seem consignable to parentheses because, to the degree that the *Essay*'s central argument has achieved the status of cultural bromide, it has become easy *not* to notice what Malthus himself understands his topic to be: population. While Adam Smith and David Hume recognize the significance of population size to social health, as Catherine Gallagher has argued, what distinguishes Malthus from those Scottish Enlightenment thinkers immediately preceding him is his willingness to imagine the health of the social body as something other than the sum of the health of the various individual bodies that it comprised.[1] In making the case that the flourishing of individual bodies might actually interfere with the flourishing of the population as a whole, Malthus insists that population be understood as a thing in and of itself, irreducible to other units, incapable of being described in terms of dynamics not specific to it.

Nor is it simply protoeconomists and social theorists from whom Malthus declares his independence. In insisting upon the force and specificity of population per se, Malthus takes aim at the tradition of critical philosophy as well. William Godwin is a prominent and explicit target of Malthus's early chapters, but we can by now supply the terms by which Malthusian population stands as a challenge to, if not quite a direct engagement with, Kant's thinking as well. For Kant, individual subjects are members of a "class," a grouping in which members are members in virtue of possessing all necessary and common characteristics. To know a single individual in a class is in effect to know all members and hence the class as a whole. The notion that humans are a class—the presumption of their fundamental and identifiable likeness to one another—at once undergirds and expresses the foundation of Kant's critical method: humans can be known insofar as they are essentially like one another, and the fact that they can be known and conceived serves as irrefutable evidence of their status as a class. Kant's racialized skin functions to shore up the status of human beings as a class by making human likeness instantaneously legible and thus canceling, or at least minimizing, the differentiating effects of human bodily functioning, for example, circulation, the processing of nutriments, and the body's aging, changing, and dying.

In challenging humans' status as a class, then, Malthus's theorization of a category of "population" challenges the fundamental analytical proposition associated with the notion of a class: that epistemology and ontology imply one another, that the possibility of thinking of an object offers proof of that object's existence, which defines it as both cause and itself capable of causing. Malthus's *Essay* implicitly generates another set of questions: To what degree is the "thinkability" of population available to the individuals whose points of view are defined in opposition to it? What is the process by which the "principle of population" might be discerned? And, finally, what is the use of discovering such a principle or principles if the dynamics of cause and effect governing populations are fundamentally distinct from—and thus beyond the reach of—the agency of individuals who might be moved to respond to such knowledge?

So while Malthus's essay has mainly come down to us as a cautionary polemic about the potentially deleterious effects of healthy individuals on populations, we might nonetheless read it as laying the groundwork of an argument for the existence of a new kind of object and for the necessity of a new discipline or methodology for studying that object. We might read it this way, but we would be acting precipitously, because as remarkable as the comprehensiveness with which the *Essay* establishes its new analytical dispensation is, the speed with which it returns to the familiar epistemological contours of Enlightenment subjectivity in its final pages is startling. While Malthus begins his *Essay* with intimations of something like sociology, he closes it by beating a hasty retreat to a philosophy of mind. I want to start by examining Malthus's *Essay* in some detail, then, not because he finally succeeds in establishing a new framework for rendering groups of people legible, but because his ultimate failure to do so helps illuminate some of the conceptual difficulties associated with establishing a "principle of population" in the final decades of the eighteenth century. By tracing the rhetoric both of Malthus's break and of his retrenchment, moreover, I hope to make apparent the ways in which the work of Malthus's most famous intellectual heir, Charles Darwin, stands not only as a fundamental rethinking of the relations between individuals and populations, but also as an elaboration of the profound epistemological implications of such a rethinking. For Darwin, as we shall see, populations are populations—they function as units or systems unto themselves—to the very degree that they are not describable by principles, at least not according to the understanding of principle embraced by Enlightenment thinkers like Kant.

The revolution of Darwin's 1859 *Origin of Species* lies at least in part in its claim that populations are both caused and discerned not by what is lawful but by what is accidental or contingent, less by principle than by the collapse of principle. In this early work, Darwin blunts the philosophical radicalism of his theory by introducing a series of abstractions and analogies—"selection," "species," the resemblance of natural selection to the artificial selection—that work to cloak the ways in which the concept of natural selection undermines the fungibility of agents, objects, and observers that is a central premise of Enlightenment universalism. To the degree to which populations are defined not by their members' shared characteristics but by the varied and contingent interactions of their different elements, Darwin's embrace of Malthus's category of population leaves him to grapple with the task that Malthus uncovered and then turned away from: figuring out by whom—or, more broadly, from what point of view—populations might productively be perceived or known. While the Darwin of *Origin of Species* details the pulling apart of the elements of a population and the point of view from which such a system might be known, and then offers what is essentially a rhetorical fix to the challenge of thinking about populations created by accident, the author of the post-*Origin* books devotes the final portion of his career, in works like *The Descent of Man* (1871) and *The Expression of the Emotions in Man and Animals* (1872), to discovering and describing the mechanism that would realign populations and those who would discern them. Darwin sets about this project by demonstrating the ways in which the history by which subjects come to recognize populations is itself a mechanism of those populations' generation. By turning the contingency of causation from a dynamic that makes populations unlawful into a quality of the group's particularity, post-*Origin* Darwin makes the accident by which populations come into being into the fundamental condition of their legibility. It is in these later works, with Darwin's insistence that species come to be recognized and to recognize themselves not according to the traits that are necessary to those species' survival but by way of traits that have no special relationship to that survival, that we discover the origins of the notion of race as sign.

Malthus's Disappearing Perspective

Malthus begins his essay with a gesture of modesty:

> The following Essay owes its origin to a conversation with a friend, on the subject of Mr Godwin's essay on "Avarice and Profusion" in his Enquirer. The discussion started the general question of the future improvement of society, and the Author at first sat down with an intention of merely stating his thoughts to his friend, upon paper, in a clearer manner than he thought he could do in conversation. But as the subject opened upon him, some ideas occurred, which he did not recollect to have met with before; and as he conceived that every least light, on a topic so generally interesting, might be received with candour, he determined to put his thoughts in a form for publication.[2]

Read in the context of what follows it, the modesty of Malthus's opening is part of its polemic. While the ambitiousness of his topic might seem to align his project with those of "speculative philosophers" like Godwin and Condorcet, whose confidence about the transformability of the world is directly proportional to the abstraction of their ideas, Malthus is eager to assure his readers that he has arrived at his subject matter and come to publish it, if not by accident, then at least by half steps. What started as a conversation gave way to an attempt to transcribe and clarify that conversation, we learn, until, as the force and complexity of the subject matter and of his own ideas became apparent to Malthus, he found himself moved to publish. What matters most about the origin of his text, it seems, is the possibility that it might not have been. Had he gone out for a smoke, say, instead of sitting down to clarify his ideas, had his thoughts taken a different turn than the one they did, then we would not be reading the *Essay* we have before us. This narrative of origin is a story not of inevitability but of its opposite.

But in simply focusing on the incrementalism of Malthus's narrative, we risk overlooking the ways in which the passage's movement effects a transformation in what counts as authority, a movement from an account of *origins* to a claim of *originality*. Malthus narrates the moment of metamorphosis—"But as the subject opened upon him, some ideas occurred, which he did not recollect to have met with before"—but what is peculiar about his turn to originality here is that it obfuscates, rather than clarifies, the issue of authorship. The passage equivocates as to whether the ideas "which he did not recollect to have met with before" are original in relation to Malthus's own existing body of ideas—ideas that had not previously occurred to him during his conversation with his friend—or whether they are new in relation to the existing body of thought on the topic of "Avarice and Profusion." The ambiguity is generated rhetorically by the sudden introjection of the "subject [matter]" as an agent ("as the subject opened upon him"), which creates the possibility that the possessor of the ideas formulated before that subject matter's moment of self-revelation is a different person than the possessor of the ideas in the aftermath of that moment.

Most significant, I think, about the role of this self-revealing subject is what it illuminates about the force of Malthus's turn to the authority of originality. In inviting us to consider the question of originality by way of an instance in which the source of the ideas remains indeterminate, the passage here suggests that what matters is not the identity of the particular thinker but rather the concept of originality per se. In making this shift from origin to originality, Malthus effectively reconceives the field in which he writes and acts—and in which ideas exist—from one that is open to one that is closed. The difference is this: In the beginning lines' logic of origin, events follow one another; nothing need happen until it happens, which means both that no future events are predestined and that all kinds of happenings are of a piece with one another. A conversation with a friend may have inspired a transcription and clarification project, but it might just as well have inspired a break for lunch, a walk to the park, or a bike ride. In Malthus's shift to originality, happening becomes discursive. The field is thus circumscribed in the sense that all its "events" are ideational, but its quality of circumscription is even more fundamental. In introducing a notion of originality in which ideas either have or have not been "met with before," Malthus suggests that all ideas already exist somewhere, preexisting their encounter with one thinker or another. Here, in marked contrast with the passage's opening, there is no question of whether the ideas the *Essay* presents will come into being: they already exist, isomorphically, with the subject matter itself. This sense of ideas' autonomy from and preexistence of those who would encounter them is consistent with the strangely elusive attribution; if ideas exist and await the moment they are met with, then when all is said and done, it finally matters very little who in particular meets with them first. The fact that the ambiguity of attribution is produced by the incursion of the active "subject [matter"] that seems to prostrate those who would think it only underscores the sense of the field's enclosure: ideas not only antedate those who would think them, but they seem to do so precisely to the degree that they are structured by their very subject matter.

In his opening, then, Malthus signals the epistemological crisis generated by the introduction of the category of population even in advance of actually analyzing his object by introducing a thinking, essay-producing subject to assume (and explore) the role of the eating, reproducing one. Whereas the individual thinker attempting to discern the dynamics of population must do so from no predetermined or reliably representative position in relation to an object whose own development is contingent and unpredictable—that is, he must work out the steps from origin to essay as he goes along—the "original" thinker with whom we are presented by the passage's end is one who can dispense with figuring out his particular relationship to his object of inquiry because that relationship is constituted and determined by the object itself, an object whose own contours and logics exist in perpetuity, awaiting only discovery by whichever original thinker encounters them first. In the isomorphism and determinacy glossed by this logic of originality, we shall see, Malthus gestures toward a return to something like a Kantian subject, a subject whose capacity to think the object in question testifies both to the fixity and lawfulness of that object and to his essential likeness to it.

What this opposition between origin and originality excludes, of course, is the possibility that ideas might be newly thought because the conditions that produce them have themselves changed. For Malthus, history happens, chance event following chance event, and already extant ideas have or have not yet been encountered; but as in the rhetoric of the opening paragraph, the two realms operate largely independently of one another as Malthus oscillates between them. In the broadest terms, this opening slide bespeaks Malthus's hesitancy about how—or whether—his *Essay* or any other essay should matter, should make a difference in the world, about whether the discursive realm in which original ideas are encountered can alter the contours of the material object that makes those ideas available. The *Essay* seems dogged throughout by the question of its own efficacy: if the fact that population increases geometrically and the food supply increases arithmetically means that human populations will wax and wane cyclically as they outstrip their food supply and then are starved into proportion, then what are we meant to do with this insight? Indeed, given that the system seems self-adjusting, need we do anything at all? But the question of whether ideas can change or respond to changes in the material world seems pointed even within the context of Malthus's epistemological lineage. If, as we have seen, Malthus's break with his Enlightenment predecessors takes the form of his insistence that there exists a material and epistemological disjunction between the condition of the population and that of the individual, then Malthus's slide from a logic of origin to one of originality—from an account of material history to a closed discursive field of already existing ideas—might be seen as both a symptom and consequence of his argument, rather than a set of methodological preconditions. A population only becomes legible to individuals at the moment those individuals' thoughts (and implicitly the individuals themselves) come to be structured by that population—that is, at the moment that population becomes something akin to a Kantian "class" composed of interchangeable individuals. Such a grouping does not require a sociology to study the variety of relations within it in order to be understood but demands only the formal interpretation that is a philosophy of mind.

As the *Essay* continues, it becomes apparent that Malthus's oscillation between a logic of origin and one of originality is symptomatic of a recurrent and fundamental ambivalence about both history and historicism—that is, both about the alterability of the material world and the ways in which such alterability renders the world susceptible or opaque to being known. Early on, Malthus figures himself as steering a middle path between the excesses of the Enlightenment's "speculative philosophers" like Godwin and Condorcet, on the one hand, and those (who remain nameless throughout) of the "advocates for the present order of things." Speculative philosophers are speculative, Malthus explains, in their commitment to the principle of the "perfectibility of mankind," a commitment that has led Godwin to conjecture that "the passion between the sexes may in time be extinguished" (and hence the problem of overpopulation solved) in the absence of all supporting evidence (19). The "friend of the present order of things," by contrast, "condemns all political speculations in the gross" and "will not even condescend to examine the grounds from which the perfectibility of society is inferred" (17). The two "postulata" that Malthus places at the center of his argument—"that food is necessary to the existence of mankind" and "that the passion between the sexes is necessary and will remain nearly in its present state"—might seem to locate him in the camp of the advocates of the present order, insisting as they do upon the unchangingness of present conditions. Malthus contends otherwise: unlike these supporters of the status quo, he does not claim as a matter of principle that nothing about the ways things are can ever change, but rather, that these particular qualities of the world have shown no sign of changing in the past and are thus unlikely to change in the future. "These two laws," he says, "ever since we have had any knowledge of mankind, appear to have been fixed laws of our nature, and as we have not hitherto seen any alteration in them, we have no right to conclude that they will ever cease to be what they are now, without an immediate act of power in that Being who first arranged the system of the universe, and for the advantage of his creatures, still executes, according to fixed laws, all its various operations" (19). What is objectionable about the speculative philosophers, in Malthus's view, is not that they argue that human beings might behave differently in the future than they do in the present, but that they do so without a modicum of evidence:

> A writer may tell me that he thinks man will ultimately become an ostrich. I cannot properly contradict him. But before he can expect to bring any reasonable person over to his opinion, he ought to shew that the necks of man have been gradually elongating, that the lips have grown harder and more prominent, that the legs and feet are daily altering their shape, and that the hair is beginning to change into stubs of feathers. And till the probability of so wonderful a conversion can be shewn, it is surely lost time and lost eloquence to expatiate on the happiness of man in such a state. (18–19)

In setting himself against the theory-driven certainties of both Godwin and his Enlightenment ilk and the glumly passive status-quo advocates, Malthus would seem to be embracing the logic of origin with which he began the *Essay*. He bothers to relate the series of steps by which some event, like the publication of an essay, comes about precisely because such an outcome could not be predicted in advance. But Malthus's adoption of this logic is somewhat less than thoroughgoing, inasmuch as he seems to understand the historical contingency associated with origins to be a condition only available in the past: things might have happened differently before, but they are unlikely to change from here on out. For Malthus, the immutability of human nature turns out to be a matter of historical fact rather than a statement of principle, a circumstance that enables him to erect an account predicated upon the regularity and predictability of the material world while, nonetheless, laying claim to an empiricist methodology.

I observed earlier that Malthus's opening slide from origin to originality was characterized in part by a slide into discursivity. Where the events of his origin narrative ranged from conversation to transcription to discovery to publication and might potentially have included other sorts of happenings as well, the framework of originality delineates a field in which everything that *happens* happens within and in relation to texts. In the polemical survey of the literature we have just examined, the field would seem, at least at first glance, to have been narrowed even further. The trajectory of (potential) events marked out by the ostrich's transmutations does not just comprise happenings within a text but includes as well the steps of an argument, while the "outcome" that may or may not be reducible to principle is the conclusion of an argument. Although we might expect Malthus to couple this narrowing of realm from text to argument with a move to contextualize that argument within a broader historical field, he in fact does the opposite. When he reprises this argument a few chapters later, he offers his description of the structure of argumentation as a model for the movement of historical events in general. Suddenly, the impossibility of coming to conclusions that have not previously been warranted by evidence—an epistemological account—returns as a descriptive framework by which we are meant to recognize the impossibility of unpredictable events in general. The patent absurdity of humans' becoming ostriches—an absurdity Malthus invents, we recall, in order to illustrate the groundlessness of the speculative philosophers' claims for the possibility of human improvement—is echoed midway through the *Essay* by the example of the Leicestershire sheep (62). The context of the sheep's introduction is again epistemological, with Malthus fulminating against those who would assert that the human life span has been prolonged in the absence of any supporting evidence. The sheep appear as an illustration by way of analogy:

> I am told that it is a maxim among the improvers of cattle that you may breed to any degree of nicety you please, and they found this maxim upon another, which is that some of the offspring will possess the desirable qualities of the parents in a greater degree. In the famous Leicestershire breed of sheep, the object is to procure them with small heads and small legs. Proceeding upon these breeding maxims, it is evident that we might go on till the heads and legs were evanescent qualities, but this is so palpable an absurdity that we may be quite sure that the premises are not just and that there really is a limit, though we cannot see it or say exactly where it is. In this case, the point of the greatest degree of improvement, or the smallest size of the head and legs, may be said to be undefined, but that is very different from unlimited, or from indefinite, in Mr Condorcet's acceptation of the term. Though I may not be able in the present to mark the limit at which further improvement will stop, I can very easily mention a point at which it will not arrive. (60–61)

Central to Malthus's rhetorical strategy here is his invitation to his readers to contemplate not simply an absurdity, but an absurdity that takes the form of a vanishing (of heads and legs). The echo of the human-ostrich transmogrification is crucial, since it is the nothingness of that evidence, less imperceptible than vanished, that enables Malthus to conflate the material and the epistemological and, in so doing, to transform a critique of the ways certain philosophers construct their arguments into an argument for the irrelevance of historically unpredictable events.

The passage begins as a rumination on the transformability of species (*can* Leicestershire sheep be bred to have smaller heads and legs until those heads and legs change into nothing?), then shifts into description of knowing-in-time that represents prediction as a kind of literal seeing (can we *see* the moment at which we will be able to know?), and finally, synthesizes the process of knowing and its object in their nonhappening, that is, the knowing of the nonarrival at nothingness ("I can very easily mention a point at which it will not arrive"). Malthus's general point is clear: there are limitations on all kinds of change, so the speculative philosophers who make the case for human perfectibility do so without adequate supporting evidence. But what would seem a straightforward argument for empiricism—don't make arguments without adequate evidence—turns out to conceal a more subtle point about the legibility of historical events per se. As Malthus would have it, the fact that a certain kind of change cannot go on forever (that it cannot be made a matter of law or principle) means that the particular degree of change that actually *does* take place is unimportant. Certainly, we might raise objections to such a conclusion: if it is an advantage to breeders to possess cattle with smaller heads, surely the difference between a cow with a head the size of a mastiff and one with a head the size of a squirrel is significant. The notion that human thinking proceeds only so long as the material world functions in regular and predictable ways is the Enlightenment's foundational premise (Kant's critical philosophy being only the most rigorous theorization of that premise), and Malthus is explicit about his embrace of this principle: "The constancy of the laws of nature and of effects and causes is the foundation of all human knowledge, though far be it from me to say that the same power which framed and executes the laws of nature, may not change them all 'in a moment, in the twinkling of an eye'" (59–60).

The Leicestershire sheep passage, then, is less remarkable for the incoherence of its claims than for the strenuousness of the efforts Malthus exerts there to bring the lawfulness of objects and the lawful process by which those objects might be contemplated into alignment with one another. The changes undergone by the Leicestershire sheep are apprehensible by rational thinkers insofar as they do not register as changes at all: they do not culminate with the disappearance of the sheep as a lawful species and thus, finally, don't matter. What becomes evident is that the recognition of the inconsequentiality of the kind of changes that produce minor and unpredictable variations in head size rests upon the notion that the passage of time doesn't change what there is to know. As Kant and anatomical medicine's standardized body taught us, dismissing the significance of such variations among sheep requires treating the differences among sheep through time as if they are the same as the variations among sheep at any given moment. Such a claim becomes especially difficult to sustain when the very dynamic that Malthus analyzes—the widening discrepancy between population and food supply—is registered over time. If the relations among individuals, their state of perfection, and the populations they make up were the same through time as they are at any given moment, there would be no population crisis in need of response. Malthus attempts to manage this difficulty by representing the object to be known as a kind of disappearance, and knowledge of the future as a literal seeing, so that the particular challenge of knowing a historically contingent future—of knowing the precise size at which the sheep's head will cease to shrink further—is rendered equivalent to the impossible ideal of the totally evanescent object, and both are made to disappear. This pulling apart of lawful objects and the process by which they are known is the not-quite-buried threat of the Leicestershire sheep section, and it will become, we shall see, the central issue upon which Darwin constructs his analytical system.

For the moment, though, I want to trace the path of Malthus's evasion. I have indicated in passing that the strains within Malthus's argument and within his *Essay* manifest themselves in part in the form of disciplinary incoherence. While the terms of his argument seem to imply the need for a new methodology, a protosociology that would speak to the irreducibility of the category "population" to the individual subjects who would know it, the *Essay* ends with a return to something much more methodologically familiar, an account of the development and operation of an individual mind. I want to suggest that the incoherencies of the Leicestershire sheep can be seen to parse this disciplinary disjunction: the necessity of treating a population as something other than a collection of lawful—which is to say, fundamentally interchangeable—individuals is the consequence of the changefulness of the population as a unit. For Malthus, a population is a population insofar as it is never identical with itself through time, insofar as its very constitution as an entity generates its changefulness. It is because populations are distinct from the individuals that compose them—that is, it is because a society of healthy, well-fed individuals produces an excess of offspring that outstrips the available food supply and, consequently, eviscerates the population—that populations are in a constant state of flux.

There is something of the tragic about Malthus's *Essay*. Populations can't help but procreate themselves into poverty and famine even when they know better; we discover populations' propensity for self-dissolution at the very moment we recognize their particularity as a category. The Leicestershire sheep episode parses this tragedy, or it would, if Malthus allowed his tragedy to stay tragic. For what is far more remarkable about the closing pages of Malthus's *Essay* than the methodological swerve to which I have been drawing our attention is the abrupt tonal shift that makes the methodological shift discernible. Populations may indeed be fated to reproduce themselves into misery, but it turns out, when all is said and done, that misery is a good thing:

> A being with only good placed in view may be justly said to be impelled by a blind necessity. The pursuit of good in this case can be no indication of virtuous propensities. . . . When the mind has been awakened into activity by the passions and the wants of the body, intellectual wants arise; and the desire of knowledge and the impatience under ignorance form a new and important class of excitement. Every part of nature seems peculiarly calculated to furnish stimulants to mental exertion of this kind, and to offer inexhaustible food for the most unremitted inquiry. (119)

The fall into famine is, it seems, a fortunate one, as the withdrawal of an unending supply of proximate provisions produces a peculiar kind of variety in its stead, a patterning of desirable objects and their lack that encourages the kind of mental exertion that allows hungry individuals to find nourishment in the "inexhaustible food for the most unremitted inquiry." But the very familiarity of this final narrative obscures the degree to which, for Malthus at least, the cast of characters has changed. Where the socioeconomic problem Malthus spends the better part of his essay detailing is predicated upon a disjunction between the qualities, interests, and points of view of individuals and those of populations, in the final chapter, the effects of this disjunction are made to disappear along with—indeed, by means of—the evaporation of the population itself. Suddenly, we are squarely back within the realm of the individual, and the events of that realm are steps in the development of an individual mind. With this final circumscription, not only is the material problem of overpopulation made invisible, but the epistemological problem associated with the disjunction between the perspective of the population and that of the individual thinker who would know that population dissolves as well. We need no longer ask how individuals might know populations defined both by their opposition to the individuals they include and by their changefulness, their nonidentity with themselves, because knowing has been implicitly reconceived not as an engagement of subject and object, but as the isolated movement of an individual mind. And as the *Essay*'s opening slide from origin to originality might have allowed us to anticipate (if only we were equipped to read it as prefiguration), the movement of the individual mind reigns paramount when the universe it would engage is already designed, closed, and directed to an extant end, as Malthus reassures us by way of conclusion:

> The idea that the impressions and excitements of this world are the instruments with which the Supreme Being forms matter into mind, and that the necessity of constant exertion to avoid evil and to pursue good is the principal spring of these impressions and excitements, seems to smooth many of the difficulties that occur in a contemplation of human life, and appears to me to give a satisfactory reason for the existence of natural and moral evil, and, consequently for that part of both, and it certainly is not a very small part, which arises from the principle of population. (124)

With this conclusion, good and evil cease to be measures of social relations—about how one ought to divide inadequate possessions, for example, or the nature of one's responsibilities to future generations—and become instead modes of mental exertion. If the epistemological problem Malthus laid out over the course of the *Essay* carries with it a moral charge regarding the proper response to a scarcity we can recognize but do nothing about, by the end of his argument "many of the difficulties that occur in a contemplation of human life" have been "smoothed away." The mere contemplation of such difficulties has become their solution. In this context, we might understand Darwin's project as a refusal to "smooth many of the difficulties that occur in a contemplation of human life." It is to this refusal I now turn.

Selecting a Point of View: Darwin's *Origins*

No one, not least Darwin himself, would dispute the influence of Malthus's *Essay on the Principle of Population* on the development of Darwin's theory of natural selection. As early as the fall of 1838, more than two decades before the 1859 publication of *On the Origin of Species*, Darwin's notebooks reflect the profound impact of his reading of Malthus: having considered the *Essay*'s account of the fragility of the equilibrium between population and food supply, Darwin announces his abandonment of his long-held position that some species' extinctions were due to the expiration of a predetermined "vital duration."[3] With all species pressing so hard upon one another and producing a delicate competitive balance, even the slightest change in conditions can plausibly bring about the loss of some species.[4] Darwin goes on to name Malthus specifically in the introduction to *Origin*, characterizing the argument of his third chapter, "Struggle for Existence," as "the doctrine of Malthus, applied to the whole animal and vegetable kingdoms."[5]

But as I have already intimated, the pressure of Malthus's thought on Darwin's registers equally significantly, appropriately enough, in their points of variation.[6] I've been arguing that the tension Malthus sets at the center of his thesis—between the conditions and interests of individuals and those of populations—entails a number of less explicitly articulated, but equally fundamental, tensions as well: between the knowledge or perspective available to individuals and to populations, between the events of knowing and the cause and effect of material change. Malthus's *Essay* is moved along by the force of these tensions, but it finally evades their implications, subsuming the material into the epistemological, transmuting the scarcity of excessive population into food for thought.

Darwin essentially takes over where Malthus leaves off—or, more precisely, where he fears to tread. Like Malthus, Darwin begins *Origin* with a narrative of his work's origin. But where Malthus almost immediately shifts registers to a closed universe of "originality," where all events are events of the mind, encounters with already extant ideas that may or may not have yet taken place, Darwin continues to insist upon the contingent relations linking the happenings of the material world, a given individual thinker's encounter with those happenings, and the forms of knowledge produced out of that encounter:

> When on board H.M.S. "Beagle," as naturalist, I was much struck with certain facts in the distribution of the inhabitants of South America, and in the geological relations of the present to the past inhabitants of that continent. These facts seemed to me to throw some light on the origin of species—that mystery of mysteries, as it has been called by one of our greatest philosophers. On my return home, it occurred to me, in 1837, that something might be made out on this question by patiently accumulating and reflecting on all sorts of facts which could possibly have any bearing on it. After five years' work I allowed myself to speculate on the subject, and drew up some short notes; these I enlarged in 1844 into a sketch of the conclusion, which then

> seemed to me probable: from that period to the present day I have steadily pursued the same object. (449)

Where for Malthus, the geography of happening is conceptual—the only space we get is that created when the "subject opened upon him"—here geography is both an object of analysis (the spatial distribution of the inhabitants of South America, the geographical relations of past and present) and a landscape to be moved through, as Darwin turns data into conjecture into publishable hypothesis.[7] Darwin informs us that he is on the *Beagle* "as naturalist," implying that he might have been in the same place in some other capacity, and had he been so, what he would have seen and known would have been different.[8] By this account, knowledge and perspective are not straightforwardly coincident with one another. What one knows depends not only on one's location in time and space, but also on the ways in which one has been trained and what one is looking for. Nor do the qualities of the subject matter wholly determine what can be known about it: Observations are made. Times and venues change. Facts are not only "accumulated" but "reflected upon" over years. Speculations are floated, tested, discarded, and reformulated.[9]

But Darwin does not simply undo the tensions that so vexed Malthus by dissolving both the material environment to be known and the qualities of the observing knower's identity into sets of unrelated contingencies. Or, more precisely, while Darwin's opening would appear to offer an account of a process of investigation in which the individual knowing subject and the species, population, or system he would investigate escape being in tension with one another to the degree that both subject and object are reconceived as contingent collections of traits, this solution turns out to be only a temporary fix. Darwin initially grapples with the "Malthus problem" in formal terms, beginning the argument of *Origin* with a discussion of "domestication" or "artificial selection" (breeding) as a means for making the case for the existence of the near-analogous process of what he goes on to term "natural selection." Darwin's goal, of course, is to make discernible the causes of variations among and within species, and in this context his decision to begin with breeding makes perfect sense. With artificial selection, the agent of change, the selector, is an individual who intends to bring about the changes he produces, and who can be seen bringing them about:

> Let us now briefly consider the steps by which domestic races have been produced, either from one or from several allied species. Some little effect may,

> perhaps, be attributed to the direct action of the external conditions of life, and some to habit; but he would be a bold man who would account by such agencies for the differences of a dray and a race horse, a greyhound and a bloodhound, a carrier and a tumbler pigeon. One of the most remarkable features in our domesticated races is that we see in them adaptation, not indeed, to the animal's or plant's own good, but to man's use or fancy. (467)

The very quality that makes domestication's process of causation visible—what makes it "remarkable"—is the opportunity it affords for aligning intentions and ends: we can see the ways in which human acts of selection produce particular outcomes to the very degree that those outcomes are pointedly distinct from the ends that would benefit the animals or plants themselves.

But what begins in Darwin's text as the muted intimation of an ethical problem not unrelated to the sort Malthus grapples with—producing "adaptations not . . . to the animal's or plant's own good but to man's use or fancy," significantly different from valuing the interests of the population at the expense of the individual?—soon mutates into an epistemological problem that threatens to undermine the usefulness of artificial selection as self-evident analogical ground. Artificial selection's alignment of selectors' intentions and ends or goals—the very alignment that purportedly has made the process of domestication especially discernible—turns out to be an inadequate representation of the comprehensive relations of cause and effect. Once Darwin begins to fill in the terms of the artificial/natural selection analogy in the chapter entitled "Natural Selection," the very perspicuousness of artificial selection's operation becomes its descriptive weakness:

> Man can act only on external and visible characters: nature cares nothing for appearances, except in so far as they may be useful to any being. She can act on every internal organ, on every shade of constitutional difference, on the whole machinery of life. Man selects only for his own good; Nature only for that of the being which she tends. Every selected character is fully exercised by her; and the being is placed under well-suited conditions of life. (503)

Here the discernibility of ends that had recommended artificial selection as an illuminating case becomes instead its analogical failing. Where we had once thought that domestication rendered the effects of selection visible—that is, where we once understood it as an analytically useful illustration—we now discover it to be a materially limited force: it can only cause effects that are visible.

Darwin's opening narration seems to offer the possibility that the causal processes by which variations within and among species come into being can themselves be made straightforwardly legible by turning knower, modes of knowledge, and the world to be known into discrete and contingent clusters of traits that need not formally exclude one another. But the awkward movement from artificial to natural selection makes manifest the difficulty of making any observations about the relations of the system qua system. It is certainly possible to observe that those involved in domestication possess certain qualities—they are farmers, say, or natural scientists, or they are poverty-stricken, or they act in the midst of an epidemic of cattle disease. And it is also possible to observe that they are breeding animals with certain ends in mind (to create cows who produce more abundant milk, leaner muscle, better disease resistance) and that the existence of these newly emergent variations might be recognized by various means (increased total annual milk production, increased life expectancy). But the moment we attempt to move from the details of any particular case to offer a general account of the ways in which we come to know how species change, it becomes impossible to characterize how we know a species without making decisions about the particular qualities that actually characterize that species.

Darwin's discussion of artificial selection in the passage above makes apparent that the decision to focus on visible characteristics is not simply a taxonomical one, for it causes things to happen in the material world, makes species different than they would otherwise have been. Malthus's Leicestershire sheep, with their shrinking but never evanescent heads, makes apparent why this is true even when such knowers' actions do not directly produce an organism's qualities. To know a species is to know it in relation to its alterations over time, and insofar as one of Darwin's (and much more provisionally, Malthus's) central insights is that species change, to know a species at a particular moment is to know one species and not another. Malthus's response to the conundrum is to declare off limits the very knowledge of species that change: if we cannot know *when* we will know that the heads of the Leicestershire sheep will have stopped shrinking, then when those heads *stop* shrinking is insignificant. Both Malthus and the domesticators presume that the process of causation by which species change must be visible in order to be significant. But where that presumption leads domesticators to circumscribe the qualities of an organism that are subject to change, for Malthus, it means that the changes that take place, but cannot be predicted or known, finally don't matter.

The revolution of Darwin's notion of natural selection lies in its refusal of either of these forms of limitation. Darwin's theory can be seen as an elaboration of the implications of the disjunction between the agency of causation and its legibility.[10] Darwin discovers this disjunction seemingly by accident as he struggles to piece together a rhetoric capable of describing the interactions of diverse species within a given environment:

> The advantage of diversification in the inhabitants of the same region is, in fact, the same as that of the physiological division of labour in the organs of the same individual body. . . . No physiologist doubts that a stomach by being adapted to digest vegetable matter alone, or flesh alone, draws most nutriment from these substances. So in the general economy of any land, the more widely and perfectly the animals are diversified for different habits of life, so will a greater number of individuals be capable of their supporting themselves. A set of animals, with their organisation but little diversified, could hardly compete with a set more perfectly diversified in structure. (523)

The point of the passage is clear: to establish an analogy between the division and diversification of labor within an individual body and the diversification of animals within a region. The narrower the functions of a particular organ or organism, the more successful that organ or organism is likely to be in doing what it does, since it is less likely to meet with competition from other organs or organisms, which themselves have been diversified to perform other, noncompeting tasks. But if we consider the analogy's logic, we are likely to find ourselves perplexed. Does a specialized organ necessarily advantage a given organism? We might easily imagine a set of circumstances—a drought, say—in which possessing a stomach that was only capable of processing vegetable matter might place an individual organism at a disadvantage in relation to an individual whose stomach could digest vegetables or meat, as need be. Indeed, the analogy appears equally unstable for Darwin: while he begins by positing the likeness of two realms of diversification, the regional and the bodily, his elaboration of the analogy offers an example—the exclusively herbivorous stomach—that fits squarely into neither tenor nor vehicle but rather falls somewhere in between. A stomach adapted to eating vegetable matter only is advantaged, after all, not in relation to other organs of the same body but in relation to stomachs of other, less exclusively herbivorous species, presumably of the same region. This stomach does not so much exemplify the likeness of the two realms as it figures the causal relation between them.

In that sense, the collapse of the analogy works to lay bare its rhetorical function. By presenting the relation between the organization of an individual body and the organization of animals within an environment as a relation of likeness, the analogy effectively brackets the question of how the two terms are related causally. The analogy thus establishes by way of axiom rather than argument: first, that the individual functions as the primary analytical unit operating within a given environment, and second, that the limits and bounds of the environment are as stable and self-evident as the limits and bounds of an individual body.[11] In hiding the causal relation between the individual body and the environment in which it exists by insisting upon their likeness, the analogy makes unaskable the question of the unit that natural selection "selects." As the strangely causal example of the herbivorous stomach makes apparent (and, indeed, as much of *Origin* goes on to elaborate), what is selected by way of natural selection is anything but self-evident. If traits (the possession of stomachs capable of digesting only vegetables) are selected, then the relation of such traits to any given organism (the division of labor among a body's organs) does not necessarily follow; if it is a species, then the species can be said to be selected only if it is not defined in terms of its possession of a stable and comprehensive set of traits. As was the case with Darwin's opening description of his own peregrinations, dissolving knowers and the material objects they would know into collections of qualities only helps resolve the difficulties of knowing populations through time so long as they aren't put back together again.

But I want to argue that if we attend to its particular content, rather than simply noticing its relation to particulars, Darwin's opening affords us a framework for apprehending a more subtle, more revolutionary lesson in his turn to analogy. For Darwin does not only disaggregate the narrative stretching from his journey on the *Beagle* to the publication of *Origin* into a series of disconnected moments that effectively render him a discontinuous subject; he also insists upon the need to follow his empirical observations of both live species and the fossil record with a period of "accumulating and reflecting on all sorts of facts which could possibly have any bearing," which is in turn followed by a period in which he allows himself "to speculate on the subject." Within the terms of this opening, natural selection is not something that can *be* discovered and known exclusively by way of observation; the bounds of relevant facts are *not* self-evidently proximate; and empirical observation *must* be followed by theorizing. Insofar as Darwin's analogy of the diversity of bodily organs and the diversity of species within an environment makes invisible the causal relation between the two terms, the passage serves to demonstrate the irreconcilability of the perspective by which relations are analyzed and of the process by which these relations come into being. There is, in a word, no point of view from which natural selection can be seen.[12] In part, natural selection's resistance to being seen lies in the fact that it takes place through time, but this diachronicity is not definitive in and of itself. Darwin's analogy does not merely render natural selection synchronic by picking out a moment at which the relation of an individual body and an environment might be read; it also picks out a particular element of the system and makes it stand in for the whole body, a body that is whole only insofar as it is like the element that represents it. In this sense, the analogy is not so much derived from a knower's point of view as it is a figure that constitutes the very possibility of having a point of view capable of apprehending relations characterized by their irreducibility.[13] The analogy's limitation likewise marks the collapse of point of view as a framework for organizing knowledge. We cannot know whether a specialized stomach will help a particular animal reproduce animals like itself, both because we cannot know whether next month will bring a drought or an abundance of rain and sunshine and because we cannot know, from any single point of view, whether this animal will be surrounded by many or few herbivorous animals, all of whose abilities to compete for plants will themselves be compromised or enhanced by an irreducible—and unpredictable—collection of other qualities.

This last example should make apparent that what I am calling the point-of-view-lessness of natural selection describes not only the challenge of analyzing the operation of natural selection, but also functions as a dynamic within the material process itself. It is not simply that we have difficulty figuring out the point of view around which natural selection is structured; rather, it is that natural selection "selects"—insofar as the relations it describes—the organization of organs within individual bodies located in variously differentiated distributions of animals through time. This organization, which we have come to know in shorthand as an "ecosystem," is itself organized around no point of view. We cannot identify a particular element or relation of elements within a given ecosystem that can be understood to comprehend the operation of that system more fully than any other part, because the maintenance or perpetuation of any one element within the system is not privileged over any other.[14] Writing a century and a half after Darwin about a self-sustaining agricultural ecosystem called Polyface Farm, Michael Pollan describes the compositional challenge of describing a system without a governing point of view.

> Industrial processes follow a clear, linear, hierarchical logic that is fairly easy to put into words, probably because words follow a similar logic: First this, then that; put this in here, and then out comes that. But the relationship between cows and chickens on this farm . . . takes the form of a loop rather than a line, and that makes it hard to know where to start, or how to distinguish between cases and effects, subjects and objects.
>
> Is what I'm looking at in this pasture a system for producing exceptionally tasty eggs? If so, then the cattle and their manure are a means to an end. Or is it a system for producing grass-fed beef without the use of any chemicals, in which case the chickens, by fertilizing and sanitizing the cow pastures, comprise the means to that end? So does that make their eggs a product or a by-product? And is manure—theirs or the cattle's—a waste product or raw material? (And what should we call the fly larvae?) Depending on the point of view you take—that of the chicken, the cow, or even the grass—the relationship between subject and object, cause and effect, flips.[15]

It is this quality of point-of-view-lessness, both as an analytical conundrum and as a conception of the material world, that constitutes Darwin's most fundamental break with the traditions of natural history and Enlightenment philosophy that precede him. When, in the summer of 1838, Darwin ruminates in his notebook about the possibility that the earth might have a beginning and an endpoint, he marks his movement away from the "uniformitarianism" of his intellectual mentor Charles Lyell, away from the premise, that is, that the causes of geological changes operating in the past must be assumed to be identical, in quality and in intensity, with those causes observed acting in the present.[16] In essence, Darwin posits a natural world driven by contingency where his predecessors saw one organized and driven by natural law. But as we have seen, for Darwin the contingency of causation in the material world cannot be extricated from issues surrounding the legibility of causation. It is his commitment to this inextricability that leads him to follow his account in *The Origin of Species* (1859) of the process by which species come to be made and to change with accounts of the process by which populations are known and individuals within those populations come to know one another—first in *The Descent of Man, and Selection in Relation to Sex* (1871) and then in *The Expression of the Emotions in Man and Animals* (1872). If *Origin* makes the case for a world not organized by law, Darwin's final two works, composed as one and published separately, concern themselves with the processes and modes of knowing both available and possible in such a lawless world.

The Point of View from Nowhere: Darwin and His Predecessors

In an ecosystem in which causation is not structured around a single point of view, we ought not to be surprised that seeing likeness and causing likeness have no necessary relation to one another. As Darwin puts it in the *Origin*:

> We must not, in classifying, trust to resemblances in parts of the organisation, however important they may be for the welfare of the being in relation to the outer world. Perhaps from this cause it has partly arisen, that almost all naturalists lay the greatest stress on resemblances in organs of high vital or physiological importance. No doubt this view of the classificatory importance of organs which are important is generally, but by no means always, true. But their importance for classification, I believe, depends on their greater constancy throughout large groups of species; and this constancy depends on such organs having generally been subjected to less change in the adaptation of the species to their conditions of life. That the mere physiological importance of an organ does not determine its classificatory value, is almost shown by the one fact, that in allied groups, in which the same organ, as we have every reason to suppose, has nearly the same physiological value, its classificatory value is widely different. (713–14)

Here Darwin makes a point of distancing himself both from the naturalists he explicitly mentions and, more implicitly, from comparative anatomists like Cuvier who saw the resemblance of functional elements among species as evidence of the presence of a higher unifying design. For Darwin, what matters most to a particular animal's functioning and survival need not, it seems, matter very much in determining the characteristics of the species of which that individual is a part, at least so long as those species are understood in terms of the processes that brought them into being and differentiated them from other species. While we might be tempted to understand fish and whales to be related to one another, owing to the importance of fins for both, they will have adapted characteristics that resemble one another because they live in similar environments exerting similar demands on organisms, not because they share any genealogical or species relation. Indeed, as Darwin goes on to explain, the characteristics that link parts of a genealogical line to one another may have been preserved precisely because they are of little use, and therefore come under little environmental pressure to change: "No one will say that rudimentary or atrophied organs are of high physiological or vital importance; yet undoubtedly, organs in this condition are often of high value in classification" (714).

For Darwin, then, the stability of a subject's or object's traits—what Kant calls its "lawfulness"—has no necessary or even predictable relation to the importance of those traits for the subject's or object's essential functioning: just because a quality is noncontingent doesn't mean that it matters. If, in the passage likening the herbivorous stomach to species jockeying for survival, Darwin implicitly defines individuals and species in terms of their common quality of "selectability" and, in so doing, turns natural selection from a process into a taxonomical principle, once causation is readmitted as a temporal process, taxonomy no longer operates as merely descriptive. In essence, Darwin can here be understood to elevate the problem surrounding the legibility of causation within anatomical medicine—the tension within anatomical medicine, I argued in my opening chapter, that animates Kant's privileging of skin as the preeminent racial sign—from a problem of individual bodies to one of the species and hence of classification. As we recall, anatomical medicine posits a likeness of bodies that undergirds its claims to be able to diagnose what ails the body. While what Darwin would call the "essential functioning" of the body is concealed from view by the skin, the presumptive likeness of bodies allows the relation between the interiors of autopsied bodies and the closed body of the patient to stand in for the actually inaccessible interior of that patient's body. As we saw, however, such legibility rests upon the bracketing of causation: the process of dying, the relations of cause and effect by which individuals get sick or well. The body seen undergoing its "essential functions" is, within this anatomical medical paradigm, a body constantly undergoing change and therefore nonidentical with itself, much less with the bodies of others whose likeness is meant to subtend any particular body's legibility. I have argued that Kant introduces racialized skin—a structure that superimposes causation and likeness within a single sign—in an effort to reintegrate causation and classification.

In this context, Darwin's insistence that constancy and significance need not go together—that the process by which the qualities of a thing are apprehended have no necessary relation to the process by which the object under scrutiny acts or makes things happen in the world constitutes his most fundamental break with the Enlightenment of Kant and of the natural historians. Darwin's turn to argument by negation in *The Origin of Species*—natural selection operates just like artificial selection, except when it doesn't, in ways we cannot see—both testifies to the essentiality of his revolution and offers a guide for navigating it. He invites his readers to reflect upon a familiar set of relations—the breeder of artificial selection whose intentions and acts produce effects upon their objects—in order to allow them to begin to contemplate a set of relations they have neither the experience nor the grammar to think: selection without a selector.

But if the abstraction of "selection" suspends the question of agency and in that sense throws a rope from the known to the unknown, the difficulty of identifying the agent or subject of natural selection suddenly alerts us to the fact that "causation" is haunted by a similar ambiguity. As ambiguities go, those surrounding "causation" have been, we have seen, remarkably philosophically fertile. As we saw in chapter 2, Aristotle conceives the tragedy's "fictionality" as a tether by which universal causation gets linked to particular agents, and he then locates such tragedies within preexisting communities for good measure. *The Woman in White* makes apparent that, without the interconnectedness of those who act and those who are acted upon (the sense that what hurts you hurts me, even if I am the agent behind that hurt), causation tends to diffuse into the errant relations of subjects and objects, less a force than an accidental collision of entities, causes, and effects. For Kant, causation's abstraction is the key to the notion's philosophical power. In his account, causation names a grammar by which subjects, objects, and knowing observers come to be understood to be in relation to one another, but *as* a grammar it essentially brings those relations into being by fixing the subjects and objects into abstract positions or functions. We understand causation to be a regular and predictable—what Kant calls "lawful"—dynamic to the degree that it is observable and knowable; essentially, it is the legibility of causation that turns it into an abstract force by transforming it into a system. In this sense, the locution "cause and effect" can be seen to express the strains within abstract causation, its entropic pull. Causation cannot be quite assigned to an agent for the very reason that it is as much a quality of the things it acts upon as of the subjects who do the acting. The continuous presence of an observer, whether actual or imputed, links the act (cause) that is done to the act (effect) that is experienced such that causation appears a force distinct from the particular subjects and objects associated with it. But Kant takes the implicit systematicity of causation one step further by insisting on its converse: not only is causation lawful insofar as it can be known or observed, but the lawfulness of any object becomes evidence of its condition of having been caused. Kant thus makes the unarticulated systematicity of causation—causes and effects only become "causation" inasmuch as they are seen—the grounds for a systematicity that is everywhere by virtue of being nowhere in particular.

It is within the context of these philosophical traditions surrounding causation that the logic and force of Darwin's revolution becomes most apparent in ways crucial for our study of the epistemological status of race. Darwin insists that the regularity or lawfulness of traits need not align with their necessity or importance to an organism, species, or line. Residual organs help trace the genealogical lines that define genera and species, help us classify and discern likeness, precisely because they aren't used much and thus experience no environmental pressure to evolve, while adaptive traits, like fins, are crucial to the (causal) functioning of animals like whales and fish that might share a common environment but possess only remote ancestral links:

> From the first dawn of life, all organic beings are found to resemble each other in descending degrees, so that they can be classed in groups under groups. This classification is evidently not arbitrary like the grouping of the stars in constellations. The existence of groups would have been of simple signification if one group had been exclusively fitted to inhabit the land, and another the water; one to feed on flesh, another on vegetable matter, and so on; but the case is widely different in nature, for it is notorious how commonly members of even the same sub-group have different habits. (711)

Darwin effectively renders explicit the unacknowledged systematicity of Kant's notion of causation. To insist that traits that enable an organism to function are distinct from traits that enable an organism to be identified precisely is to insist upon the distinction between the causation that makes subjects possess the traits they do and the causation that makes subjects legible.

In this making explicit, and in his effort to reaggregate disconnected processes of causation and classification, Darwin emerges as an architect of the ruins excavated, and in some ways created by, two of his contemporaries: Wilkie Collins and John Stuart Mill. In *The Woman in White*, Collins turns the classifiability of bodies from his novel's condition of possibility to its manifest topic of investigation. The novel's plot, when all is said and done, is the story of the process by which one woman's sick body comes to seem like, and hence becomes interchangeable with, another woman's dead body. But in detailing the process of cause and effect by which the classification and interchange come to take place, *The Woman in White* undermines the claim for the bodies' likeness. Like Darwin's adaptations, the more fully we recognize the embodied subjects before us to have been shaped under the pressure of distinct trajectories of events, the less like one another they appear to be. Even as Collins's novel demonstrates the unraveling of likeness from the perspective of those characters witnessing and undergoing the interchange, it also demonstrates how its own formal structure, by producing a perspective ontologically distinct from those characters and events, operates to render such classification possible. Insofar as the novel's fictionality invites readers to imagine the bodies of characters they don't actually see, those imaginings effectively render those characters' "vital functioning" imperceptible and irrelevant to the task of classifying types. Readers are able to discern the sameness of characters even as those characters age, change, and die, because readers aren't actually seeing the bodies themselves. Rather, they are experiencing their own perspective apart from those bodies: their unchanging, because essentially contentless, capacity to imagine and to classify. Collins's novel thus leaves its readers toggling between the array of unassimilable particulars constituted by the novel's multiple plots and typologies whose classificatory force extends no further than the imagination of a given reader.

For Mill, by contrast, human subjects and the objects they apprehend are so fundamentally constituted by their placedness in time—by their location within causal chains of events—that the very enterprise of classification, of finding the common characteristics of objects that can themselves be commonly recognized, must of necessity stand as an affront to those subjects, an assault upon their own particularity. The opportunity afforded subjects to abstract their perceptions of the world from the causal circumstances that have generated them—an opportunity made available by the development of technologies of perceptual abstraction like photography—suggests to Mill the possibility of experiencing a commonness caused at no moment in particular, and hence equally available to everyone.

Darwin not only insists upon the distinction between the causation that creates particular traits in subjects and the causation that makes those traits apprehensible, but also links the difference between the process of causing objects in the natural world and the process of knowing those objects to the diffuseness of cause and effect that becomes explicit in a system in which the effects visited upon one group of organisms function as causes visited upon another set. In essence, there is no identifiable "selector," no agent of selection, in natural selection for the same reason that natural selections' relations of causes and effects resist being abstracted into a transcendent "causation." Darwin's causes and effects remain linked to the particular organisms from which they are generated and upon which they act because such actions and effects make species change or disappear, rendering species perpetually nonidentical with themselves. Kant posits a system in which the legibility of causation works to subsume the particularity of acting subjects and the particularity of acted-upon objects into the regular, lawful, and *universal* operation of causation—causation that operates the same way no matter who sets it into motion and no matter who it acts upon. In contrast, Darwin's insistence that causes and effects *take place within* and are not simply apprehended by way of an (eco)system makes impossible both the abstraction of causation and—what is essentially the same thing—its apprehension by way of a unified point of view. For Kant, objects are both caused and identified by what is regular, predictable, and lawful about them; for Darwin, the motors of change are events that are contingent, unrepeatable, and unpredictable.

In positing a material world made and transformed by accident, then, Darwin's account of natural selection not only challenges the lawfulness of the material world and humans' capacity to act effectively and predictably within it, but also undermines the modes and processes of knowing predicated upon such a lawfully organized world. While the first is a truism about natural selection, the implications of the second, epistemological challenge have been less fully explored. Indeed, it is this latter set of consequences that seems to trouble Darwin himself most profoundly. While he leaves the principles of natural selection largely intact from the publication of *Origin* to the end of his life, it is possible to read—and I will be arguing we ought to read—the work of the remainder of his career as a series of efforts to undo the most epistemologically revolutionary aspects of his theory of evolution by making natural selection legible.

Darwin's two final works, *The Descent of Man and Selection in Relation to Sex* (1871) and *The Expression of the Emotions in Man and Animals* (1872), put forth two very different solutions to the problem of knowing a world created and framed by natural selection. In *Expression*, Darwin theorizes a type of sign—what he calls "expression"—that synthesizes the adaptive and genealogical qualities into a single figure as a way of constituting a comprehensive point of view capable of apprehending both sorts of qualities at once. But, as we shall see, the very capaciousness that recommends this figure becomes its limitation as well: it effectively turns all species capable of the same modes of expression into versions of one another. In *Descent*, Darwin, responding to the nonidentity of the process of knowing and causing species' essential traits, posits a mode of discernment in which the capacity to identify a partial set of traits that stands in metonymically for the species as a whole itself becomes an identifying trait of the species. In what Darwin terms "sexual selection," traits are selected and passed on not according to the ever-shifting pressures of survival imposed by the interactions of competitive species, but according to the desires of the individual (usually female) members of the species. Not only does "survival of the fittest" give way to "survival of the sexiest," but species come to be known by what they find attractive. In this second, necessarily self-limiting metonymic mode, we will discover a theorization of the kind of "linguistic" racial sign that characterizes most contemporary understandings of race.

The epistemological conundrums posed by natural selection surface most immediately as problems of evidence. While Darwin makes clear the importance of differentiating between the adaptive traits that manifest the process by which organisms are created and changed and the genealogical traits by which they are classified, he is much less forthcoming about how precisely such distinctions are to be recognized or, more fundamentally, about the degree to which we are to understand the distinction to remain stable over the course of the history of a species or local population. We cannot tell, simply by looking at a whale, that its fins are adaptive, that they are brought into being under the pressure of its immediate environment (an environment it shares with the fish it outwardly resembles), and that its lungs or skeletal structure are genealogical. It is for this reason, Darwin concluded, that we must turn to the fossil record. But with fossils too, he explains in the *Origin*, the precise relations among species are far from self-evident:

> Those who think the natural geological record in any degree perfect, and who do not attach much weight to the facts and arguments of other kinds given in this volume, will undoubtedly at once reject my theory. For my part, following out Lyell's metaphor, I look at the natural geological record, as a history of the world imperfectly kept, and written in a changing dialect; of this history we possess the last volume alone, relating only to two or three countries. Of this volume, only here and there a short chapter has been preserved; and of each page, only here and there a few lines. Each word of the slowly-changing language, in which the history is supposed to be written, being more or less different in the interrupted succession of chapters, may represent the apparently abruptly changed forms of life, entombed in our consecutive, but widely separated, formations. On this view, the difficulties above are greatly diminished or even disappear. (647)

The "difficulties" to which Darwin refers here are "imperfections in the geological record," but such deep-seated imperfections present a particular type of challenge: how does one make them disappear? For Darwin, the answer is not to perfect the imperfect but rather to redefine the nature of the imperfection. The tradition he confronts, one that includes "all the most eminent paleontologists [and] geologists"—"Cuvier, Owen, Agassiz, Barrande, Falconer, Forbes . . . Lyell, Murchison, Sedgwick" (646)—conceives of the fossil record's imperfection as a problem of nonexistent forms. For these naturalists, the impossibility of "finding in successive formations infinitely numerous transitional links between the many species which now exist or have existed" stands as definitive proof of the immutability of species: because there is no evidence to be found of species' changing, we must conclude that species do not change. In Darwin's view, such a conclusion misconstrues the nature of the imperfection: what are missing are not the formations but the records of the formations.

But as the passage proceeds, Darwin's gesture comes to seem more than a simple sleight of hand designed to transmute a problem of fossils into a problem of records. What is remarkable about his claims here are not merely negative: he does not simply suggest, as we might expect, that the absence of a fossil record does not *rule out* the possibility that intermediate species might have existed. This negative claim would rest on understanding the fossil record as a kind of text, a collection of representations of past life that might itself be disrupted or rendered incomplete without necessarily disturbing the continuity of the underlying life-forms represented. And, certainly, there is much in Darwin's rhetoric to support such a reading: of this "history of the world imperfectly kept," "we possess the last volume alone . . . of this volume, only here and there a short chapter . . . and of each page, only here and there a few lines." But Darwin goes beyond this textual metaphor. If the history of the world is imperfectly kept, its failings are as much linguistic as they are secretarial or archival, written as it is in "a changing dialect," a "slowly-changing language." By the logic of this second, linguistic metaphor, fossils are not the representations of life-forms but are rather the life-forms themselves. The records being kept are of the languages themselves, and these languages are the entities that mutate and produce slowly changing intermediate forms. Because both the textual and the linguistic metaphors feel representational, it is easy to overlook their difference from one another, and indeed, Darwin himself does not acknowledge the shift—more of a twitch—preferring to classify what he is doing as a unitary "following out" of Lyell's metaphor. In this sense, then, Darwin's argument—his intervention as well—depends not so much on substituting the records of the forms for the forms themselves than on showing there to be no difference between them. Darwin is able to turn his negative argument (the absence of a fossil record of intermediate forms does not necessarily stand as evidence of the nonexistence of those intermediate forms themselves) into a positive argument (the incompleteness of the textlike fossil record, inasmuch as it is of a piece with the slowly changing language, stands as *evidence for* the existence of intermediate forms) by elaborating a conception of fossils that understands them to be both life-forms and the records of life-forms at one and the same time. If we translate this back through the rhetoric of genealogical and adaptive traits, we might understand the function of the doubled fossil metaphor this way: suddenly, a description of the nature of adaption—what changes (an adaptive as opposed to a genealogical trait) is likely to be important—is made equivalent to an analytical observation about the quality of taxonomy. What is important changes. It is this doubleness that allows Darwin to turn his opponents' most damning arguments to his own benefit, and it is this doubleness that will enable him, however paradoxically, to turn a world of species made and made over by natural selection into something those opponents might comprehend.

Encompassing as they do both shells (fragments of skeletons, of life-forms, arrested into rock) and the impresses of these bodily shards (the records of life-forms, splayed, millennium upon millennium, across a bluff's face), fossils can well be seen, as Darwin's oscillating metaphors invite us, to render continuous and thus imperfectly distinguishable organisms themselves, their traces, and still further, their representations. An account of representation as contiguous with, rather than ontologically distinct from, the things represented not only organizes the evidence by which Darwin and his naturalist cotravelers are able to distinguish species' genealogical and adaptive traits, but does so in a way that blunts the epistemological challenges posed by natural selection. In part, the solution offered by Darwin's fossils is a temporal one: in juxtaposing organisms with the record of their transformations over time, "the fossil record" lets organisms and their development be viewed at a single instant, from a single point of view. But Darwin's decision to figure both organisms and the record of their development in representational terms—the changing language, the incomplete text—suggests that he understands the epistemological difficulties before him to be not exclusively temporal. If the problem of knowing the ecosystem were simply an issue of being able to know an organism through time, it would be a problem of subjectivity alone. What makes the difficulty of knowing an ecosystem animated by natural selection different from the difficulty of, say, calculating the elliptical geometry of Mars's orbit is that not only does the subject's temporal and spatial relationship to the phenomenon in question change, but the phenomenon itself changes. In deriving an account of the transformations of a species in relation to the always-transforming species around it by way of his observation of the (incomplete) fossil record, Darwin describes a species that is, insofar as it is no one thing, no particular organism and no consistently identifiable collection of traits. By figuring a mutating species as changing language whose traces are incompletely gathered into a set of tattered volumes—by figuring both the species and its record in representational terms—Darwin suggests that in order for a species to be legible, its interpretive logic, the perspective or language through which it is known, must itself be constantly mutating, even as its variations are assimilated within the unifying framework of a text. To the degree that, for Darwin, a species is a species not because it shares traits in common, but because it doesn't, because the traits that identify it are never quite the same from one generation to the next (not to mention from one individual to another), his notion of species is essentially a positivistic one: lions are what are called lions. In that sense, the species itself is a representation, one that represents effectively insofar as *how* its language means is never quite the same. But in insisting that such a constantly mutating interpretive framework is nonetheless comprehended within a single textual apparatus, Darwin suggests that the representational quality of species is not simply an effect of subjectivity, the choice of one taxonomy rather than another, but instead ought to be understood as an essential, discernible, even objective and lawful quality of species life itself. It is the elaboration of the truth of this claim that becomes the task of his final two works.

Figuring Legibility: Darwin's *Expression*, *Descent*, and the Solution of Race

As is apparent from its title, Darwin's 1872 work, *The Expression of the Emotions in Man and Animals,* professes to demonstrate the fundamental continuity of animal and human species by demonstrating the development and the fundamental likeness of their expressive practices. In theorizing a general account of the ways in which specific fleeting yet habitual expressions come into being and come to be universal, Darwin departs both from a physiognomic tradition that sought to "recogni[ze] character through the study of the permanent form of the features," and from the emergent discipline of philology, which traced modern language "families" back to their ancient linguistic antecedents in order to establish the capacity for language as an exclusively and constitutively human quality.[17] The contours of Darwin's project become apparent in the context of these departures: expression is discernible externally, but it is neither a fixed sign of inner character nor a deliberate effort to communicate inner thoughts. Of all those who attempted to describe the mechanics of expression, the physiologist Charles Bell, who in his 1844 *Anatomy and the Philosophy of Expression* insisted upon the physiological intimacy between the movements of expression and those of respiration, stands as Darwin's most obvious precursor in the mechanism he presents to account for why expressions are the same everywhere. In linking expression to the ongoing operation of the human body, Bell went a long way toward integrating expression within the mechanisms that produce other physiological traits; in restricting his interest to respiration, he did not go far enough, or so Darwin would have it.

In Darwin's view, particular expressions come into being by way of a regular and predictable series of steps. The origin of a given expression can be traced, as with most of an organism's salient qualities, to an external threat to that organism's survival. In one of his most well-known examples, Darwin finds the source of the domestic dog's expressions of anger—uncovered canine teeth, ears pressed close to the head—to be an actual encounter with an enemy: such actions are intelligible because they follow from the dog's intention to attack his enemy. What is more surprising is that a dog's gestures of affection have precisely the same origin: gestures that would otherwise appear to be of no service to the animal—a body sunken downward with head raised, a lowered head and tail—come to express affection because they are the antithesis to the self-evidently intelligible movement and attitudes assumed by the dog when it intends to fight. This "principle of antithesis" is a subcategory of what Darwin calls the "principle of serviceable associated Habits." He elaborates: "Certain complex actions are of direct or indirect service under certain states of the mind, in order to relieve or gratify certain sensations, desires, &c.; and whenever the same state of mind is induced, however feebly, there is a tendency through the force of habit and association for the same movements to be performed, though they may not then be of the least use" (1277). Thus, in Darwin's view, expressions become "habitual" at the moment they cease to be "of the least use," which is to say, at the moment they are no longer performed in response to an actual and present threat. Adults contract the muscles around their eyes when they feel grief, he suggests, because as infants, they developed the habit of squinting to protect their eyes from the sun while screaming in distress. It is because there is no way of distinguishing an habitual "useless" response from a response to a direct threat that expressions turn out to be universal; if expressions were to retain specific marks of the circumstances that generated them, then there would be as many types of expressions as there are threatening situations.

But while Darwin's insistence upon expression's fundamentally habitual character works to ensure the generalizability of its forms, his characterization of habit and antithesis as versions of a single principle testifies to the complexity of the conceptual tasks for which expression is being enlisted. Darwin's singling out of Charles Bell's physiological model of expression as the one to which he himself is most indebted makes a great deal of sense within the context of his larger oeuvre, since in tying expression back to the ongoing functioning of the body, both Darwin and Bell lay the groundwork for understanding expression as simply another version of adaptation to an essentially competitive environment. So long as a dog's tail-wagging can be traced back, through however many steps, to a moment in which an animal's survival—and hence its reproductive viability—is under threat, then tail-wagging can be understood as an advantageous adaptation. But Darwin's investment in making expression universal is at least in some tension with his impulse to understand it as adaptive. Inasmuch as a behavior is conceived as habitual by virtue of its indifference to its particular circumstances—the dog bares its teeth in order to express anger even when it has no intention of attacking anything in its immediate environment—it is difficult to understand in what regard such behavior continues to be adaptive (that is, in what ways it can be seen to be ongoingly responsive to the pressures of its environment). How can a given behavior offer advantages within a particular environment if it functions, as habit does by definition, without regard to its environment?

I want to suggest that Darwin's classification of both straightforward "habit" and "antithesis" as versions of a common "principle" (that of "serviceable associate habits") implies a framework within which we can begin to understand the kind of conceptual work his notion of expression is doing in relation to the larger argument of his oeuvre.[18] Although Darwin is careful not to define expression as a form of communication—at no moment does he claim the successful operation of a dog's growling rests upon apprehension of the meaning of such growling by that dog's enemy—he nonetheless does seem to understand expression to function semiotically. Indeed, what defines antithesis is its status as a sign. The affectionate dog's arched back and tail-wagging are remarkable precisely insofar as they make no sense, serve no function, *except in relation to* the set of behaviors they reverse. But while antithesis is unambiguously semiotic, habit is a much more complicated case. If habit functions semiotically, at what moment precisely can it be said to become a sign? At the moment it ceases to be generated in response to an immediate threat? What if that moment is just minutes after the original response, just after the enemy has fled? Darwin also insists that habit characterizes behavior not only over the life span of an individual animal but across a species, from one generation to the next. Does each animal respond instinctually and usefully to an immediate threat only to reiterate that behavior semiotically in subsequent experiences, or can the movement from instinct to sign trace the history and development of a behavior across a species, such that all behavior after an ancestor's originary encounter with an enemy ought properly to be understood to be semiotic?

I would argue that Darwin's interest is less in resolving these ambiguities than in generalizing them. In classifying both habit and antithesis as versions of the same thing, Darwin lays out a model of representation—and an implied framework of interpretation—in which signs do not exist within a system that is ontologically distinct from the material objects to which they refer but rather are continuous with such material objects. By this logic, the meaning of signs lies in their development out of, rather than their difference from, the material world, and particular signs ought to be read not merely as announcing anger or affection or fear, but also as making apparent the genealogical relation of the various individuals who would use them. Such signs render otherwise diachronic genealogical relations legible at a single instant, and they do so by transforming the "environment" framing a behavior's significance from that to which it is well or poorly adapted to that in which the reading or interpretation of the sign takes place. In this regard, Darwin's expression can be seen as an instantiation of the interpretive logic of the fossil record, the transformation of that record from evidence in support of an argument about the relations of species to one another over time (the "record imperfectly kept") to a demonstration and generalization of those relations (the shifting dialect).[19]

But if expression can be seen as the logical conclusion of Darwin's double claims for fossils—fossils do not only give us information about how species change but are themselves the instantiation of changed species—then it is likewise subject to the same limitation as the fossil record. Both expression and fossils offer the possibility of perceiving development in an instant, but they do so at the cost of being able to understand this development as a mode by which species, or even individuals, might be differentiated from one another. In synthesizing species' development and expressive signs into a single semiotic system, expression makes the generation of expression just one step among many in the transmutations of species through time. But inasmuch as expressions become signs at the moment they are generated without regard to the threats posed to an individual expressive animal by that animal's immediate environment, not only do such expressions cease to function as traits that might be selected for by natural selection, but they become equally characteristic of all species, in theory as well as in fact. In making the development of species continuous with the use of expressive signs, expression effectively makes explicit the sense in which species are like signs, distinguished by their iterative relations to one another, their quality of beforeness and afterness, rather than by any other qualities of historical or classificatory particularity. Indeed, Darwin's conception of expression seems to offer us no basis for differentiating between the semiotic relation between the action of a prehistoric wolf who learns to wag its tail at the arrival of a familiar member of its pack only moments after baring its teeth at an enemy and the tail-wagging of its distant domesticated cousin on the occasion of the refilling of his dinner bowl, or between the tail-wagging of the same dog at dinner and then again at breakfast the following morning. All tail-waggers effectively come to be related, common descendants of Darwin's original angry ancestor dog, as alike—or different from—one another as they are from themselves, from one moment to the next.

And if the example of tail-wagging makes evident how little ground expressive signs offer for distinguishing relations of descent (the prehistoric wolf's relation to the domestic dog) from temporally coeval dogs or even from the behavior of a single dog over several days, other forms of expression are even more capacious. In Darwin's telling, dogs and cats assume remarkably similar postures to express hostility (*Expression*, 1290–91), while Indian elephants and humans are known to contract their eye muscles in virtually the same positions when they weep (1355–56). So while Darwin's expressions abstract particular physiological (re)actions from their proximate environmental causes and in so doing make diachronic relations of descent available in a single instant, they offer genealogies of connection that potentially confuse as much as they clarify in their capaciousness.

This is Darwin's dilemma: how to make the movement of natural selection apprehensible from a single point of view, by way of an embodied consciousness, without reducing all elements in the ecosystem to versions of the same, punctuated moments on a temporal scale of distant past, recent past, present. I end this chapter by examining what I understand to be Darwin's solution to this dilemma—race. By reading *Descent* as offering a solution to a problem formulated in *Expression*, I am suggesting that the two works, which as we recall were originally conceived as a single project but were published separately in subsequent years, continue to inform one another in fundamental ways. In *Descent*'s account of race and sexual selection, we find the origin of the conception of race most familiar to us today, one in which particular traits are understood to stand in for raced subjects as a whole by virtue of their partiality and conventionality, their status as constructions of culture. The particular epistemological challenge posed by natural selection lies, we remember, in its nonalignment of the causation by which traits are selected and species are transformed and the process by which such traits or species are apprehended. Where Kant makes the alignment of knowing and causing the foundational premise of his critical philosophy—the possibility of perceiving the lawfulness of a given phenomenon is evidence of the fact of its having been intentionally caused—the Darwin of *Descent* turns the capacity to *recognize* a given species' reproductively advantageous traits into a reproductively advantageous trait itself. Darwin effectively elaborates a category of reproductive advantage—"sexual selection"—that operates independently of environmental forces beyond a given species' reproductive circle by virtue of being the consequence of species' members own acts of recognition and choice. In sexual selection and, in a slightly different way, in race, Darwin offers a corrective to the formalism of *Expression*'s "habit." Insofar as the "habit" described there provides a model for abstracting and classifying individuals as distinct from the always shifting environmental forces by which they are constituted by differentiating the original act from its subsequent iterations, the taxonomies grounded in expressions are simply too capacious. In effect, the only designations available are early and late, that is, the originary encounters and their (expressive) inheritors. Darwin's sexual selection, by contrast, abstracts from within by designating certain "useless" traits as metonymic, representative of the species as a whole and, in so doing, builds a point of view from which the ecosystem's diffuse diachronicity becomes legible by a kind of administrative fiat: these are the traits that designate species because we say they are. Darwin returns the power to cause a species' defining and knowable traits to the species itself and thereby effectively realigns the power to cause and the capacity to know the process of causation. But to the degree to which the possibility of such alignment rests upon the demonstration of a given trait's independence of the selective pressures of the ecosystem, both the taxonomic and the reproductive significance of the trait in question must be shown to be partial and arbitrary.

We can begin to parse the differences between the system of expression and that of race/sexual selection by looking to their respective accounts of their observers (and would-be taxonomizers). If the problem of expression as a semiotic system was that in making the fact of species development instantaneously legible, it eliminated the criteria for distinguishing among them, this turns out to pose a problem for the would-be interpreter of expressions as well as for those whose likenesses are discerned through its lens:

> When we witness any deep emotion, our sympathy is so strongly excited, that close observation is forgotten or rendered almost impossible. . . .
>
> . . . From the reasons above assigned, namely, the fleeting nature of some expressions; our sympathy being easily aroused, and our attention thus distracted; our imagination deceiving us, from knowing in a vague manner what to expect, though certainly few of us know what the exact changes in the countenance are; and, lastly, even our long familiarity with the subject,—from all these causes combined, the observation of Expression is by no means easy, as many persons, whom I have asked to observe certain points, have soon discovered. (*Expression*, 1267, 1270)

Here the observation of expressions of affect also turns the observer into an expresser of affect, so similar to what is observed as to be incapable of any further discriminations. The observational problem has a temporal aspect as well, as "long familiarity" with (that is, the experience of earlier iterations of) an expression seem to render any particular iteration difficult, if not impossible, to discern.

Consider, by way of contrast, Darwin's introduction to his discussion "On the Races of Men":

> Now let us apply these generally-admitted principles [of classification: constancy of traits, fertility of offspring etc.] to the races of man, viewing him in the same spirit as a naturalist would regard any other animal. In regard to the amount of difference between the races, we must make some allowance for our nice powers of discrimination gained by the long habit of observing ourselves. In India, as Elphinstone remarks, although a newly-arrived European cannot at first distinguish the various native races, yet they soon appear to him extremely dissimilar; and the Hindoos cannot at first perceive any difference between the several European nations. Even the most distinct races of man, with the exception of certain negro tribes, are much more like each other in form than would at first be supposed. This is well shewn by the French photographs in the Collection Anthroplogique du Museum of the men belonging to various races, the greater number of which, as many persons to whom I have shown them have remarked, might pass for Europeans. Nevertheless, these men if seen alive would undoubtedly appear very distinct, so that we are clearly much influenced in our judgment by mere colour

> of the skin and hair, by slight differences in the features, and by expression. (*Descent*, 900)

In the case of race, familiarity with the subjects of observation, whether a result of the observer's experience of her own similar traits or a consequence of previous observations of other like objects, turns out to be necessary for rather than a hindrance to the discernment of the racial subject's differences. Yet even as Darwin asserts the efficacy of such observations, we find ourselves faced with what by now is a familiar conundrum of Darwinian taxonomy: it's not clear from the language of the passage whether the acculturation Darwin describes, which allows an observer at a certain point to recognize differences where earlier he could not ("yet they soon appear to him extremely dissimilar"), results in the discernment of a variety of (heretofore) indiscernible groups or, in the dissolution of group likeness altogether, in favor of an array of particular individuals ("these men if seen alive would undoubtedly appear very distinct"). In this regard, the concept of acculturation Darwin introduces in this passage would appear designed to address the familiar tension between knowing and causation within an ecosystem under the pressures of natural selection. (Still, it is worth noting that while Darwin points to the merely heuristic status of the category of "species" frequently throughout his work, a category that allows us to trace the way in which traits are preserved or eliminated by natural selection, in this passage, the difficulties of knowing where races begin and end are in no way presented as in any way undermining the realness of the perceived differences or of racial distinctions more generally.)

What, then, does the concept of acculturation accomplish, and what does it have to do with the realness of race? While being like the object of one's observation seems an advantage in discerning race in a way it was decidedly not in discerning expression, one notable aspect of racial knowing is that people get better at it over time. This notion that observers might be acculturated into seeing what they couldn't before is not limited exclusively to racial observation. Jonathan Smith, for one, has detailed the ways in which Darwin represents observers of barnacles as getting better with practice.[20] Still, given the difficulties of knowing the ecosystem already discussed, the usefulness of such an acculturative model is evident. In suggesting that experience matters, Darwin implies that the qualities being observed do not themselves change; we only learn about something by seeing it again and again, so long as the things we are seeing remain the same over time. Given that natural selection's resistance to being reduced to a single point of view is a consequence of a disjunction between the temporality of the process by which objects act or are acted upon and the temporality of the process by which those objects come to be known, the recharacterization of the observer as less a subject who knows over time than a subject who comes to be capable of knowing over time is crucial. In positing a knower who must be acculturated, Darwin relocates diachronicity from a quality of the object (the constantly transmuting species) or of the process of observation (the qualities of lawfulness discerned over time) and turns it into a quality located entirely within the subject. Experience is made the precondition of observation rather than its consequence, and the figuration of objects by way of juxtaposed, synchronic, and unchanging traits emerges as a logical necessity of this new model of knowing.

The only problem with this acculturative solution to the problem of knowing the ecosystem under natural selection is that it seems to have nothing to do with the ecosystem under natural selection. That is, although Darwin's initial account of acculturation would appear to solve the problem of knowing an ecosystem organized around the nonprivilege of any particular point of view, such a "solution" depends upon making the ecosystem unrecognizable. So long as what the acculturated observer learns to recognize are sets of traits that stand for a species or race by virtue of their stability over time, then Darwin's acculturation turns out to be a perfectly unremarkable instance of induction, where subjects come to recognize what is regular and lawful about the objects of the material world by way of repeated observations of that world.

I want to suggest, however, that if we read Darwin's account of acculturation and racial knowing in the context of what follows it in Darwin's text (part 2: *Selection in Relation to Sex*) rather than in terms of what precedes it, (part 1: *The Descent of Man*), we will discover a theory of the formation of the observer in which observation and selection are effectively understood to be forms of one another. By his own account, Darwin pulled the observations that make up *Descent* into a published argument only reluctantly: "During many years I collected notes on the origin or descent of man, without any intention of publishing on the subject, but rather with the determination not to publish, as I thought that I should thus only add to the prejudices against my views." Indeed, Darwin had hoped initially that he might simply address the relevance of natural selection to human development by way of implication: "It seemed to me sufficient to indicate, in the first edition of my "Origin of Species," that by this work "light would be thrown on the origin of man and his history" (777). However, the emergence at midcentury of a scientistic discourse of polygenesis—the idea that human races originated as separate and distinct entities—impelled him to make explicit a case for the common emergence of humans from lower organic forms. But if *Descent* can thus be seen as an act of defense, designed to protect both his theory of natural selection and the category of the human by demonstrating their inextricability from one another, *Sexual Selection* ought to be understood as Darwin's gesture of affirmation, one that turns the new culturally pressing perception of racial difference made manifest by the debates over polygenesis into an occasion for refining what ought to be known as selection and who is capable of doing it.

In suggesting that we might understand Darwin's model of the acculturated observer in the context of his theory of sexual selection, I am inviting us to consider another element of acculturation: not only is it the power to discern traits developed over time, but it is a power that effectively locates the observer within the circle of the race or species being observed. In this regard, acculturation can be seen to reconceive the project of knowing the ecosystem. The problem of knowing an ecosystem driven by natural selection is the challenge, we recall, of establishing a place and moment from which to know when knowing and causing are distinct from one another because no particular point of view is systemically privileged. In acculturation, we shall see, Darwin offers us an account of a system in which the privileging of a particular point of view is paramount—one has to be of or like the object of one's observation to know it—but in which the agency of causation and the point of view of observation, both of which exist within a specific species, nonetheless remain distinct from one another. In short, what Darwin does is theorize the creation of an observer as a particular element of species life, as a trait that species, qua species, must possess.

Sexual selection, as Darwin explains it, concerns itself "only with that kind of selection . . . [that] depends on the advantage which certain individuals have over other individuals of the same sex and species, in exclusive relation to reproduction" (923). In sexual selection, that is, some individual members of a species with certain traits are advantaged over other individuals of that species with different traits, but the pressure that produces that advantage comes not from other proximate species competing for the same food supply or depending upon an existing environmental camouflage, but from preferences expressed by members of the species themselves in their selection of reproductive mates. Darwin posits the existence of sexual selection as a means of accounting for traits that seem to offer no special advantage in the struggle for existence, traits like "ornaments of many kinds" or the "organs for producing vocal or instrumental music" (924), or even a certain skin color. But while he surmises that certain traits in male organisms must make them more attractive to females, he is initially stymied as to the mechanism by which such heightened attractiveness translates into actual reproductive advantage. While a peacock possessing elaborate plumage is more likely to be chosen to mate before one without such fancy feathers, it is difficult to see how such primacy translates into a reproductive advantage—the production of a greater number of offspring—so long as there are adequate numbers of females to go around.[21] So Darwin first hypothesizes that there must not be enough females for everyone, that the population of males in any given species must consistently and predictably outnumber that of females, only to abandon the hypothesis when the data fail to support it.

It is in the wake of this failure that Darwin turns to other forms of gender differentiation in his effort to theorize a version of selection that is motored from within a given species rather than by way of that species' competitive relations with other adjacent species. Males, it turns out, are more modified than females: "Throughout the animal kingdom, when the sexes differ from each other in external appearance, it is the male which, with rare exceptions, has been chiefly modified; for the female still remains more like the young of her own species, and more like the other members of the same group" (932). To the degree that sexual selection describes the advantages some individuals hold over other members of the same species, "it would be no advantage and some loss of power if both sexes were mutually to search for one another" (933). Darwin's argument is essentially this: the more actively both males and females are engaged in seeking out one another, the less fully traits associated with one sex only offer a decisive reproductive advantage. If females as well as males are active in searching out mates, then the less appealing males will be less disadvantaged than they would be if their reproductive success were exclusively dependent on their own exertions. In order for the power of selection to be circumscribed within a species, Darwin concludes, the male must be most "eager" in seeking out females, while the female, "though comparatively passive, generally exerts some choice and accepts one male in preference to others" (933).

In essence, Darwin offers a version of sexual differentiation—and an account of sexual selection—that looks a lot like the relation between observers and their objects. Darwin's females must be at once passive and discerning, and their capacity to recognize the qualities of the mate that make him most attractive—and hence that will most frequently be passed down—is part and parcel of their membership in the species. Indeed, the passiveness of the females would seem to stand as testimony to the permanence of the traits and to their uselessness, their status as things to be noted as marks of a particular yet unchanging genealogical record, rather than qualities for better living, instruments to enhance survival. But although the large movements of Darwin's oeuvre appear to be predicated upon a clear distinction between natural and sexual selection, his detailing of the particular dynamics of selection in actual species undermines the clarity of that distinction. Darwin dubs the traits subject to sexual selection "secondary sexual characteristics"—traits that appear only in particular sexes yet are not directly connected to the act of sexual reproduction—but acknowledges the difficulty of cordoning such characteristics off from the primary reproductive characteristics on the one hand and the traits of natural selection on the other:

> As the male has to search for the female, he requires for this purpose organs of sense and locomotion, but if these organs are necessary for the other purposes of life, as is generally the case, they will have been developed through natural selection. . . . When the two sexes follow exactly the same habits of life, and the male has more highly developed sense or locomotive organs than the female, it may be that these in their perfected state are indispensable to the male for finding the female; but in the vast majority of cases, they serve only to give one male an advantage over the other, for the less well-endowed males, if time were allowed them, would succeed in pairing with the females. (923)

For Darwin, the fact that a male insect's prehensile legs aid it in holding the female in place for the sex act make those legs categorically continuous with the organs of reproduction themselves, while this very difficulty of distinguishing what is essential to the act of reproduction from what is ancillary to it makes it hard distinguish what ought to count as sexual selection from what counts as natural selection. In this sense, the epistemological difficulty we saw earlier with the example of the herbivorous stomach—the difficulty of attributing legible traits to organisms or units organized by their causal functions—makes a return appearance here, at once revealing the logic by which sexual selection circumscribes and stabilizes the energies of natural selection, while at the same time threatening to puncture that circumscription.

But in this moment of staging the threat to sexual selection's corrective logic, Darwin also offers a framework within which sexual selection is itself stabilized—by being turned into a theory of the acculturated observer of race. At the close of the passage we have just been examining, Darwin reminds us of the temporal structure of the threat to sexual selection—too much time—"for the less well-endowed males, if time were allowed them, would succeed in pairing with the females." Sexual selection, we recall, only works as a limiting case when the time for reproduction is finite; the more time is allowed for coupling, the more opportunity there is for females to act more like seeking partners and less exclusively like observers, and for the traits that make one individual more attractive than another to seem like characteristics for survival.

I draw attention to this requirement of temporal finitude because it helps make sense of what Darwin gains when he implicitly aligns the passive female admirer of male traits with the acculturated observer, what he gains, that is, by making the functions of observing distinct from the functions of everyday survival. We remember that Darwin represents the passivity of the female partner in sexual selection in explicitly temporal terms, but I would argue that passivity functions not simply to limit the time in which coupling takes place by turning such coupling into a sprint to seize inert female objects. It also, simultaneously and paradoxically, operates by transforming the traits that differentiate individual males from one another from instrumental characteristics that make a given individual better able to function reproductively—that is, better able to produce more offspring like itself—into figures, signs of nothing more than the individual's species identity and desirability. The more passive the female, the more her "exertion of some choice" functions as an expression of desire, an observing or marking of the significance of a quality, rather than actual steps that bring about a reproductive end (and render sexual selection virtually continuous with natural selection).

If this is the logic of the female of Darwinian sexual selection, where the condition of the desiring female becomes the asymptotic end point of passivity, then how much more so is it the logic of the observer? More precisely, what we have in the structure of the acculturated observer is a kind of formalization of the passivity of the female within sexual selection: the acculturated observer's activities do not matter within the species life of those she observes because she is not quite of them. In such an accounting, the figurativity of traits, the marks of desire that identify and stand in for the species in their partiality, their discontinuousness from the activity of survival, turns out to be the logical consequence of the structure of the acculturated observer, itself a consequence of the far less sturdy structure of sexual selection. If sexual selection continually threatens to become simply a version of natural selection, with the extravagant plumage and prehensile legs that passive female observers find attractive appearing only tenuously distinguishable from the traits that offer advantage over other species, the acculturated observer, who begins outside the species and only eventually becomes part of it by virtue of a demonstrated capacity to exercise the species-defining discernment of its female members, works to anchor those traits firmly in the realm of the nonfunctional, the (merely) semiotic.[22] Insofar as acculturation signals the existence of a changing subject observing a stable set of traits—the subject only succeeds in coming to know the traits she observes better so long as those traits remain unaltered—it testifies to the evolutionary uselessness, and classificatory centrality, of the traits she picks out. Insofar as acculturation announces the observer's ultimate membership in the species she observes, it renders the capacity for species members to recognize and know one another by a defining characteristic of the species. The double, passively watchful, insider-outsider quality of the acculturated observer from what she observes is what characterizes the traits she recognizes as at once figurative and partial, standing in for the species as a whole and rendering that species recognizable precisely because they do nothing else.

The trait as sign—the characteristic that marks the species insofar as it *does* nothing—is this not what we have come to recognize as the modern logic of race? As we saw in the introduction, it is the figurativity and partiality of the racial sign that stands as the register of its contingency, and this contingency both becomes the condition of race's vulnerability to transformation and sets the terms of its mandate. In one sense, Darwin brings us back to where we began, back to *The Sneetches*, where the recognition of the arbitrariness and partiality of the terms that identify a group stands as an invitation to alter these terms so that one can be a member too. Insofar as this notion of an arbitrary racial sign and the discourse of racial constructionism built around that sign emerge from the context of Darwinian natural selection, the arbitrary sign can be seen as a kind of domestication of the radicalism of Darwin's idea, turning group membership into something that might be known, and in being known, chosen, made, and made again. This Darwinian genealogy tells a story in which the invention of the racial sign stands as a vehement assertion of the particular power of human beings to know themselves, and in knowing themselves, to know and control both the conditions of their being and the terms of their associations in the face of a natural selection that would dissolve them into shifting clusters of traits, an intersection of forces. This story of assertion is, notably, one in which the arbitrary racial sign and its critique come into being with one and the same gesture. In insisting upon the particularity of the human, the legacy of Darwin's racial sign has been to transform humanness into a catalog of particularism, a falling away from the possibility of imagining there is a human sameness that we cannot quite see.

FIVE

Structures of an Instant: *The Wire* and the Institution of Race

The first glimpse we get of that iconic image, the jittery jagged line that seems to dance to sounds only it can hear (not quite the rhythm of the series' theme song, the Blind Boys of Alabama's "Way Down in the Hole," a beat behind the remote and silent voices it traces) is not on the screen of the police monitor from which *The Wire* draws its name. The jagged line we first see is a rivulet of blood, fresh enough still to be wet, beginning at an undistinguished patch of asphalt and making its crooked way to the black male body that is its apparent origin, lying face up by the curb. This line of blood doesn't quite move like the police equalizer's nervous dancing one, but only appears to, illuminated intermittently by the rotating light of a police car parked in the unseen foreground.

With this opening gesture, *The Wire* embeds its declared interests—the relations of a variety of urban institutions, especially as those relations are produced and mediated by technology—within a far less explicit analytical framework: the (dead) body of a black man. In its proleptic evocation of the jerking police monitor we have not yet seen, the line of blood flickering in the light positions the black body it meets as both object and medium. And if there is perhaps nothing more familiar than the first, the second is still likely to give us pause: what might it entail to tell a story of this black, dead body by way of the body's logic, to consider the body as a mode of organizing the world and our knowledge of it rather than simply as a thing within that world?

We might consider the conversation that follows to be a gloss of that question, conducted as it is off screen between voices the teleplay identifies as "obviously white" and "obviously black" as the camera lingers over the flickering:

MCNULTY: So your boy's name is what?

WITNESS: Snot.

MCNULTY: Snot.

WITNESS: Huh.

MCNULTY: You called this guy Snot?

WITNESS: Snotboogie, yeah.

MCNULTY: Snotboogie.

CAMERA finally finishes its low-angle scan of the terrain to reveal HOMICIDE DET. JAMES "JIMMY" MCNULTY, white, mid-thirties, Irish, notebook in hand, questioning the WITNESS, black, early twenties. They are sitting, MCNULTY casually and the WITNESS nervously, on the steps of a vacant rowhouse.

MCNULTY: He like the name?

WITNESS: What?

MCNULTY: Snotboogie. [Moves toward body.] This kid, whose mama went to the trouble to christen him Omar Isaiah Betts, he comes out of the house one day, maybe six or seven years old, and, ah, you know, he forgets his jacket. And so his nose starts running. And some asshole, instead of handing him a Kleenex, he calls him Snot.

WITNESS: Huh.

MCNULTY: So he's Snot forever. [Pause.] Doesn't seem fair.

WITNESS: Life be that way, I guess.[1]

To suggest that Snotboogie's childhood reduction to errant bodily fluid prefigures his fate as a crooked line of blood splattered across a darkened Baltimore street is to miss the force of the condensation the scene works to pull apart: to be Snotboogie is to be barred from the possibility of prefiguration altogether. Snotboogie is not merely characterized by a bit of bodily interior (a humor) turned outward, but his entire being is contracted to what ought rightly to have been the passing bodily state of an instant, the childhood cold of one Omar Isaiah Betts caught and recuperated from. Snotboogie cannot end up a line of blood on the street for the reason that he has been it all along, snot and blood the externalizings of a murky interiority that should have been left unseen and undistinguished. Here, too, the rotating police light, iterating a single, inert view so that it assumes the guise of movement and change, like the jittery line of the wiretap's equalizer. *Life be that way.*

It has been the project of this book thus far to offer an alternative history of race, one that does not begin by presuming race to be a system of signs whose epochs are marked off by the replacement of one arbitrary set of meanings by another, but rather, one that understands the regime of the arbitrary racial sign to be just one moment in a longer-standing epistemological effort to explore the degree to which the body is able to function to subtend and make manifest the universal likeness of human beings. I have been arguing that the history of anatomical medicine, with its foundational notion of a standardized body that is at once common to all humans and not directly observable by any of them, offers a framework for making sense of some of the central logics and incoherencies of Enlightenment and post-Enlightenment thought, including, but not limited to, its theory of race. In this account, skin is elevated as the primary mark of race in the final decades of the eighteenth century as a structure for making the newly conceived likeness of human bodies perceptible in an instant. Such racializing works to circumvent (if not quite resolve) what I have suggested is the fundamental tension within modern anatomical medicine's conception of the body: the passing diagnosis of a sick body is made possible thanks to that body's ongoing and fundamental likeness to all other bodies (including the autopsied bodies from which expert physicians would have learned their skills and with which they imaginatively compare any sick body). Yet sick bodies are only treatable so long as the state of sickness—a runny nose?—is different from the standard body to which it is compared, a passing, contingent treatable condition, here today, gone tomorrow. As I detailed in my first chapter, Kant theorized a racialized skin that makes the ongoing likeness of human bodies instantly legible in a single glance, obviating the need for comparing different people's bodies or for tracing a single body through its various states of sickness and health. This instantaneity would circumvent the conceptual pitfalls associated with the scientific model of a body that is always like other bodies and that nonetheless gets sick and requires healing. In offering, in its opening scene, the story of a passing and contingent bodily moment made permanent ("So he's Snot forever"), *The Wire* establishes the anatomical bodily logic of race as its own and makes the exploration of that logic its project: the racial body as both object and medium. Over the course of the series, we shall see, various characters attempt to establish ways of inhabiting and reconfiguring the institutions they find themselves in so as to thwart their own reduction to instantaneously legible objects. In most instances they fail in their efforts to establish their own opacity, to insist upon their essential diachronicity as subjects. That the concentration of the life and death of Snotboogie into a spurt of bodily fluid is presented to us at once as a moment to be witnessed—the jagged line of blood in the street flickering into and out of visibility, revealing its sameness over and again—and a narrative recalled secondhand and after the fact, instantiates the inextricability of what is immediately perceptible and what is learned indirectly and through time as the structure of *The Wire*'s not-quite-narrative genre.

Caroline Levine has written compellingly of what she terms *The Wire*'s "infrastucturalism," the series' interest in investigating institutions' particular recalcitrance to change, and the ways in which this recalcitrance tends to produce a "social life . . . governed by many overlapping and discordant institutional tempos."[2] For Levine, institutions are not simply inert, but self-reinforcing as well, governed as they are by rules and patterns of behavior that tend to render other rules and patterns of behavior unimaginable. While the Baltimore represented in *The Wire* certainly boasts more than its fair share of inert and self-reinforcing institutions, to frame the series' project primarily in terms of its relationship to institutionality per se is to risk overlooking the ways in which modern, skin-based race itself functions as a kind of institutionalizing, and by extension, the degree to which *The Wire*'s various institutions operate as responses to and manipulations of the institutionalizing that is race. This book has been impelled from the outset by an attempt to make sense of what has long been recognized as one of the central paradoxes of the Enlightenment: that the same philosophical and political tradition that produced the most comprehensive theorization of universal equality that the world had theretofore seen also generated theories of race that transformed "human variety" from a set of qualities that were assumed to be circumstantial and contingent into deep and comprehensive qualities of the self.[3] I argued in chapter 1 that the emergence of race is less a betrayal of Enlightenment ideals than an attempt to fulfill them in ways that allow the commitment to the universal equality of individuals to be squared with the undeniable fact that those individuals change (mature, age, die) over time. Kant reconciled these two claims, I suggested, by way of a notion of race that allows the likeness of individuals to be immediately perceptible in the very skin of their bodies, in a way that turns likeness from a quality that needs to be thought into one that can be seen and perceived. In transforming the *idea* of equality into the *sensory experience* of likeness, modern race can be seen to function as a kind of institutionalizing, an institutionalizing that, in circumscribing the universal by making it present, turns it into something less capacious, something subject to hierarchization. Born of the impulse to witness likeness, race becomes the mark of difference.

This dual quality of institutionalization has narrative implications as well.[4] In taking up the internally tense logic of the racialized (anatomical) body as its own, *The Wire* transforms the instantly witnessed event, act, identity from a self-evident unit of measure, the thrum of narrative rhythm, into an object of investigation. Such instantaneity is not only revealed to be contingent—the name Snotboogie sparks McNulty's speculation of how it might have been otherwise—but it is also shown to be a practice, one way of knowing the world significant in its relation to other ways not only of knowing, but of organizing the world. So we not only hear a possible account of how one boy might have come to seem fully legible as he was on one tissueless winter's day, but we are invited to understand the transformation of Omar Isaiah Betts into Snotboogie as coincident with and thinkable through his presence as a drying trickle of blood under a flashing police light, not a precondition but an element of that presence.

In advancing the case for understanding *The Wire* as an exploration of the epistemology and politics of instantaneity, I am not in any way meaning to discount the significance of institutions. While I mean to argue that the particular centrality and significance of instantaneous legibility follows from the logic of the racialized anatomical body, the *practice* of seeing instantaneously is frequently, though not exclusively, organized and performed by the police. David Simon, *The Wire*'s executive producer and head writer, has termed his work a "visual novel," one in which "all the visual cues and connections . . . need to be referenced fully and at careful intervals."[5] Simon has also spoken repeatedly and at length about his decision to organize the show's five seasons as serial explorations of distinct urban institutions: the police and drug trade, the organized labor of the Baltimore ports, city and state politics, the public school system, and print journalism. What I am suggesting is that we consider these assessments to be stringently, and not just accidentally, linked to one another. The visual cues that structure *The Wire*'s patterns of significance order a genre that is more geometrical than linear, our movement from one ongoing institution to another registering shifts in attention rather than a logic of causal development, the movement of story. When the second season opens and presents us with a cast of characters we have never seen before—the mostly Polish-American shipyard workers of East Baltimore who, faced with the mechanization and globalization of their labor, take up drug smuggling and human trafficking—we do not in any way believe that their activity is a consequence of Westside drug lord Avon Barksdale's having been sent to jail at the close of season 1. Although Jimmy McNulty's demotion from drug investigations to harbor patrol might occasion the shift in our attention from the Westside low-rises to the docks, the stevedores' smuggling doesn't begin when Jimmy climbs aboard his patrol boat, nor are we given any reason to assume it ends when Jimmy is invited back from his exile. We're just attending to something we weren't attending to earlier. In Simon's visual novel, perceiving visual images does not simply stand in for reading about linguistic ones; rather the world of the visual novel is organized such that legibility and causation—the capacity to be seen and the power to act and make happen—need not imply one another.

But while I hope the argument I have offered thus far has paved the way for recognizing the intimacy of racial seeing and institutionalization, there remains an aspect of the presence of this chapter in this book that has yet to be accounted for. Given that I have been presenting this project as one of historical recovery—a call to recognize a racial logic that has, since Darwin's late work in the 1870s, been largely overlooked, if not wholly supplanted, by the paradigm of racial construction I have been calling "linguistic"—an obvious question emerges: How do I make sense of the existence, in the first decade of the twenty-first century, of a narrative structured around the intersecting logics of race and medicine? I have made the case throughout for analyzing genres and discourses seemingly distant from the operation of race by insisting that the abiding force of racial ways of seeing and knowing can only be understood by way of their imbrication within and usefulness to more general philosophical, political, and cultural logics. But *The Wire* is created and set well over a century after the last of the other works this study examines, and it engages the dynamics head-on, not sidelong. Much has been written about *Wire* creator David Simon's deep familiarity with the urban landscape out of which he pieced together his serial drama—Simon was a homicide reporter for the *Baltimore Sun* for twenty years before he turned to writing for television—and he himself has insisted that *The Wire* is "not about Jimmy McNulty . . . Or crime. Or punishment. Or the drug war. Or politics. Or race. Or education, labor relations or journalism. It [i]s about The City."[6] Simon is eager to generalize his story about metropolises not only to the aging US industrial cities that resemble Baltimore, like Cleveland, Detroit, Buffalo, and Pittsburgh, but also to European cities like Manchester or Amsterdam. Although Simon is perhaps not wrong about the generalizability of his urban object, he may be overlooking the conditions of possibility of his own insight into that object. In Simon's Baltimore, modern anatomical medicine and race come together with a starkness unequalled by any other urban metropolis: Johns Hopkins University and Medical Center, located in the heart of African American East Baltimore is the city's biggest nongovernmental employer, as well as its biggest nongovernmental landowner. As Rebecca Skloot has recently detailed in her best-selling *The Immortal Life of Henrietta Lacks*, the reach of Baltimore's medical institutions and discourses into the social, cultural, and political workings of the city and its residents is pervasive and profound.[7] It is this shaping power, I suggest, that enables Simon, in his commitment to uncovering the deep logic of the City of Baltimore, to excavate the otherwise diffuse and cloaked interrelations of modern race and medicine.

We attend, rather than have our attention drawn along by the causal chain of a narrative, because *The Wire* offers a world in which visibility registers not only the circumscription of subjectivity to a single instantaneously perceptible moment, but the circumscription of agency as well. Having conjured a stunningly self-obliterating biography for Snotboogie, McNulty and the witness lament its foreshortening:

WITNESS: Motherfucker did not have to put a cap in him.

MCNULTY: Definitely not.

WITNESS: He coulda just whipped his ass, like we always whip his ass.

MCNULTY: I agree with you.

WITNESS: He gonna kill Snot when Snot been doin' the same shit since I dunno how long. [Pause.] Kill a man over bullshit. [Pause.] I'm saying every Friday we in the alley behind the cut-rate, we rollin' bones, you know? All the boys from 'round the way. We roll 'til late.

MCNULTY: Alley crap game, right.

WITNESS: And like every time, Snot, he would fade a few shooters, you know. Play it out until the pot's deep. Then he would snatch and run, you see what I'm sayin'?

MCNULTY: Every time?

WITNESS: Couldn't help hisself.

MCNULTY: Lemme understand this. Every Friday night, you and your boys would shoot crap. And every Friday night, your pal Snotboogie would wait until there was cash on the ground. Then he would grab the money and run away. [WITNESS nods.] You let him do this?

WITNESS: Naw. We catch him and beat his ass. But ain't nobody go past that. [MCNULTY stands, turns and watches as the body, now bagged, is hauled into the back of the morgue wagon.]

MCNULTY: I got to ask you. If every time Snotboogie would grab the money and run away—if he did that every time—why did you even let him into the game?

WITNESS: Huh?

MCNULTY: If Snot always stole the money, why did you let him play?

[WITNESS looks at MCNULTY like he's an idiot]

WITNESS: Got to. [Pause.] This America, man. (1:1)

So Snotboogie, a man forever frozen as his runny-nosed child-self, traces a life no less immediately discernible for its dilation through time: day in, day out, he bides his time until the pot is deep, then snatches the money and runs. That we are offered no account, speculative or otherwise, for the perfect reiterativeness of his behavior is surely part of the point, since the condition of being Snotboogie is to be denied the possibility of coming to behave like Snotboogie. The formal resemblance of his name and his behavioral repertoire stand in for the story of a self, or even the story of a compulsion: for Snotboogie, there is no distinction between identity and activity. And so, too, the comprehensiveness of the instant, the single action, endlessly replayed, ramifies outward, as not only Snot himself but the gangbangers he plays with and robs organize themselves into interlocking cycles of repetition (playing, robbing, beating) in respect for the integrity of a self—and the idea of a self—dignified by its freedom to act as its selfhood dictates, in the spirit of America.

As sociology, of course, this account of circumscribed agency is nothing new. *The Wire* certainly does not refrain from showing us—and making us care about—characters whose opportunities and geographical horizons are so narrowly constrained that they do not know what they are missing. The first season alone features drug hoppers Bodie, who takes his first trip to Philadelphia, a mere hundred miles north of Baltimore, when he is sent on a drug run, and Wallace, who has never heard of an iconic seafood restaurant less than two miles from the abandoned rowhouse where he distributes a breakfast of juice boxes and single-serving bags of chips to the similarly abandoned children he has taken under his care. But it is *The Wire*'s particular rigor (and, I will be arguing, its form of politics) to insist that for every reiteration of what we already know—to be young and poor and black is to be radically constrained in what one can accomplish or even aspire to accomplish—we attend to something we are likely not yet to have noticed: the circumscription of black subjectivity and agency are not simply social relations to be noted and mourned, but form the epistemology around which a range of Baltimore's institutions are structured. This is not an elaborate way of saying that these urban institutions, in particular the police, are constraining forces upon the black population they police, or that such institutions, under the guise of neutrality, act upon African American citizens with particular brutality, though both of these things are doubtless true. The story *The Wire* has to tell is not a story of formally neutral institutions that are deployed in differential ways; rather, it narrates the ways in which the differential practices of racial seeing undergird and organize the formal structures of the institutions themselves. In *The Wire*'s Baltimore, not only the police and the policed, but also the government officials, the commercial real estate brokers, and the ordinary citizens who inhabit the urban space are organized around the practice of seeing racially—that is, making bodies legible in an instant. As a consequence, these institutions of law and lawfulness cannot help but sustain a fundamentally racial social organization, even (indeed, especially) when they are functioning at their most neutral.

Even as *The Wire*'s opening scene registers the circumscription of a life and sphere of activity condensed into a single instant, endlessly replayed, the show builds into its framework an alternative model of repetition in which what is reiterated is not a moment of selfhood or a singular activity but a kind of observation, a pedagogy that demands that attention be extended over time, an invitation to look again and learn more. I will be arguing that *The Wire*'s interrogation of the logic of instantaneous racial seeing, its understanding of the functioning of institutions, and its eschewal of linear narrative are all of a piece. "The first thing we had to do," David Simon recalled, "was teach folks to watch television in a different way, to slow themselves down and pay attention, to immerse themselves in a way that the medium had long ago ceased to demand."[8]

And certainly, the teaching begins with the series' opening scene. Jimmy McNulty's conversation with the witness is an interrogation, surely, but it is also a review and translation, as Jimmy underlines and repeats, schooling viewers in how to attend even as he translates the witness's idioms and mumbled black English for those members of the HBO audience who might benefit from such a translation. Even as the repetitions, which persist with a patterned intermittence over the length of the opening scene, offer viewers multiple chances to make sense of an encounter that otherwise begins in medias res, the pedagogical mode is not solely directed toward the audience. The next scene in the opening episode begins with yet another iteration, as McNulty repeats the witness's words to his partner Bunk Moreland of the homicide unit as the two of them walk together into the downtown Baltimore courthouse. We witness this repetition on the screen of a security monitor positioned behind the guard's desk at the courthouse's entrance, and this repetition via the monitor interpellates both the viewers and Bunk and McNulty into equivalent positions, implicitly transforming the pedagogical mode from a method of engaging viewers into a formal structure that borrows its logic from the social interaction it represents. In place of a narrative built around the tracing of cause and effect, one event leading to another, we are presented with a world of encounters organized around telling, teaching, retelling.[9] This pedagogical mode is extended even more broadly a moment later, as Jimmy settles himself onto a backbench in the courtroom of the trial he has come to observe. We watch, along with Jimmy, as the trial is pared down to the demand for another repetition and the attempt to retract the authority of a version of knowing built out of the dilation of an instant of knowing into a kind of attention and familiarity that extends through time. The prosecuting and defense attorneys question the prosecution eyewitness in turn:

HANSEN (PROSECUTOR): Mr. Gant, do you see the man you identified from that photo array sitting in the courtroom today?

GANT: He's right there.

HANSEN: For the record, the witness has identified the defendant, D'Angelo Barksdale. [To LEVY] Your witness.

LEVY: Just one question, Mr. Gant. Had you ever seen this young man before the day in question?

GANT: No.

LEVY: Your honor, no further questions.

As the lawyers' back-and-forth makes apparent, the authority to offer persuasive evidence rests not simply on a witness's capacity to repeat himself, but on his capacity to demonstrate the sort of familiarity that comes with sustained engagement. This version of repetition, the repetition of sustained attention, matters precisely because it cannot be presumed to be transparent: there is no guarantee that the object one observes over and again will continue to be the same. But if the opening scene's overlapping of the circumscription of a life to an instant and the repeated recounting of that circumscription offers the epistemology of a subject and its pedagogical repair, the trial scene reveals the extent to which the institutionalization of such repair in the form of legal testimony generates its own proliferating vulnerabilities. The witness who follows Gant refuses to repeat her testimony after a threatening glance from the drug lord Stringer Bell, and the episode closes as it opens, with the dead body of a black man—this time Gant's—splayed awkwardly across the asphalt. Sensitive to the danger that the revelation of the instantaneously discernible likeness of the black bodies that frame the opening episode might function to underscore their anonymous interchangeability—another dead black man felled on television's mean streets—the scene's writers remind us again what it is we should understand ourselves to be seeing. The body is turned over by the homicide investigator to reveal Gant's name on the tag of his uniform, while we hear, in the series' only voiceover, a repetition of the voice of the prosecutor asking Gant to identify the defendant, D'Angelo Barksdale. The narrative frame that will be scrupulously maintained for the remainder of *The Wire*'s run is broken here,[10] not by the voiceover of some omniscient narrator who insists upon our positioning outside the fictional world of Gant, D'Angelo Barksdale, and Snotboogie and the knowledge that follows from that positioning, but by the repetition of something we have already heard and seen, something we might have seen if we were sitting beside Jimmy McNulty in the courtroom. The breaking of the frame functions here then, paradoxically, to alert us to our immanence within the world of the narrative. As we are prompted by the prosecutor's voice not only to identify Gant's willful naming of D'Angelo with the splayed body before us but also to note the likeness of that body to the body of Snotboogie that opened the episode, we are likely to be struck with how much has passed, how much we have come to know, between our first sighting and this new one.

Here, then, in its opening episode, the series highlights a commitment it will retain throughout, a commitment to what I am calling its pedagogical form, structuring itself less around the tension and revelation of an unfolding plot than through a series of efforts to look and look again, over time and from different angles. In part, *The Wire*'s adaptation of this pedagogical mode can be seen as a registration of the inappropriateness of narrative to the world being represented. To the degree to which the condition of *The Wire*'s institutions and individuals is to see and be seen in an instant, an organization both predicated upon and generative of a radical circumscription of agency, plottedness seems thoroughly beside the point. To put the formal challenge in slightly different terms: how does one go about telling a story—that is, giving an account of the relations of cause and effect—when the world to be represented is one in which seemingly everyone is unable to cause effects, in which what is legible comprises discrete moments rather than the relations between them? In this spirit, I organize this chapter as a series of examinations, at once diagnostic and descriptive, of various efforts to escape and manipulate the relations of instantaneous legibility being described and criticized. But insofar as this pedagogical mode—a kind of attending over time structured not around the relations of cause and effect but instead around the discernment of likeness and particularity in repetition and the passage of time—engages with a world whose subjects are constrained by the conditions of their own legibility, *The Wire* presents its pedagogy not merely as an instrument for learning about the world it represents, but also as a kind of politics, a mode of ethical engagement for viewers and characters alike.[11]

Racing Space and the Logic of "Real Estate"

With pedagogy in mind, I want to tarry, for one more moment, with Snotboogie. It is the condition of being Snotboogie to live as someone it does not take a lot of time to know. Last week, this week, next week, he plays, snatches, runs, gets whupped, the apparent sequentiality of his busyness foreshortened, by its repetition, into a single act, endlessly rehearsed. But while we are not likely to learn more of Snotboogie by looking longer, nor to discover how it is he came to be someone who could be comprehended so fully in an instant, the fact that Snotboogie exists outside a developmental narrative does not relieve us of the burden of puzzling over his translation from a runny-nosed instant to an equally instantaneous line of blood in the street. Just as the formal resemblance of Snotboogie's identity and his repertoire of action signals both the relation between the two and the absence of any mechanism by which one can be said to have changed the other, the formal juxtaposition of snot and blood, of a momentary condition of one body and that same body, dead and arrayed across space inhabited by others, evokes a sense of likeness without getting us from here to there. Kant theorizes racial skin, we recall, in an effort to make the changes of a body, the movement from sick to well, from living to dead, legible by way of the presumption that all bodies are alike, always. Racial skin makes the likeness of bodies visible in a moment, presenting that likeness as the effects of a cause while nonetheless insisting that those bodies not be subject to changes, the sorts of changes that would make them different from one another. We are asked, in the opening scene of *The Wire,* to understand the movement from the living Snot to the dead one, from an intact body to a body splayed across space, both as a singularly horrible event occasioning our ethical and political scrutiny and as no change at all. (We don't even see it happening.)

And just as we are meant both to register and discount the likeness of the instantly legible intact body and the line of blood splattered across space, we must discover Snotboogie's exemplariness formally, via the resemblances he organizes, rather than by understanding him and the drug hoppers he robs and who mourn him to be the common outcomes of a common developmental narrative. And certainly that makes sense: Snotboogie, forever knowable as a single instant, cannot quite be understood to have been formed by psychological or social forces that turned him from what he was to what he became, and inasmuch as he isn't "shaped," he cannot be like those around him in virtue of their having been shaped by common forces.

Later in the episode that opens by presenting us with a body defined by its instantaneous legibility, we are presented with a characterization of instantaneously legible space. D'Angelo Barksdale, a ranking member of the Barksdale drug clan recently demoted to supervising the drug trade in less profitable low-rises, cautions Wallace, an underling, against making the sorts of drug transactions that would be observable in an instant:

> D'ANGELO: You can't serve customers straight up after taking the money. Somebody snapping pictures, they got the whole thing. See what I'm saying, you get paid, you send them off 'round the building, yo. Then you serve.

Here instantaneous legibility is presumed, produced, and thwarted. The illegality of the exchange of drugs for money is, for the police, made manifest in the instantaneity of the exchange, the moment in which the fact that one is being given for the other becomes something that can be seen. That the police perched on rooftops snap photographs of the exchange to submit in court as definitive evidence of a crime certainly contributes to investment of instantaneity with significance. The police choose to photograph drug transactions because those transactions' illegality is made manifest in a moment, and the illegality of the drug transaction is made manifest in a moment because the snapshots of exchanges capturing an instant are what the police offer in court as evidence of illegality. It is this instantaneous structure of illegality that motivates the adjustment D'Angelo urges Wallace to make. Rather than handing customers the drugs they have purchased in the same instant he receives the money, the savvy hopper sends his customers away, directing them around the building to serve as their own decoys and waiting for them to return before handing over the product. We can easily imagine a way of framing this scene as a narrative: D'Angelo, catching wind of a new police practice of photographing drug transactions from roofs, calls a meeting of the hoppers he supervises to introduce them to a new, dilated, and spatially diffuse way of delivering drugs to customers, designed to thwart hidden police photographers in their project of gathering evidence. In place of such a singular occasion of insight and development, we are presented with another example of what I have identified as *The Wire*'s fundamentally pedagogical mode. D'Angelo instructs Wallace on the "best practices" of the local drug trade, but we are never allowed to imagine that we are witnessing the moment of invention of such practices, or that they will somehow supplant the structuring instantaneity of the drug transaction. Just as neither the police surveillance by way of snapshots nor the instantaneity of the drug exchange can be said definitively to precede or produce the other, the practice of thwarting the instantaneity of the transaction by diffusing it through space doesn't so much disrupt the logic of instantaneity as coexist with it. The implication of this coexistence is that the dilation of the drug transaction spatializes instantaneity by creating something like a thoroughly homogeneous space. In place of an exchange of drugs for money that takes place in a moment, we are presented with a space in which all that happens is the exchange of drugs for money: "You get paid, you send them off 'round the building, yo. Then you serve." This formal alignment of the condition of the body at a single moment and the reduction of all action to a single type of course resembles the alignment we saw with Snotboogie, whose characterization by way of that single runny-nosed moment of childhood seems to necessitate, without quite causing, his ceaseless and inalterable act of play-snatch-grab. Insofar as Snotboogie's instantaneity precludes a causal explanation for his narrow repertoire of behavior, that absence of causation eliminates the possibility of conceiving of Snotboogie's exemplariness or generalizability as undergirded by his formation by shared historical circumstances. D'Angelo's advice to Wallace offers a structure of generalizability, the hand-to-hand transaction converted to a space filled with many people's functionally identical actions. *The Wire*'s drug hoppers do one thing and one thing only, not because they have been identically constrained by a common traumatizing event, but because they occupy a space structured around the presumption that what needs to be known about bodies can be seen in an instant and by the resistance to that presumption.

It might be tempting to understand *The Wire*'s representation of a space in which surveillance has no origin and no end point in Foucauldian terms. But to slot too quickly into this familiar analytical structure the relationship between the Baltimore police and the various drug operations they trace by way of rooftop photos and ever more elaborate wiretaps is to miss the ways in which a much more specific bodily and racial history of looking structures both the modes of engagement and the various, strenuously imaginative attempts to escape and transform those modes of engagement. While the yard of the McCulloh low-rises where Wallace and D'Angelo strategize could certainly not exist outside of a modernity conceived in broadly Foucauldian terms, the prisoners of Bentham's Panopticon, having assumed their captors' intermittent but invisible gaze as their own, would never contemplate the possibility that sending one's customers around the side of a building might take the transaction in question beyond the disciplinary gaze. D'Angelo's literalized sense of the police gaze, his notion of it as something that might be evaded if only one put a building between oneself and it, is not naïve as much as it is experienced. Only someone with a long history with actual police—with "real police" and other, less elevated sorts—would know that the eyes behind the camera that can snap a photo of just visible wads of bills and baggies and glass tubes filled with some indeterminate something passing between hands are located within a body that can be positioned here as opposed to there, can get bored, can miss a shot when it sneezes, or can go to the far side of the roof to pee. More to the point, such actual police conduct their surveillance in a world in which lots of different kinds of looking occur, not least the complex concentration of looking that I have argued is constitutive of the modern racial body. This is not merely to say that virtually all of the drug hoppers under police observation—as well as those who plot their escape from that observation—are black, although that certainly is the case. (Early in season 2, the low-level white police detective known as Herc is deployed to do undercover drug buys in the mainly white, working-class neighborhood of Locust Point. He reports back, disgusted, that the white drug dealers who sold him their wares just handed the drugs over when he gave them the money, not bothering with any of the strategies of indirection or spatial diffusion employed by the black dealers: "Need affirmative action for these white boys," he concludes.) The Foucault of *Discipline and Punish* conceives of a logic of surveillance in which the disciplinary gaze has a kind of dematerializing function: the idea that subjects could be being watched at any time by an unseen external gaze leads those subjects to discipline themselves, to act preemptively as their own self-scrutinizing, self-disciplining force. In *The Wire*, by contrast, it is the unevenness and opacity of the field—the differences between the bodies and the spaces they act within, the particular relations of legibility and opacity with both the bodies and the space—that both invites observation in general and structures the various forms it takes. Racialized skin is culturally and politically useful for the late-eighteenth-century Enlightenment moment in which it comes into being, we recall, not simply because it renders immediately visible a kind of bodily likeness, but because the likeness it makes visible is not disrupted by the fact that such a body acts and is acted upon, ages, and changes. In this regard, the concept of race responds to the threat to identity and self-knowledge posed by the model of the anatomical body: that bodies, especially interiors of bodies, can function in ways the subjects inhabiting those bodies know nothing about; that such bodies are consequently vulnerable from incursions from without; and that such bodies can act in ways that change themselves beyond recognition. What makes the world according to D'Angelo an elaboration of the logic of the racial body is thus not that the boys and men selling the drugs are black, or that the exchange of drugs and money can be captured in the instant of a snapshot, but rather that the action and the instant are rendered equivalent. The instantaneous visibility of the drug transaction and the homogeneous space in which all possible action is reducible to the exchange of drugs for money are made to stand in for one another.

This equivalence also exposes a certain deadness at the heart of the concept of modern, skin-based race. By the end of *The Wire*'s first season, Wallace will be dead; by midway through the second, his instructor D'Angelo will have joined him—both killed by members of their own crew for the infraction of imagining the possibility of doing something other than slinging drugs. The habits of home are explicitly epistemological and temporal: Wallace returns from the safe haven of his grandmother's house on Maryland's Eastern Shore when he discovers himself to be unable to think of ways of passing the time other than the way to which he is accustomed. With the rupture of the congruence between the action and apprehension structured by the homogeneous space of the low-rises-under-surveillance—a moment of looking at one action, endlessly reiterated—Wallace finds himself faced with the experience of undirected looking and passing time: "I got bored with all that scenery and shit. Life too slow for me" (1:12). I have made the case that the invention of modern, skin-based race ought to be seen as a response to the pressure within anatomical medicine to reconcile the differences between living and dead bodies by making their likeness apprehensible in an instant. Inasmuch as racialized skin renders the two congruent by producing the appearance of changelessness in the live body, race can be seen as a kind of deadening. "This is me, yo, right here," Wallace says to his friend Bodie, wielding a gun against him in what will turn out to be their final conversation. Consigned to a space in which only one sort of thing is done, Wallace's death, like Snotboogie's, is less an inevitability than a fait accompli.

Moreover, the equivalence of body and space that is for Wallace at once a declaration of identity and an autobiography operates as the unit by which *The Wire*'s Baltimore is mapped, space transmuted into "real estate," an instantiation of identity. "Real estate" is the term of art used by players up and down the gangs' institutional hierarchies to name and mark out the space they lay claim to. There are Barksdale corners and Proposition Joe corners; later, Marlo Stanfield will claim control over both kinds, disrupting the delicate détente. It is the tussle over real estate, the question of if, where, and how the Barksdale's Westside drug empire will encroach upon Proposition Joe's Eastside operation, of whose corners sell which drugs provided by which supplier, that structures what little there is of recognizable plot over the course of *The Wire*'s first three seasons. "Real estate" effectively formalizes the homogeneous space of the diffused hand-to-hand exchange in which D'Angelo tutors Wallace. So long as only one type of activity of significance can happen there, the putatively public space of the street can come to be identified with a single entity. Not only is "real estate" the category through which the dynamics of the racialized body are most sustainedly explicated by the show's characters themselves, but it is by way of a series of reformulations of real estate that *The Wire* stages its most ambitious efforts to escape the logic of racial knowing it assiduously identifies and analyzes. I examine, in turn, these efforts at reformulating this conflation of instantaneously legible space and identity, from the differently utopian strategies of the entrepreneurial drug lord Stringer Bell and the battle-worn Western District commander, Major Bunny Colvin, to the calmly dystopic project of Marlo Stanfield, who envisions the escape from scrutiny to offer the opportunity for the uninhibited proliferation of death. Where each of these would escape the constraints of instantaneous legibility by diffusing the bodies into the space with which they are identified, the reformulation that is ultimately allowed to stand is one—Jimmy McNulty's—that returns to the not fully or coherently legible interior spaces of the body itself.

Examination 1: Opacity for Sale; Stringer Bell's Real Estate

> "Naw, man. We're done worrying about territory, man, what corner we got, what projects. Game ain't about that no more. It's about product."
>
> —Stringer Bell

In the world according to Stringer Bell, the problem with territory is the bodies. The commitment to real estate is followed by a series of consequences, a causal chain that unspools with the clarity and inevitability of a logical corollary: "real estate" brings dead bodies; dead bodies bring police scrutiny; police scrutiny brings arrests and the disruption of the Barksdale drug trade. Eliminate the premise and you eliminate what follows from it: no real estate, no bodies, no police, no arrests, no disruption. The drugs flow easily from hand to hand, as unremarkable as the exchange of cash for candy or packs of cigarettes at the corner store. In his insistence on the necessity of the relationship between dead bodies and the corners and projects that map the topography of the drug slingers' real estate, Stringer comes closest of all *The Wire*'s players to offering an explicit theorization of what I have been arguing is the mutually constitutive relation between bodies and homogeneous identitarian space that structures the show's interactions and legibility: the notion that the imperative that bodies be perceptible in an instant is the same imperative that reduces all possible action to a single type within the spatial bounds of drug "real estate."

But Stringer Bell is not content merely to forgo the spatial organization of the Barksdale drug operation and all that follows from it in the service of turning the heroin his charges peddle into just another commodity. As Stringer makes the case for imagining a system for distributing "product" that dispenses with the need to control particular corners or housing projects, he is at the same time deeply engaged in pursuing a parallel career founded upon another form of real estate, as the CEO of B&B (Bell and Barksdale, Barksdale and Bell) Enterprises, a commercial developer of harborside condominiums. The Stringer Bell whom Jimmy McNulty secretly observes taking night classes in management at a local community college is undeniably a capitalist. But the quasi-magical power he imputes to his alternative—which is to say, thoroughly mainstream—form of real estate suggests that he is not simply content with clearing the way for the unfettered circulation of commodities, but recognizes the possibility of transforming the fundamental social relations organized by real estate by means of his advocacy of an alternative form. Here the genealogy of Stringer's enterprise is telling: while we are not privy to Stringer's thoughts in the run-up to his launch of his real estate venture, his movement into the orderly market circulation of condominiums involves more than a renunciation of the struggle over corners. Prior to his entry into the legitimate real estate market, Stringer negotiates a deal with the Eastside drug lord known as Proposition Joe to establish a citywide drug co-op by which Stringer's Westside gang cedes control over some of the city's most valuable, highly trafficked drug corners in exchange for regular and reliable access to Prop Joe's superior "product." In its bartering of control of space for the already fungible "product," Stringer and Prop Joe's co-op effectively synthesizes a market in real estate without the legitimizing force of property law, simply by combining the formal elements of such a market.[12]

If developing and selling condominiums to people one doesn't know is somehow the alternative to a version of real estate that produces dead bodies as a matter of course, what is the nature of commercial real estate's peculiar liveness? We come to know well past our initial introduction to his entrepreneurial ambitions that Stringer is not just pursuing but is pursued as well. Because he can obtain preferred access to properties via a federal program designed to encourage minority developers, he is able to court and has been courted by several white developers hoping to monetize the advantages conferred by this affirmative action program. Stringer's willingness to trade away the perks his identity confers bespeaks, I suggest, not his cynicism about the conditions of this government program but what he understands to be its utopian aspect: the freedom afforded by the possibility of trading away one's identity. It is the detail and specificity of Stringer's materialism that distinguishes his faith from the sort of naïve belief in the abstracting powers of the market debunked by Marx in his critique of the supposed "tautology" of commodity circulation in *Capital*.[13] For Stringer, in fact if not by design, real estate properly understood becomes not just the occasion for bartering away the fact of his black identity but the specific instrument of escape from that body's constraints. Where the "real estate" of corners and low-rises becomes entirely homogeneous (admitting only one kind of person capable of doing one kind of thing and structured as it is out of hoppers' efforts to render themselves invisible by dilating the action of their drug transactions through time and space), for Stringer, what makes condominiums the space of free activity is the fact they are conceived as being inhabitable by anybody.[14] Because they are fungible, because they might be bought by anyone, they are a space in which anything might happen. But the freedom afforded by the fungibility of real estate is not simply identitarian. While actions do map onto inhabitants (a variety of potential inhabitants implies a variety of potential activities within the space of domestic habitation), as we trace the rise and fall of Stringer's venture into legitimacy, we come to see that the fact that a space might be inhabited by anyone constitutes that space as one in which any *particular* inhabitant might do a variety of different kinds of things. In this conception, commercial real estate is freedom inducing because it is understood to be inhabited *through time*. Unlike the rental engaged for a particular occasion or passing need, owned domestic space is space that allows its inhabitants to do whatever they like within it, one thing after another.

Moreover, this quality of likeness, this interchangeability of inhabitants of the condominium space, is at once guaranteed by and implies that space's opacity. In this regard, Stringer's is not simply a fantasy of domesticity, a belief that the private space of the home is somehow protected from public observation and regulation. Rather, in aligning the opacity of the space of commercial real estate and the freedom of action within those interiors with the likeness of those spaces' inhabitants, Stringer's real estate can be said to borrow its structures of legibility from the anatomical body, to imagine that something like the body's interior, with its opacity and attendant freedom of action, might be made a habitable space. Real estate, according to this vision, is not merely an instrument for circulating opaque spaces of freedom, but an instrument for generating those spaces. Like the standardized body of anatomical medicine, which supplanted the thoroughly individualized bodies organized by humors, the opacity and the standardness of the space cannot be extricated from one another. This quality of inextricability forms the basis of Stringer's reframing: likeness turns as much on the structure of opacity and the freedom of action it implies as upon legibility. The surveillance of the drug hoppers constitutes a version of the anatomical body that is all instantly legible surface; Stringer Bell's fantasy picks up the elements that surveillance would render moot, an architectural reconstruction of interchangeable anatomical bodies that are all diachronic interiors, opaque to the outside world.

Stringer's belief in the power of the real estate market to constitute the equality and freedom to act through time of those who possess and inhabit property is not without at least some historical precedent. This precedent is intimately linked to the complex history of segregation in Baltimore City, and the surprising role of real estate brokers within that history. On 15 May 1911, Baltimore mayor J. Barry Mahool signed into law the first legislation in the United States mandating the segregation of residential housing by race. By the end of the following year, similar ordinances had been adopted in Mooresville, Winston-Salem, and Asheville, North Carolina; Richmond, Norfolk, and Roanoke, Virginia; Atlanta, Georgia; Madisonville, Kentucky; and Greenville, South Carolina.[15] Ordinance 692 claimed to be aimed at "preserving peace, preventing conflict and ill feeling between the white and colored races in Baltimore City, and promoting the general welfare of the city by providing, so far as practicable, for the use of separate blocks by white and colored people for residences, churches and schools" (289). But the law was initiated by a hapless white lawyer, Milton Dashiell, after a far more prominent African American lawyer, George W. F. McMechen, purchased a home just three blocks from Dashiell on the theretofore all-white McCulloh Street—the very same stretch of the very same McCulloh Street that, nearly a century later, comes to boast the low-rises where Stringer's minions D'Angelo and Wallace ply their wares.

While the establishment of racially divided residential zones might, at least theoretically, have enabled the development of two parallel real estate markets, the particular provisions put into place to ensure segregation led real estate brokers to be concerned about the ordinance's potential to shrink the market for property. The bill passed by the Baltimore City Council on a party-line vote (Democrats in favor, Republicans opposed) mandated that "no negro can move into a block in which more than half of the residents are white," and that "no white person can move into a block in which more than half of the residents are colored." At the same time, as reported in the *Baltimore Sun* on 20 December 1920, existing conditions were not to be disturbed: "No white person will be compelled to move away from his house because the block in which he lives has more negroes than whites, and no negro can be forced to move from his house if his block has more whites than negroes." The proposed ordinance seemed predicated upon the notion that residential segregation might function like the (albeit illegal) segregation of public transportation or schools, according to which the racial community one joins is entirely presentist, constituted anew with each new "member." However, the lurking, incompletely repressed diachronicity of the possession and inhabitation of real estate structuring the market for these commodities ("Existing conditions shall not be disturbed") led the brokers who traded in them to be wary of the proposed legislation. One broker wrote Mayor Mahool in advance of the bill's signing to express his concern that the ordinance might discourage or preclude blacks from moving into a block in which blacks already lived but were in the minority. In the wake of the bill's passage, others pointed to the peculiar situation of one white man who had vacated his house temporarily while it was under repair, thereby pushing the block's white population under the 50 percent benchmark: was he to be faced with the choice of permanently abandoning his home of longstanding or being subject to criminal charges? (302–3) The brokers who joined the population of black homeowners in opposing the legislation in advance of its passage and pushing for its rollback in its wake recognized the difficulty of defining the "population" of a block or neighborhood where the inhabitation of homes over time foreclosed the possibility of either a defined instant of measurement or a temporally circumscribed commodity to circulate in the market.

Stringer's utopic vision of commercial real estate seems at first glance to be founded upon the same diachronic quality of the inhabited home that drove his professional forebears to oppose the 1910 segregation bill. But while the architecture of habitation has remained largely unchanged from 1910 Baltimore to the Baltimore of the early twentieth-first century, the fact that such habitation takes place within the context of institutionalized practices of police surveillance (practices that are themselves, I have been arguing, elaborations of particular habits of seeing racialized bodies) means that Stringer's conception of the power of the diachronic space of real estate is ultimately compromised by the temporal contradictions associated with and emanating from the efforts to make such bodies legible. As we shall see, these contradictions undermine both his most optimistic projections concerning its freedom-inducing potential as well as the capacity of this new "legitimate" form of real estate to supplant the corrosive logic of the old.

We are told in no uncertain terms that Avon Barksdale's decision to put out a hit on his lifelong friend who functions as the CEO of his vast drug empire is motivated by their disagreement concerning the proper way to run that operation, by the conflict between one conception of "real estate" and another. But the limitations of Stringer's paradigm are not made to hang solely upon the contingent outcome of this particular power struggle. Stringer and Avon betray one another virtually simultaneously: the scene in which Avon engages the men who will kill Stringer is followed immediately by the scene in which Stringer gives the renegade police commander Bunny Colvin the address to Avon's safe house. Stringer's betrayal of Avon—the culmination of an extended, uncharacteristic drunken tirade set off by Stringer's discovery that the "rain money" he has paid the shady state senator Clay Davis has done nothing to advance his application for federal grant money—is animated by the collapse of the promise of commercial real estate as an alternative to and escape from the deadly and endless vying for corners. Maury Levy, go-to attorney for the drug kingpins and their underlings, bemusedly lays out the mechanism of Clay Davis's scam:

MAURY LEVY: He rain-made you. A guy says if you pay him, he can make it rain. You pay him; if and when it rains, he takes the credit. If and when it doesn't, he finds reasons to get you to pay more.

STRINGER BELL: Naw, he got these building permits. . . . He got me $35,000.

LEVY: How much'd ya pay him, $400,000?

BELL: He's bribing the motherfuckers. . . .

LEVY: There are no bribes. You really think a state senator is going to risk his salary and his position by walking into a government building with a suitcase full of drug money?

BELL: I saw him get Chunky Coleman a grant.

LEVY: Chunky Coleman gets his grant money like everyone else. He fills out his application, makes sure his buildings meet spec, and then he prays like hell. (3:11)

If Stringer Bell's limited experience makes him vulnerable to the manipulations of a Clay Davis—"They saw your ghetto ass coming a mile away," Avon puts it matter-of-factly—it is his schooling in the logic of the space of the corner that finally does Stringer in. His error lies in mistaking the diachronicity of the grant process for evidence of the sort of causation driven by the local acts of individuals. In misidentifying what is essentially the application of a rule ("like everyone else" you get grants by filling out an application, making sure your buildings meet spec, and praying like hell) for a series of independent and contingent events, Stringer manifests his acculturation to the epistemology of the instant and its accompanying architecture of homogeneous space. Stringer is vulnerable to being scammed in the way he is because he understands the defining characteristic of the rule (including, obviously, the paradigmatic rule of law) to be its legibility and applicability in an instant: the hand-to-hand exchange of drugs for money, captured from afar by a police snapshot. Clearly, it is Clay Davis's capacity to shuttle back and forth between the culture of West Baltimore drug enforcement and that of downtown developers that gives him the insight necessary to engineer such a scheme. (When, an episode earlier, Stringer presses Davis about the lack of movement on the building permits he has paid Davis to procure, the senator reproaches him for his impatience: "buggin" is street behavior.) Stringer's conflation of law and instantaneous legibility leads him to imagine that he can intervene in advance of the operation of the rule of law to make that law work differently, hence the superfluous bribe money to Davis. Maury Levy's parsing of the formal logic of Davis's deception allows us, and presumably Stringer, to recognize retrospectively the degree to which that presumption turns out to have structured Stringer's efforts at reforming the practices of the Barksdale crew by eschewing the premises of drug real estate. Stringer's belief that he can intervene in advance of the moment in which the rule governing the grant disbursement goes into effect resembles nothing so much as his belief that he can intervene in advance of the police scrutiny so as to head that scrutiny off: "No corners, no bodies, no police."

The same association of agency and freedom with the diachronicity of cause and effect that leads Stringer to hire Clay Davis can be seen to undergird his fantasy regarding the transformative power of commercial real estate, but the redundancy of his bribe highlights a pointed difference between the two structures. Stringer's vision of real estate presumes the likeness, the interchangeability, of the inhabitants as the foundational premise of the opacity of that space and its freedom-endowing qualities. But the likeness associated with the process of disbursing grants turns out to be context-specific and radically circumscribed. The applicants for federal grants are neither presumed nor demanded to be like one another in any comprehensive or foundational way. They merely make themselves temporarily like one another for the purposes of the process by acting according to the prescribed rules: they fill out applications, bring their buildings up to spec, pray. Its diachronicity notwithstanding, participation in the grant process does not endow them with freedom; at best, with luck, it gets them a grant. Stringer imagines he can act to redirect the grants by paying Clay Davis to pay someone else off because he understands himself to be possessed of the agency invested in him by his ownership and inhabitation of the interior space of his condominium, without quite understanding that the power of the condominium's opacity is predicated upon its specific relation to the logic of the drug corners. What he fails to recognize, in other words, is the way in which the instantaneity governing drug real estate, with its hand-to-hands, and the diachronicity of his commercial real estate venture, with its promise of opacity and freedom, are in fact elements of a single, if complex, structure of recognition. When, in the immediate aftermath of Stringer's assassination by a pair of hit men in Avon Barksdale's employ, a grief-stricken Jimmy McNulty rummages through the objects left in Stringer's luxuriously appointed condominium, he is startled to find a well-thumbed copy of Adam Smith's *The Wealth of Nations* on the bookshelf. "Who the fuck is this guy?" he marvels (3:12). With Jimmy's articulation of the logical conclusion of the real-estate-as-standardized-body model of legibility, we are made to realize with a start the degree to which Stringer failed to achieve the opacity to which he aspired. Stringer's misreading of the grant process makes apparent that the terms of his imagined liberation are derived entirely as a negation of a certain specific practice of drug surveillance and that both practice and negation are part of a comprehensive epistemology of the racialized anatomical body—not a consequence of surveillance per se, but of a particular context and logic of surveillance. What makes real estate's condominiums freedom endowing, in other words, is also what assures their inextricability from the instantaneous policing of the hand-to-hand drug transaction and the corner wars. Stringer may indeed contain multitudes, and Jimmy, physician-like, may be positioned to appraise the depths of Stringer's depths only after he has died and the opaque walls of his apartment are opened to view, but we viewers have been convinced all along that there is more to know about Stringer than what can be apprehended in an instant. The freedom Stringer buys himself turns out to extend no further than Jimmy and the structure of instantaneous legibility it inverts. For extradiagetic viewers, positioned literally outside the context of police surveillance, the only surprise is how little the posthumous view reveals. Indeed, it is the jolt of surprise we are likely to feel at the nonrevelation offered by Stringer's autopsied apartment that provides the framework for understanding our shock at his vulnerability to Clay Davis's machinations. Taken in by his belief that the simple fact of events' unfolding through time is evidence of those events' manipulability, Stringer turns out to be just as quickly known as those around him.

Examination 2: The Semiotics of the Paper Bag

While the full range of Stringer's complexity only becomes apparent to Jimmy McNulty after the would-be mogul has died, our perspective is forcefully distinguished from the view Jimmy assembles out of rooftop snapshots, muffled audio recordings, and exchanged courtroom glances. The Stringer revealed by his death is, we recall, not just betrayed but betraying: his abandonment of Avon's apparently unshakeable commitment to presiding over an empire of corners and low-rises is quietly, if sadly, principled. We see something more of the strength of his investment in the logic of harborside real estate than Jimmy does in one of Stringer's final conversations, a meeting with Bunny Colvin, who has only days earlier been demoted and forced to retire from his commandership after the revelation of his project to decriminalize petty corner drug-dealing in the name of public safety. As Stringer and Colvin wander among gravestones—they have presumably chosen to meet late at night in a cemetery to avoid observation—Stringer explains his decision to come to Colvin with information about the location of Avon's safe house: "Look like you and me both trying to make sense of this game" (3:11).

If Stringer's effort to "make sense of the game" is finally scuttled by the force of a racialized bodily logic he himself is structurally prohibited from apprehending, Bunny Colvin is animated by a radicalism born of expectations limited from the outset. Facing pressure from the mayor's office and central police administration to raise the rate of arrests for drug crimes in the wake of an intensification of drug-related violence, Colvin sends the police under his command out into the field to do "rip-and-runs"—that is, to arrest the low-level drug dealers whose hand-to-hands have been captured on film—the result of which is an officer with near fatal injuries sustained in an effort to commandeer three vials of heroin. A quietly seething Colvin strides into the morning meeting of his officers the following day, places a small paper bag on the edge of his podium, and begins to speak:

COLVIN: As of this time, all hand-to-hand undercover operations in the Western District are suspended.

Sometime back in the dawn of time, this department had on its hands a civic dilemma of epic proportions. The City Council had just passed an ordinance that forbade alcoholic consumption in public—on the streets, on the corners. But the corner is, was, and always will be the poor man's lounge, where a man wants to be on a summer's night, cheaper than a bar.

But a law's a law. The Western cops rolling by: what were they going to do? If we took notice of every dude out there tipping back a High Life, there'd be no time for any other kind of police work. And if they look the other way, they open themselves up to all kinds of flaunting, all kinds of disrespect. [Picks up the paper bag, and replaces it on the podium.] This is before my time, when it happened: somewhere back in the 50s or 60s, there was a small moment of goddamn genius by some nameless smokehound who came out of Cut-Rate one day and, on his way to the corner, he slips that just-bought pint of Elderberry into a paper bag.

A great moment of civic compromise. A small wrinkled-ass paper bag allowed the corner boys to have their drink in peace, and gave us permission to go and do police work, the kind of police work that's actually worth it, that's worth taking a bullet for. Dozerman, he got shot last night trying to buy three vials—three! There's never been a paper bag for drugs [Pause.] . . . until now. (3:2)

Colvin's "paper bag for drugs" takes the form of what comes to be known as "Hamsterdam," a two-block strip of a blighted West Baltimore street in which the sort of drug-dealers formerly subjected to rip-and-runs are allowed to sell their product undisturbed under the watchful eyes of Baltimore's finest in exchange for a willingness to halt their drug sales anywhere outside the zone. ("Vincent Street is like Switzerland. Or Amsterdam," one hopper explains to an understandably wary compatriot.) As Colvin suggests, such an arrangement frees the police to go and do real police work elsewhere, but it also allows the residents in the remainder of the neighborhood to go about their own business of living, unconstrained by the operations of a drug market outside their doors. (Colvin has arranged to have the few remaining residents of Hamsterdam relocated outside the zone.) In this sense, Colvin creates a paper bag for drugs by transforming a logic of surface and interior—the wrinkled paper bag that covers a bottle of liquor—into a logic of space. But in designating a zone in which the selling of drugs is condoned, Colvin does not so much divide the space of police work from the space of its absence as he fractures what counts as police work internally and distributes the separate practices across space, creating new forms (and new objects) of policing.

The police do not ignore or overlook Hamsterdam. Rather, they supervise it, and in supervising it they create for themselves a new kind of police authority: the authority of meaning making. Indeed, I want to suggest that the reconception of police authority that takes place with the establishment of Hamsterdam actually depends upon uninterrupted maintenance of the hand-to-hand drug selling within its boundaries. "Look: we grind and y'all try to stop it. That's how we do. Why you got to go and fuck with the program?" a skeptical midlevel member of the Barksdale organization known as Fruit complains on hearing of the new police plan to relocate and consolidate drug sales. Fruit has got it half right: the context of the police transformation of their own power is a set of circumstances in which "how we do" is self-evident and largely unchanging. In ringing the zone's perimeters, Colvin's police are less concerned with making sure that no unauthorized activity takes place than they are in reauthorizing, resignifying, what *does* occur, transforming the buying and selling of drugs from illicit into legal behavior. For the police to go from the business of enforcing laws, however ineffectually, to making meaning, the object of police regulation needs to change from modes of behavior to types of signs. In this regard, it is the demonstration that the buying and selling of drugs is unaltered by the kinds of associations that are attached to it that functions to establish this buying and selling as a sign contingently deemed legal or illegal, rather than a behavior.

At the same time, by insisting upon the mutual exclusivity between what takes place within Hamsterdam's borders and without, Colvin's plan splits the freedom to make meaning from the freedom to do everything else and, in so doing, effectively turns semiotic play from an action of language into an activity in the world. Where the police who snap photos of drug transactions from the rooftops ringing the McCulloh low-rises observe the hoppers beneath them in such a way as to render them instantaneously apprehensible and thus engage and extend an epistemology of the racialized anatomical body, the supervisors of Hamsterdam effectively create a semiotics without an epistemology, having relocated the activities of policing and living elsewhere. These Hamsterdam police need not observe the drug transactions happening in front of them, even for the instant it would take to snap a photo, since it is their presence, their authority, rather than their knowledge, that constitutes their relation to what takes place. In this shift from racial epistemology to semiotics, agency, such as it is, is effectively transferred from the drug hoppers—who must, under normal circumstances, decide whether to pass their packets of product to the customers in the same moment they are paid or to dilate the transaction into invisibility by sending customers around the block—to the police, who determine how the hoppers' behavior ought to be designated. In its withdrawal of the role of the observer, Bunny Colvin's Hamsterdam project transforms the drug hoppers from agents whose behavior, however constrained, nonetheless demands to be identified and evaluated, into something like figures who function how they function because it is their nature to do so. In this way, the establishment of Hamsterdam revises the structure of law enforcement by recapitulating in miniature the historical movement of race from a mode of knowing changing bodies to the arbitrary content of a linguistic sign so as to invoke the familiar constructionist critique: race is constructed, and therefore its meaning can be changed. Colvin attempts to escape the inertial pull of interwoven institutional histories organized around the observation of bodies by grasping for the police the radical power of resignification: no courts, no politics here. In transforming the work of police from the observation of activity to its resignification, Colvin renders not simply the drug hoppers' activities, but the hoppers themselves, radically contingent, their value in the world entirely dependent upon the terms in which the police designate it at any given moment.

But if, as I have been arguing, the status quo Colvin's Hamsterdam disrupts is one in which the hoppers' instantaneous legibility instantiates a kind of deadness, it is this quality of deadness that ultimately interrupts the Hamsterdam hoppers' ceaseless signifying, the frenzied immortality of human figures, and turns them back into observable bodies. The activity of hoppers can only remain plausibly "signlike" so long as it is—and by extension the hoppers themselves are—unchanged. When a dispute just outside the borders of Hamsterdam erupts into gunfire that leaves one slinger lying dead just inside the free zone's boundaries, Colvin's loyal deputy Ellis Carver asks his own police running-buddy "Herc" Hauck to help him relocate both the body and its accompanying evidence back outside Hamsterdam. The investment of police authority with the power to append new meanings on old behaviors depends upon transforming the observation of bodies into the reading of signs, and *that* can only take place once the police are no longer in the business of discriminating among various kinds of activity, and only so long as those engaged in the activity to be revalued do not live, or shoot, or grow old, or get shot, but ceaselessly do one thing, over and over again. The Hamsterdam experiment does not immediately collapse the moment it is revealed, largely because the police themselves remain engaged in the resignifying business. In the gap, the lag of institutions, there opens up the tantalizing possibility that Colvin's resignifying might be transformed and legitimized via the executive power into the rule of law, as the embattled Baltimore mayor and his advisors chew over the political implications of converting the Hamsterdam experiment into public policy. It is only when, thanks to a phone call to the *Baltimore Sun* by a disgusted Herc, the business of observation previously the work of police is then reassigned to the reporter who heads across town to investigate that the full force of the transformation of police work is made apparent and undone. If the ultimate fate of Hamsterdam thus seems as arbitrary as the veering of a plot this way instead of that, surely that is the point: a transformation that rises upon the demonstration of the arbitrariness of the authority to make meaning has no case to make for its own sustenance.[16]

Examination 3: Vacant Real Estate

Stringer Bell finds a spiritual comrade-in-arms in Bunny Colvin, united as the two are in their dedication to "making sense of the game" in a way that searches out freedom from (and in various forms of) police attention. But the most canny student of the failed utopia of real estate is someone with no apparent interest in freedom at all: Marlo Stanfield, the chillingly laconic drug lord who builds his dominance in the wake of the Barksdale empire's collapse. To call Marlo a student is perhaps not quite right, since the term implies a kind of intersubjectivity that is inconceivable to him. But I suggest that it is precisely his imperviousness to the claims of particularity and perspective undergirding the very notion of intersubjectivity, a perfection of disinterest, that enables Marlo to recognize, in the same dwelling places Stringer would make available to anyone, a certain power to obliterate. Stringer's fantasy, we recall, was that the real estate market could function to make fungible the freedom associated with inhabitation. Where the model of police observation structured around the racialized anatomical body presumed that drug hoppers could be fully known in the snapshot-instant of hand meeting hand to trade drugs for money, and where the hoppers' efforts at circumvention produced the homogeneous space of "drug real estate" among the Barksdale low-rises and Eastside corners, Stringer's real estate promises more than the privacy and freedom that a home might afford its inhabitants to act and be in ways too complex, changing, and unpredictable to be legible in an instant. It also implies that this freedom might be instantiated in the architecture of the homes themselves and thus in theory available to all buyers, real and potential. It was the second part of this fantasy—the desire not just to seek self-determination and freedom from police scrutiny in the opacity of private dwellings but also to imagine that freedom might be proliferated and distributed via the market in private real estate—that led Stringer to formalize the link between private space and freedom, a move that effectively located the power of dwelling in the walls of the dwellings themselves. Because he believed that the right kind of home would *inevitably* secure the freedom to act and change through time rather than simply make such freedom *possible*, Stringer mistook the diachronicity of the federal grant process for its vulnerability to manipulation and imagined that his complexity as a subject might matter in the world even as it went unrecognized in his lifetime.

Stringer's error appears to follow, then, from a misplaced faith in an intersubjectivity so pervasive as to be lodged in the walls of condominiums and the invisible hand of the market. Such pervasiveness, in Stringer's understanding, eradicates the need for actual subjects. For Marlo, by contrast, the presence or absence of other minds or observers is less an experience of the world than an analytical hypothesis to be ventured and withdrawn as the information, or the occasion, suits. Thus when Marlo takes up Stringer's foundational credo—"no bodies, no police"—he understands his project to be not the elimination of the turf battles over corners that produce the bodies that draw the police, but rather the elimination of bodies from police view. He dispatches his deputies, first to shoot the interlopers who would venture onto his turf (as well as his own employees who would act other than directed) and then to hide the bodies in one of the many rows of vacant houses in West Baltimore, prying off the government-issue boards from the doorways and then reattaching them moments later, bodies entombed, with a high-end nail gun. If Marlo's chilled indifference allows him to contemplate the possibility of splitting the existence of dead bodies from police observation of them, so too does it allow him to follow Stringer's formalization of freedom in the architecture of real estate to its logical conclusion. Stringer seemed to attribute to the very walls of the buildings he inhabited and traded a magical power to repair the fundamental contradiction of a structure that shields its dwellers from the scrutiny that inhibits and reduces them to a moment's legibility while simultaneously offering a framework for making that opacity legible and hence socially and politically significant. But if Stringer's "solution" operates by making the freedom of inhabitation a necessary attribute of the dwelling walls themselves and thus obviating the need for inhabitation by actual people, Marlo essentially calls the bluff ventured by that solution: just walls, no people, or more precisely, no freely acting people. In Stringer's real estate, dwelling space is necessarily diachronic, endowing its inhabitants with the freedom to act and change by shielding them from the scrutiny that would inhibit their inborn capacity to act and change. Marlo uses this same logic of architectural diachronicity—a logic whose very principle seems to refuse any distinction between vacant and furnished, fully operating interiors—to shield the bodies of his victims from police scrutiny as they rot. Empty houses containing dead bodies look a lot like full houses containing live bodies.

With walls standing, like so much skin, as evidence of the unseen, always changing life of the interior, Stringer's and Marlo's respective uses of dwelling space can be seen as finally irreconcilable readings of the two paradoxical aspects of the anatomical body. On the one hand, we have Stringer's, in which the universal capacity of the outer surface to make manifest the always changing freedom to live and to act in particular ways and moments in history is sustained only by the exclusion of dying itself from the range of possible activities; on the other, Marlo's, the expression of that excluded dying. (We should recall in this context the skepticism of early critics of anatomical medicine like Thomas Sydenham and John Locke regarding autopsies. The conundrum of how to distinguish the changes of the bodily interior that cause death from those that are the effects of death, less solved than repressed by anatomical medicine, reemerges, three-and-a-half centuries later, as the difficulty of distinguishing Stringer's unseen inhabitants from Marlo's corpses.) Stringer's attempt to formalize the freedom-endowing power of dwelling space in the architecture itself implicitly seeks to transform the relationship of buildings and bodies from an epistemology dependent upon the presence of observers and not-quite-visible inhabitants into an analogy in which the staging of the likeness of buildings and bodies magically bestows upon each the qualities of the other. Marlo, undistracted by any effort to imagine other minds, much less to presume their likeness with his own, is perfectly positioned to recognize and exploit the logical consequences of Stringer's slide from epistemology to analogy, his transmutation of the apartments from walls blocking inhabitants from view to something like brick bodies. And so the dead bodies in dead houses pile up, unmissed—three, five, eighteen, twenty-two. Dwellings can indeed ensure the freedom of the unseen inhabitants inside to act and change as they wish by shielding them from the constraints of immediate legibility, but they can do so only so long as there are actual, living dwellers inside. The dwelling space of real estate can enable the diachronic time Stringer associates with freedom only so long as that diachronic time, the time of dwelling, is itself contingent. It is this doubling of dwellers inside dwellings, of bodies inside bodies, that makes apparent the way in which the fact of living itself undergirds the capacity of the standardized anatomical body to ground a universal capacity for freedom, even as that living must be taken on faith.

But if Marlo's indifference to the fact of living itself, to the force that would distinguish the likeness of buildings and bodies from the inhabitation of one by the other, renders him supremely calculating, we would be wrong to think it makes him cynical. Cynicism presumes an elevation of one perspective over others, and Marlo is as uninterested in his own life as he is uninterested in the lives of others. Within Marlo's purely calculating vision, the analogy of buildings and bodies, of space and the diachronic time that enable change, becomes not just an instrument for getting away with murder but also a mode of existence itself. Having refused the opposition between the spatial logics of Avon Barksdale's real estate of corners and low-rises and Stringer Bell's market in harborside condominiums in favor of the power to make bodies disappear into abandoned rowhouses as if into thin air, Marlo himself becomes strangely elusive, both to the deputies of his drug empire and to the police assigned the task of tracking his whereabouts. Soon after seizing power in the wake of the police raid on the Barksdale crew's safe house at the end of season 3, Marlo announces he is canceling the regularly scheduled strategy sessions of the citywide drug co-op, limiting his encounters with his underlings to hastily arranged "meet-ups" that move, without apparent pattern, from one place to another. The same team of police investigators that managed to bring down the Barksdale empire with snapshots and increasingly sophisticated wiretaps find themselves baffled by the communiqués of Marlo and his underlings they manage to intercept. Marlo and his crew do not speak to one another at all by phone, but instead send one another photographs of clock faces with various times. The pictured times do not correspond to the hour of transmission or meeting, yet they seem to generate meetings at designated spots, in clusters of two and three. It is only when one detective, Leander Sydnor, loses the trail of a member of Marlo's crew he has been tracking and reaches for a map book in hopes of reencountering his quarry that the code gets cracked. The pictured clock face does not designate time at all: rather, Sydnor announces triumphantly, the clock's second hand shows the map book's page number, while the hour and minute hands designate the quadrants of longitude and latitude respectively. The meetings, Sydnor and his supervisor Lester Freamon surmise, take place within an hour of the moment of the transmission of coordinates, just long enough for the participants to get from here to there. With this code, time and space are figured as entirely abstract and hence fully translatable coordinates of one another. The equation of space and time that would render analogous the diachronicity of free activity and the dwelling space in which such time passes are made into the coordinates of the crew's inhabitable world.

But this analogizing marks less the triumph of Stringer's fantasy of a freedom distributable to all via the market than the diffusion of Marlo's alarmingly depopulated vision. In this vision, time is rendered equivalent to space only insofar as all activity is reduced to the process of translating between them. Within the parameters of this system, Marlo and his crew do little besides move from the places at which they receive their instructions to the places they are to meet; and the meetings themselves, only moments long and shot largely in middle distance and outside our earshot, seem designed to do nothing further than to convey instructions for the next meeting. Stringer's dream of the liberating potential of the opaque space of inhabitation was structured as an escape from the logic of the instantaneously legible racialized body—the sort of escape attempted by drug hoppers when they refuse hand-to-hands and instead send their customers off to circle buildings. But it was also an attempt to turn that negation of racial knowing into both a program for reform and a mode of social organization. Stringer's investment in making that positive vision stick, making it independent of the particular actions of those who would inhabit and observe its spaces, thus ultimately leads to Marlo's conceptual landscape of human counters, push-pins on the page of a map book. Where Stringer imagined the possibility of remaining with and in bodies whose particularity was drawn out by the space whose own diachronicity it organized, with the coordinated space-time codes of Marlo's map book, the racialized body is not dilated but made to disappear altogether. So long as the traversal of space and the passage of time fully entail one another, bodies become not only unnecessary but inconceivable, except as they occasion the shift from time to space and back again, the asymptote at which bodies disappear into abstraction.

Coda: Requiem for a Body Disappeared

Marlo, having had a deal cut on his behalf by prosecutors and police that will allow him to stay out of jail in exchange for his willingness to walk away from his drug empire, attends a party of downtown developers and, feeling out of his element, escapes to the street, where he encounters a pair of unnamed hoppers:

MARLO: Fuck y'all lookin' at?

HOPPER #1: You, nigga.

MARLO: You know who I *am*?

HOPPER #1: You know who *I* am?

Here, then, the world overturned, and yet unchanged. Out of the overlapping coordinates of time and space, embodied subjectivity contracts to a single point—will, agency, shrunk to identity: "You, nigga." Sociability reduced to the demand for recognition: "You know who I am?" Then, more: The second hopper pulls a gun on Marlo, who punches him and knocks the gun loose. Marlo reaches for it. The first hopper slashes Marlo's arm with a razor, and the two running buddies flee down the street. *The Wire*'s final image of Marlo: He touches his wound, tastes the blood on his finger, and smiles slightly, brow wrinkled, perplexed by the taste of his own particularity, inside turned out, the self in a drop of blood. Or snot.

Examination 4: Jimmy McNulty's Suspended Bodies

Marlo becomes a gloss on his own enterprise, bodies neither transcended nor dilated, but made to disappear. But *The Wire*'s final season runs another gloss alongside Marlo's, an attempt to tell the story of those bodies inside vacant houses, to tell the story of the insides of bodies. The first telling, to put us on notice, comes in the form of a joke in the season's opening episode: Three homicide detectives, Bunk Moreland, Jay Landsman, and Ed Norris, bring a reluctant corner boy in for questioning about a recent shooting. The suspect vociferously denies any involvement, so the detectives set up their "lie detector"—in truth a photocopying machine loaded with paper on which "true" or "false" has been written—to aid in their interrogation. The detectives center the suspect's hand on the glass of the copier:

CORNER BOY #1: So it feel my heartbeat?

LANDSMAN: Your pulse. Yeah.

CORNER BOY #1: If Marcus say I had the gun, he lyin'.

LANDSMAN: This machine tells the tale, son.

BUNK: We ready, Professor?

The cops ask the corner boy his name and address, both of which he answers truthfully, at least according to the just-loaded pages marked "true" that the copier spits out each time Landsman pushes its button. Finally, Bunk leans in for the kill:

BUNK: And did you and Marcus shoot your boy Pookie down on Carey Street just like Marcus said you did?

CORNER BOY #1: Naw.

NORRIS [grabbing sheet from the photocopying machine and showing it to CORNER BOY #1]: False.

NORRIS: Lie. You lyin' motherfucker.

LANDSMAN: Machine is never wrong, son.

CORNER BOY #1: Fuck, man. Nigga can't never shut his damn mouth, you know? I shoulda busted a cap on Pookie my ownself, left Marcus home an' shit. He just a bitch is all. (5:1)

In unspooling the story of the insides of bodies (the boy's "heartbeats") as one among its many pedagogical enterprises, this final season does not content itself with imagining the possibility—so ingenuous it needs to be passed off as a joke—that bodily interiors might be rendered so transparent as to function as self-evidently true, indeed, to function as a kind of figure for self-evident truth itself. The appeal of this transparency is its simplicity, and *The Wire* clearly recognizes the allure of such simplicity—the resting too soon or too comfortably—in setting its own aesthetic, moral, and political vocation against it. In the terms the series presents, I have been arguing, knowing quickly, in an instant, is itself a reaction to a complex and internally contradictory set of demands and produces a ramifying series of epistemological, institutional, political, and social complexities. What makes the story of bodily interiors an important one, we would do well to remind ourselves, is precisely its nontransparency: skin color comes to be useful as a structure for making the fundamental likeness of bodily interiors legible because they are *not* transparently knowable (and because they change over time, as bodies sicken and get well, age and die). In this regard, the project of telling the story of how bodies change and die functions as a corrective to the various injustices of racial seeing that *The Wire* has spent the first four seasons of its run elaborating. But while most of the earlier efforts to loosen the constraints imposed by the instantaneity of racial seeing took the form of engineering strategies to translate changing, moving, contingently acting bodies into architectural and urban spaces that might hide them or render them opaque, the strategy with which the series concludes is one that would escape race by returning to those bodies' complex and incompletely legible interiors.

As the fifth and final season opens, the investigation into the twenty-two dead bodies Marlo's crew dispatched, discovered only in the previous season's final episodes, has been suspended in response to a city budget crunch. For the police officers in charge of investigating the vacant houses, the decision to direct budget dollars elsewhere—first off, to the investigation of the perpetually scheming state senator Clay Davis—bespeaks a disturbing undervaluation of black bodies: "One thieving politician for twenty-two dead bodies. Quite the exchange rate," Cedric Daniels, the supervising major disgustedly observes in episode 1. In the episode that follows, McNulty, Freamon, and Bunk, expansive with drink, elaborate on Daniels's exchange rate:

MCNULTY: Guy leaves a couple dozen bodies scattered all over the city and no one gives a fuck.

FREAMON: It's who he dropped.

BUNK: True that. You can go a long way killing black folk in this country. Young males, especially. Misdemeanor homicides.

MCNULTY: Now if Marlo was doin' white women.

FREAMON: White children.

BUNK: Tourists.

MCNULTY: One white ex-cheerleader tourist missing in Aruba.

FREAMON: Ho, shit.

BUNK: Trouble is, this ain't Aruba, bitch.

FREAMON: You think if three hundred white people got killed each year in this city, they wouldn't send in the Eighty-second Airborne? Negro, please.

MCNULTY: Gotta be something that'll make 'em turn on the faucet.

BUNK: Go 'head, Jimmy. You're the smartest boy in the room. You come up with something in this broke-ass city. (5:2)

This exchange neatly embeds a narrow project—to "make 'em turn on the faucet"—within a much larger, more fundamental one: figuring out a mechanism for investing dead black bodies with a value equivalent to dead (and by implication, live) white bodies, for turning the theory behind anatomical medicine's standardized body into a social and institutional practice. The "something" that Jimmy will spin into a solution to both—a solution whose construction and unraveling will organize the final season—turns out already to have been presented to him. In what is perhaps the most explicit invocation of the epistemology of anatomical medicine, the key to making the dead bodies of the vacant housing matter turns out to be discoverable in the autopsy room of the Baltimore medical examiner's office.

Jimmy, arriving at the ME's to check up on an unrelated murder, comes upon a heated exchange between the assistant medical examiner and two Baltimore Country police officers. The ME, it seems, has just classified as a homicide a death the cops are certain is due to a heroin overdose, infuriating one officer, who is loathe to have an unsolvable murder on his docket. Nancy Porter, the second officer, fills Jimmy in on the history and science behind the error:

PORTER: New cutter's dug her heels in, saying it's a murder. It's not, but I can see why she'd think strangulation. [The two move together toward the body.] Guy's got a fractured hyoid, petechia in both eyes. But it's a freak thing. If we hadn't been there to see it, I wouldn'ta believed it myself. [PORTER points out bruising on the neck.] All post-mortem. He fires a speedball, then blacks out, falls down between toilet and bathtub. Manages to get himself wedged back pretty good. I couldn't make this shit up. Medics come and pronounce him right then and there. But get this: They can't pry the guy out without grabbing him by the neck for leverage. We watched 'em do it. This Dundalk medic and the morgue guy, they grab his neck and just start yanking. Finally get him out and he comes down here looking like a strangle job.

MCNULTY: They can't tell that it's post-mort?

PORTER: On a fresh body, no way you can. Grab a guy hard enough and you can create petechia, break the hyoid and even leave bruising. All after death. (5:2)

On a fresh body, there's no way to tell the difference between injuries sustained before death and injuries sustained "post-mort," between cause and effect. This ambiguity becomes the foundation of McNulty's scheme to "make 'em turn on the faucet." Thus, when Jimmy comes upon the recently dead body of a homeless man, unbeknownst to anyone, he stages a set of injuries that make it seem as though the man has been murdered, and he then does it again and again, injuring each dead body he comes upon the same way so that he is able to make the case that a serial killer is on the loose, preying on vagrants. The ensuing panic predictably leads the mayor to redirect funds that had been budgeted to the school system to respond to this law enforcement emergency, and McNulty, having been placed in charge of the (bogus) homeless murder investigation, is able to redirect many of the emergency funds to police investigations that had been suspended for budgetary reasons, including, most crucially, Lester Freamon's investigation of twenty-two dead bodies in vacant houses.

That we learn of the scientific ambiguity that undergirds McNulty's scheme *in advance* of the bar conversation that first spells out the usefulness of the scheme suggests, in ways in keeping with *The Wire*'s pedagogical structure throughout, that we are meant to engage this ambiguity as an autonomous analytical structure, rather than as an "event" whose relevance to the grievances expressed by Jimmy and his drinking buddies rests on the contingent unfolding of a plot. And indeed, I hope by this point, the autonomy—not to say the historical richness—of this ambiguity need not be argued for, since it is precisely the ambiguity at the heart of anatomical medicine, the very ambiguity, I argued in chapter 1, that generates instantaneously legible, skin-based race as its "resolution." The impossibility of determining whether a particular set of internal injuries is the cause or the effect of death in a given body is the consequence of the abiding tension between the two foundational postulates of anatomical medicine: first, that bodies are fundamentally like one another; and second, that the diseases or injuries responsible for sickness and death are localized in particular internal structures (organs and skeletons) that are inaccessible to direct observation and thus must be discerned by way of a comparison of the sick or autopsied body with a theoretical "standardized" body that shares the qualities of likeness of both but is literally neither.[17] Herein lies the tension: since the legibility of the sick or injured body is premised upon its likeness to the dead bodies whose interiors are revealed via autopsies, the process by which a body comes to be dead, which presumes a *difference* between sick and dead bodies, is illegible within the epistemological structure of anatomical medicine. The medical examiner cannot tell whether a fractured hyoid and petechia in both eyes are signs of a cause of death (the dead man has been strangled) or marks of the effects of death (he has died, fallen, and gotten his neck wedged between the wall and the toilet, so that the paramedics must twist his neck to release him) because the standard, normal body against which the deviations are measured is not itself presumed to change over time and, as a consequence, cannot register the process of causation that produces a given body's deviation from the standard, only the fact of the deviation itself. In order to preserve the notion that human bodies are fundamentally like one another—the presumption that makes diagnosis possible at all within the paradigm—anatomical medicine must ignore the fact that bodies themselves change over time. In chapter 1, I argued that the late-eighteenth-century invention of a model of race centered upon skin color ought to be seen as an attempt to address and resolve the incoherence within anatomical medicine I have been describing. By making the likeness of bodies instantly recognizable, race circumvents the tension within anatomical medicine that treats sick and autopsied bodies as if they are alike (and hence comparable to one another) and different (certain things must happen for a sick body to become a dead one).

In drawing our attention back to the causal narratives that skin-based race makes disappear, then, Jimmy McNulty's fictional serial killer scheme would seem to resolve the predicaments before him in one fell stroke: he finds a way of getting funding resumed for the investigation of the bodies in the vacant houses with the very same gesture that returns those bodies to the condition prior to their racialization, the condition in which all bodies are like one another, but nevertheless must therefore be observed over time for that likeness to be confirmed. For Stringer Bell, the market in real estate offered a release from the constraints imposed by the condition of living within an instantaneously legible body insofar as it traded in architectural spaces that functioned like the exteriors of anatomical bodies, allowing inhabitants to act, free from observation, even as the fungibility of these spaces operated to guarantee their dwellers' essential likeness to one another. By tying their freedom to the disjunction between the inhabitants themselves and the visible exteriors of their dwelling spaces and the illegibility produced by this disjunction, Stringer's vision produced in architectural form anatomical medicine's perpetually alive (because never dying) standardized body. It is precisely this exclusion of death created by the market in habitable space that Marlo Stanfield exploited in employing the vacant interiors to secret the bodies of his victims. Just as anatomical medicine establishes the likeness of all bodies by excluding the process of cause and effect by which sick bodies come to be dead, Stringer's apartments allow inhabitants to do whatever they like inside by presuming that the one thing they are not doing is dying.

Rather than resolve this ambiguity between the evidence of architectural exteriors and the presumptive activity within interiors by producing some new index of the relation between them, Jimmy McNulty's serial killer fraud attempts to release the bodies of Baltimore from the constraints of race by rejecting the various strategies of urban spatialization, of institutionalization, and returning to the narratives of the anatomical body itself. In spinning a plot in which we are invited to scrutinize the process by which a live body comes to be dead, this final season of *The Wire* bears some significant resemblances to Wilkie Collins's *The Woman in White*, discussed in chapter 2. But where Collins's novel makes the events undergirding and hidden by anatomical medicine's standardized body (the narrative by which the sick body of one woman is interchanged with the dead body of another) the key to resolving the novel's central mystery, what is at stake in *The Wire* is not a truthful determination of the events by which the hyoids of a series of dead bodies come to be ruptured but the very fact of the ambiguity surrounding those events. That is, *The Wire* is less interested in dramatizing either of the versions of bodily cause and effect it offers than it is in lingering with the difficulty of choosing decisively between them, turning that suspension into its own quality of drama. We do not cast our affective lot with the sorting out of circumstances—Who is the serial killer? How will he be found? What if there is no serial killer? Instead we follow out the effects of the indistinguishability, underscored first by the fact of the deaths' seriality and further underscored by the short burst of "copycat" murders Jimmy's staged series spawns.[18] There is no mystery here.

The roots of this difference are doubtless in part historical: published in 1859, *The Woman in White* emerges at a cultural moment at which the opacity of the anatomical body to the subjects inhabiting it is only emerging as an anxiety, the worry that individuals' bodies might be acting (and acted upon) in significant ways they know nothing about. This anxiety was heightened, I have suggested, by the 1856 murder trial of physician William Palmer, the notorious Rugeley Poisoner, who took advantage of this opacity by poisoning his patients under the guise of medicating them. (Interestingly, in the sixth season of the television series that first brought him and Baltimore street life into the national spotlight, *Homicide: Life on the Streets*, David Simon wrote two episodes centered on the effort to discover the fate of a drug dealer named Wilkie Collins.) But *The Wire*'s historical belatedness in this regard allows us to begin to account for generic differences between the two works that can be seen as the expression of markedly distinct goals. *The Woman in White* is written early enough in the history of the modern anatomical body for it still to seem possible to imagine that the uncertainty surrounding how bodies change, act, and die can be eliminated if only the right people look vigilantly enough. By the time we arrive at the moment of *The Wire*, discovering the best mode of "living with," a kind of suspension of uncertainty rather than alteration or resolution, has become the goal.

This suspension manifests itself as a tentativeness that is at once narrative and tonal, and rather than signaling the absence of a vision for reform, it becomes, I want to suggest, a defining quality of the type of reform that is imagined possible. Where Colvin's Hamsterdam attempts to overturn standing law and a host of institutional practices by sheer force of will, and Stringer Bell presses for a self-transformation so fundamental that it promises to carry other people along by way of its exemplarity, the unspooling of Jimmy's scheme is presented in ways that point up its limitedness. I have been arguing that *The Wire* discerns the various ways in which Baltimore's institutional, social, and political practices are organized around the modes of instantaneous legibility associated with the racialized body.

But while Colvin's and Stringer's efforts to remake those modes of bodily knowing are conceived as institutional revisions as well, Jimmy's return to narratives of the body's interior seems in many ways to be a scaling back of attention to individual bodies. This smallness of scale is both a condition of possibility and an outcome of his scheme. Jimmy is able to return attention to the condition of bodies prior to their racialization and surveillance because the homeless men on whom the fictional serial killer preys exist almost entirely outside institutional structures (and possess no real estate of any sort). However, this isolation means that the critique and reorganization of relations invited by the return to bodily interiors does not automatically extend either its critique or its organizational implications to social or institutional structures. And, too, while Bunny Colvin's and Stringer's projects finally fail to bring about the transformations to which they aspire, Jimmy's plan is frankly fraudulent: its invitation for a revaluation of the relations of the world rests upon a misrepresentation, albeit an indiscernible one, of what has already taken place.

While it is this fraudulence that ultimately leads to the discovery of Jimmy McNulty's scheme, it is not quite the scheme's undoing. In what we are meant to understand as the journalistic equivalent of the superficial, rip-and-run policing that targets the low-level drug hoppers engaged in photographable, hand-to-hand transactions while leaving the larger infrastructures of distribution intact, callow *Baltimore Sun* reporter Scott Templeton, in pursuit of a Pulitzer Prize, pretends to have been contacted by Jimmy's fictional serial killer and subsequently concocts a high-profile series of fictional interviews with the nonexistent killer. (Jimmy, initially surprised by Templeton's articles, eventually goes about impersonating the killer himself in several phone calls to the reporter, who is himself nonplussed at having been contacted by an interview subject he knows himself to have made up.) Jimmy, uncomfortable at seeing a number of his closest colleagues devote valuable energy to investigating a fictional string of crimes, confesses his doings to one after another of them, until one, Kima Greggs, is sufficiently angered by his actions to report him to his superiors. Although Jimmy, along with accomplice Lester Freamon, immediately come clean when confronted, once the mayor and the police brass convene a series of hastily organized emergency meetings, they determine that the intertwined fictions of reporter and police investigator have created an illusion too vast and politically incendiary to be undone. (The revelation would of necessity reveal the complex of compromised institutional practices of the police, city government, and newspaper that made the construction of the fictions possible.) Jimmy and Lester are allowed to retire quietly, while in the final montage of the series, we are shown a grinning Scott Templeton receiving his Pulitzer.

The preservation of the hoax effectively transforms the indistinguishability of death-as-cause and death-as-effect characteristic of the anatomical body from an epistemological conundrum neutralized by racialized skin into a version of plot in which the story of what has happened is pushed aside in favor of an accounting of how people turn their reading of what has happened into a ground for action, the basis of further plotting. But as pointed out by the many critics, both popular and scholarly, who have faulted *The Wire*'s fifth season for the busyness and implausibility of its interlocking narratives, the convolutions and coincidences of plot necessary to create a situation in which the revelation of Jimmy McNulty's fiction is more politically costly than its maintenance make the narrative—and by implication, the institutional—edifice upon which this balancing rests a shaky one indeed. There is no question that the existence of Jimmy's fictional serial killer works to free up the funds necessary to resume the investigation into the dead bodies in the vacant housing, even as the bodily events motivating and justifying the expenditure turn out, finally, to have taken place after the bodies in question have died. And though the terms of the reordering are more subtle, there is also no question that the carrying out of that investigation to its end point can be seen as a radical redistribution of value, an investment in the worth, the social and political significance, of dead bodies that effectively eliminates the distinction between the living and the dead. Kant and anatomical medicine, we have seen, provide the framework for recognizing how the elimination of this distinction renders unthinkable the distinctions of race. *The Wire* imparts a dramatic heft to this equalizing, having devoted a good part of its run to excavating the fundamental deadness at the heart of instantaneous racial legibility, the circumscription of life and subjectivity implicit in the presumption that what matters about an individual can be perceived in an instant. With McNulty's fiction rendering the unseen actions of live bodies indistinguishable from the actions visited upon dead ones, Snotboogie, laid out dead on the Baltimore pavement before our story has begun, consigned endlessly to replay a single moment of selfhood, is granted an afterlife outside our purview, the richness of life as Omar Isaiah Betts.

So while the conditions enabling this revaluation are not the large-scale reorganizing of institutions but the tenuous crossing of the acts and interests and ambitions and resentments of one life and another, surely that is the point. Considered as a narrative, the neat coincidence of the fictionalizings of one angry, self-aggrandizing Baltimore homicide cop and one lazy, feckless journalist seems a near impossibility. *The Wire* itself flags that impossibility as such as it draws to a close with a scene of the recently fired Jimmy McNulty as a guest at the "wake" his colleagues throw for him in a local bar to memorialize the death of his police career, rising with a smile from the flower-strewn platform upon which his "lifeless" body has been laid out.[19] We recall, of course, that anatomical medicine vests authority in the physician—and the not-quite-empirical standardized body—precisely because patients are barred from the position of seeing themselves when they are dead, a perspective that would enable them to see the chain of cause and effect by which they went from being sick to being dead. Only someone capable of attending his own wake could see both elements of McNulty's fiction: the causal chain by which he goes from being alive to being dead and the events that follow from his death.

But if McNulty's fiction can be realized only by way of a near impossible set of narrative contrivances, I suggest that we consider both the fiction itself and the contingencies of plot that operate to make that fiction irrefutable not as a program for reform, but as the articulation of an ethical framework. In making the case for understanding the tenuousness and contingency of McNulty's "solution" as an articulation of political value, I must make clear that I am *not* arguing that the series means to align its own position with Jimmy McNulty's, to suggest that institutional reform ought to give way to the strenuous transformational powers of a visionary individual or two. While McNulty concocts the story of a serial predator because he believes that only he possesses the clarity of vision required to make an inertial, rule-bound system of interlocking institutions sufficiently flexible to serve the citizenry, *The Wire* offers us the narrative of Jimmy McNulty's fraud because the system of interlocking educational, political, legal, and economic institutions is only functioning as it ought so long as it affords citizens the freedom and imaginative pliancy to generate such schemes, however misbegotten or subject to punishment, in ways that produce effects in the world. It is not Jimmy McNulty's scheme that makes for an inhabitable world; rather, an inhabitable world is one in which the hatching of such a scheme is possible.

But while the fragility of the "success" of Jimmy's plan articulates the *content* of the values the institutions in question ought to aspire to protect, I want to conclude by suggesting that it offers a vision of the formal structure of institutionality—that is, institutions in practice—as well. In this elaboration of institutional life, we find the aspiration to pedagogy that is not merely an instrument for making sense of a discrete object but a way of inhabiting the world. Here we need to attend, one final time, not just to the contingency and unlikelihood of the events that allow Jimmy's hoax to stand, but also to the peculiar and paradoxical doubleness that structures the legibility of the modern anatomical body and undergirds Jimmy's hoax. Autopsies cannot distinguish between the causes and effects of death within a given body because the legibility of such bodies presumes both their likeness to one another—always and forever—and their contingent changeability, the literally vital significance of the movement from health to sickness, from sickness to death. Skin-based race comes into being, I have argued, in order to reconcile these contradictory claims within this modern conception of the body. Jimmy McNulty, animated by a commitment to do right by abandoned and unidentified dead bodies—both by treating black and white bodies as if they are fundamentally alike (equally valuable) and by investigating the process of cause and effect by which they came to be dead—undoes the reconciliation that is race.

What is finally most remarkable about *The Wire* as a dramatic form is the way in which it, like Jimmy's hoax, holds these two seemingly contradictory claims in suspension. Time and again, we are shown that all institutions, the licit and the illicit, are fundamentally like one another and identical to themselves through time, too big or entrenched, too rigid or frozen by inertia, to be transformed. As rogue cop replaces rogue cop, one too-gentle-for-this-world junkie is rehabilitated only in time for another to be born into numbness. At the same time, Jimmy's scheme succeeds—is assimilable to the ongoing and unchanging operation of institutions—not because he follows institutional protocol but because he demonstrates the ways in which the bodies that staff and get observed by those institutions act and appear like nothing but themselves. But to the degree that this quality of irreducible particularity is not presented as a theoretical postulate but as the consequence of a scheme that is allowed to stand only because it intersects with the vision, interests, and desires of others, including but not limited to the *Sun* journalist Scott Templeton, it emerges as an ideology of a set of overlapping institutions in a given time and place and, from the perspective of *The Wire* itself, an argument for a certain vision of institutionality. This vision, I contend, is to be found not in Jimmy's self-aggrandizing heroics or at the moment of his wake, but in the steady vigilance of the beat cop Nancy Porter, who stays by the crime scene in which a strung-out heroin addict overdoses, falls head first in the space between toilet and wall, is tugged out by his neck, and is discovered, via autopsy, to have a broken hyoid. Nancy Porter knows the truth of a story she would not otherwise believe because she understands her job to be the job of staying and watching, carefully and over time. And if *The Wire* trains its viewers, over time, how to watch it, the essence of that training may just be how to watch over time, how to watch, that is, like Nancy Porter. The vision of institutional life that emerges from such sustained vigilance is certainly not cause for unalloyed celebration: it is only when we watch over the span of years, a collection of interrupted lifetimes, that we are able to notice the patterns of likeness that make institutions seem immoveable and unalterable. But neither does this long view give us only cause for despair. Inasmuch as it embeds a particular set of values within an unfolding network of interests and actions—the value of the freedom to scheme, the freedom to act in unexpected, unpredictable, and even illegal ways to instantiate one's vision of the world and to be punished for the excesses of one's behavior—this fragile and unlikely realization presents the opacity of the individual as an argument, one version and vision of institutional practice and not another. We come to recognize, over time, institutions as an aspirational corrective to the problem of the too-speedy legibility of race, to the reduction of the subjectivity of the black citizens of Baltimore to a version of likeness so circumscribed that it can be apprehended in a moment. In and by way of institutions, we find the invitation to an enduring and durable attendance, a structure within which alteration over time and the likeness of individuals described by those institutions are noncontradictory. If the world of Baltimore politics and policing and drug dealing and laboring with which the series ends does not appear radically different from the one with which the series begins—if we have not learned how to distinguish Snotboogie from the friend who sits on the corner and tells Snotboogie's story, and to care about that distinction—this may be because we are looking in the wrong places for signs of change.

NOTES

INTRODUCTION

1. "Agency of NATO and United Nations to Distribute Dr. Seuss Story to Foster Racial Tolerance in War-Torn Bosnia," *Business Wire*, 10 August 1998. For more on the relation of Dr. Seuss's project to its immediate cultural context, see Donald Pease, *Theodor Seuss Geisel*, Lives and Legacies series (Oxford: Oxford University Press, 2010), and Louis Menand, "Cat People: What Dr. Seuss Really Taught Us," *New Yorker*, 23 December 2003.
2. Dr. Seuss, *The Sneetches* (New York: Random House, [1953]).
3. President John F. Kennedy, televised address, 11 June 1963, reprinted in *Ebony*, September 1963, special issue commemorating the hundredth anniversary of the Emancipation Proclamation, 233. In an unsigned editorial note, the *Ebony* editors called Kennedy's address "the most important document about the Negro ever delivered by a President of the United States."
4. The most sustained elaboration of this logic is of course represented by the work of John Rawls, particularly his 1971 *A Theory of Justice* in which he first proposes the test of "the veil of ignorance." This "veil" is the formal structure of counterfactualism by which the fundamental justice of a given institutional structure is tested and measured: an institution is only just so long as one would be willing to participate without knowing which particular role or position one would occupy within it. What Rawls's "veil of ignorance" fails to consider, in my view, is the extent to which the capacity to imagine oneself in positions other than that which one occupies is itself unequally distributed and is the mark of a fundamental imaginative freedom.
5. (Kwame) Anthony Appiah, "The Uncompleted Argument: Du Bois and the Illusion of Race," *Critical Inquiry* 12 (Autumn 1985): 21–22; later republished in Appiah's *"Race," Writing, and Difference*, edited with Henry Louis Gates Jr. (Chicago: University of Chicago Press, 1986). More recently, Paul Gilroy has invoked contemporary work on DNA sequencing to make a similar case for the biological incoherence of race. See Gilroy, *Against Race* (Cambridge: Harvard University Press, 2000).
6. The abiding influence of Gates and Appiah's anthology, as well as that of the other text I examine in some detail in this introduction, Michael Omi's and Howard Winant's *Racial Formation in the United States*, is testified to by the decision to offer

a series of reflections on the two works in the October 2008 special issue of *PMLA*, *Comparative Racialization*.

7. In his philosophically inflected survey of social construction discourse, *The Social Construction of What?* (Cambridge: Harvard University Press, 1999) 20, Ian Hacking calls this the "argument against inevitability":

> Social constructionists about X tend to hold that:
> 1) X need not have existed, or need not be at all as it is. X, or X as it is at present, is not determined by the nature of things, it is not inevitable. Very often they go further, and urge that:
> 2) X is quite bad as it is.
> 3) We would be much better off if X were done away with, or at least radically transformed.

Hacking's accounts of both the logic and the rhetoric of "social constructionism" are largely in line with my own. I make no claim to originality in that regard; rather, the specificity of my argument rests upon what I understand to be the particular comprehensiveness of the claims for social constructionism enabled by race. Insofar as categories of race lay claim to the possibility to explain, predict, or describe all aspects of a subject, and to the degree that it is understood to function as an essence of the subject—Hacking calls essentialism "the strongest version of inevitability"—I am suggesting that race does not merely offer an occasion for the deployment of a social constructionist logic, but also provides the structure through which social constructionism comes to be rendered formal, comes to comprehend everything and hence to be linked to no particular content.

8. This move is what Karl Mannheim called "the unmasking turn of mind." The notion here is that once the "extra-theoretical function" of an idea is exposed, the idea will lose its "practical effectiveness." Here what is at stake is not a claim about the truth or falsity of a given account, but rather the authority from which it is derived and to which it is put. See Karl Mannheim, *Essays on the Sociology of Knowledge* (1925; London: Routledge and Kegan Paul, 1952), quoted and discussed in Hacking, *The Social Construction of What?*, 20.

9. Appiah, "The Uncompleted Argument," 35–36.

10. I want to make clear that my misgivings with the contemporary critical tendency to conflate—or invert—race and culture are quite different from those expressed by Walter Benn Michaels and the many critics influenced by his line of thinking. For Michaels, cultural practices are implicitly racialized at the moment they are accorded diachronic authority—at the moment, that is, that individuals feel moved to behave in certain ways (follow certain rituals, listen to certain music) because others whom they understand to share the same (cultural) identity as they do follow those rituals. In his construction, any model of identity that conceives of itself in relation to what precedes it is racial. As will become apparent, I depart from Michaels on both counts of his argument: first, his presumption that the properly self-conscious subject is one whose selfhood emerges with no reference to the past and is expressed entirely in the present, and, second, his assertion that to recognize a subject racially is to understand that subject to be defined by her genealogical links to ancestors, real or putative. Even if we bracket the complex role played by the past in any psychoanalytical or psychologically inflected account of the subject, I understand the experience of embodiment relevant to racial (self-)perception as being constituted by the complexity of its movement through and legibility in time. Race, on the other hand,

is by my account a mechanism for the production of the kind of instantaneously legible subject Michaels seems to celebrate. For an early explication of his position, see Michaels, "Race into Culture: A Critical Genealogy of Cultural Identity," *Critical Inquiry* 18, no. 4 (Summer 1992): 655–85. For his most sustained account of the position, see Michaels, *Our America* (Durham: Duke University Press, 1998).

11. Michael Omi and Howard Winant, *Racial Formation in the United States: From the 1960s to the 1980s* (New York: Routledge, 1986), 62.
12. Ibid.
13. Kwame Anthony Appiah and Amy Gutmann, eds., *Color Conscious: The Political Morality of Race* (Princeton: Princeton University Press, 1996).
14. In its effort to historicize the notion of the racial sign, my project can be seen to be of a piece with Elizabeth Abel's important and revelatory recent work, *Signs of the Times: The Visual Politics of Jim Crow* (Berkeley: University of California Press, 2010). Abel assembles an archive of photographs of Jim Crow–era signs in order to analyze the ways in which the interactions of photographic technology and the signs organizing racial segregation operated to turn biological qualities into signs whose arbitrariness undermined the force of racial categories even as it constituted those categories. My project similarly seeks to identify a moment in which the idea that race functions as a sign comes to the fore, but it does so in order to clear the way for a prehistory of that moment.
15. In her wonderfully thought-provoking article "The Fourth Dimension: Kinlessness and African American Narrative," *Critical Inquiry* 35 (Winter 2009): 270–92, Nancy Bentley links the emergence of the notion of the arbitrariness of racial signs to the residual force of a paradox of African American slavery: the fact that the condition of kinlessness associated with slavery is itself passed from slave mothers to their children. Bentley argues that this paradox illuminates the "coexistence of a distinct realm of experience with a three-dimensional world that remains oblivious to it" (281). Bentley points to the proliferation of late-nineteenth-century novels (including an unpublished fragment by W. E. B. DuBois) that "detach blackness from any schema of human consanguinity" (280) by creating versions of counterfactual worlds in which white characters suddenly come to possess the racial marks of black characters, and vice versa. These are fictional narratives built, in essence, around the positing, as thought-experiments, of the arbitrariness of racial signs. Bentley's interest here is the way in which the paradox of African American kinlessness illuminates the legal and historical underpinnings of the supposedly natural and universal condition of kin-relations: rather than serving as the foundation of other forms of sociality, kinship is actually a civil creation. In *The Fugitive's Properties: Law and the Poetics of Possession* (Chicago: University of Chicago Press, 2004), 247–51, Stephen Best also analyzes the proliferation of Reconstruction-era racial counterfactual narratives, a phenomenon he ties to the Fourteenth Amendment's linguistic ambiguity regarding the meaning of equality.
16. Only within the context of a racial knowing—and, in some cases, a racism—structured around likeness does the force of the "getting to know people personally" make sense as a mechanism for overcoming individuals' racism.
17. Saidiyah Hartman, *Scenes of Subjection: Terror, Slavery and Self-Making in Nineteenth-Century America* (London: Oxford University Press, 1997); Jacqueline Goldsby, *A Spectacular Secret: Lynching in American Life and Literature* (Chicago: University of Chicago Press, 2006); Brent Hayes Edwards, *The Practice of Diaspora: Literature, Translation and the Rise of Black Internationalism* (Cambridge: Harvard University Press,

2003); Elizabeth McHenry, *Forgotten Readers: Recovering the Lost History of African-American Literary Societies* (Durham: Duke University Press, 2002).

Recent theoretical approaches have likewise tended to engage the category of race sidelong. I'm thinking in particular of Stephen Best's *The Fugitive's Properties*, which examines the relationship between the property in human chattel and evolving conceptions of contract and property more generally; Hortense Spillers's *Black, White and in Color: Essays on American Literature and Culture* (Chicago: University of Chicago Press, 2003), which investigates, among a variety of other topics, the transformations of bodies into flesh that is the consequence of slave women's absence of a legal relationship to their offspring; and Fred Moten's *In the Break: The Aesthetics of the Black Radical Tradition* (Minneapolis: University of Minnesota Press, 2003), which reads jazz performances of artists like Cecil Taylor and uses the notion of improvisation as a formal structure for illuminating the contours of the relationships between philosophers ranging from Heidegger to Husserl and Derrida and black radical thinkers like Frederick Douglass and Samuel Delany. An interesting effort to characterize the theoretical topography of contemporary race studies is Utz McKnight's *The Everyday Practice of Race in America: Ambiguous Privilege* (London: Routledge, 2010), esp. chapters 1 and 2.

18. Kenneth Warren, *What Was African American Literature?* (Cambridge: Harvard University Press, 2011), 1, 10.

CHAPTER ONE

1. For a descriptive, though not particularly analytical account of the emergence of dermatology as a distinct field of medical specialization, see William Allen Pusey, *The History of Dermatology*. Baltimore: Charles C. Thomas, 1933 (New York: AMS Press, 1979).
2. Robert Willan, *On Cutaneous Diseases* (Philadelphia: Kimber and Conrad, 1809), 8. References to this work are cited parenthetically in the text hereafter.
3. On the need for a new attentiveness to the particular qualities of embodiment, see Elizabeth Grosz, *The Nick of Time: Politics, Evolution and the Untimely* (Durham: Duke University Press, 2004), 3.
4. The body of historical work that gets closest to what I'm after is work about the history of the racialization of the slave trade, but again this work tends to emphasize the outcome—that the alignment of slavery and blackness had the effect of making these sets of people slaves or generating these sets of justificatory rhetorics—rather than analyzing what the emergence of one racial sign as opposed to another might reveal about this political or epistemological or social conundrum race emerged to address. As Elazar Barkan puts it in *The Retreat of Scientific Racism* (Cambridge: Cambridge University Press, 1992):

> Race theories and racism have been presented as an almost natural outcome of the power relationships between various groups. This is in the case of the blacks' enslavement in the United States. Yet, the South American experience suggests that it was not an inevitable outcome. There, the free black was accorded a substantial degree of social equality. In the United States, in contrast, race outlived slavery and became an independent ingredient "fatally united with the physical and permanent fact of color" (Tocqueville, *Democracy in America*). Race perceptions were greatly influenced by race relations, but the precise reciprocity was not predetermined. (18)

The locus classicus of the debate over the relative priority of race and slavery is the exchange between Oscar and Mary Handlin and Winthrop Jordan that extended over most of the 1950s. For more on the historiography of racism and enslavement, see Theodore Allen, *The Invention of the White Race*, vol. 1 (London: Verso, 1994), and Edmund Morgan, *American Slavery, American Freedom* (New York: Norton, 1971).

5. My discussion throughout this section is indebted to Jay F. Rosenberg's lucid and incisive *Accessing Kant: A Relaxed Introduction to the Critique of Pure Reason* (Oxford: Oxford University Press, 2005), as well as Ernst Cassirer's *Kant's Life and Thought* (New Haven: Yale University Press, 1981).
6. Rosenberg, *Accessing Kant*, 59.
7. Ibid., 114.
8. George M. Frederickson, *Racism: A Short History* (Princeton: Princeton University Press, 2002), 11.
9. For a useful, if frustratingly brief, anthology of Enlightenment writings on race, see Emmanuel Chukwudi Eze, *Race and the Enlightenment: A Reader* (London: Blackwell, 1997).
10. Nancy Leys Stepan, *The Idea of Race in Science: Great Britain, 1800–1960* (New Haven: Macmillan Press, 1982), 1.
11. Frederickson, *Racism: A Short History*, 11.
12. Notable exceptions to this general tendency to ignore the significance of skin are the works of Roxann Wheeler, *The Complexion of Race* (Philadelphia: University of Pennsylvania Press, 2000); Claudia Benthien, *Skin: On the Cultural Border between Self and World* (New York: Columbia University Press, 2002); Stephen Connor *The Book of Skin* (London: Reaktion Press, 2004); and most recently, Anne Anlin Cheng, *Second Skin: Josephine Baker and the Modern Surface* (Oxford University Press, 2011). Wheeler's historicist project remarks upon the significance of the shift from a humoral to an anatomical logic for the history of race and identifies this moment as one in which skin gains in significance as a racial sign, but she leaves the logic and dynamics of the transformation largely unanalyzed. Benthien, Connor, and Cheng discuss skin from within a generally poststructuralist framework, with distinct chapters analyzing the various contexts in which skin has been conceived, race being just one among many.
13. As Wheeler has noted, Samuel Johnson's dictionary offers a series of definitions for the word "complexion" that manifest an essentially humoral logic: "complexion" refers not only to skin color but also to character, and to a kind of emotional sensibility. On the establishment of race as a signifier and the explosion of studies on racial difference by the end of the century, see Wheeler, *The Complexion of Race*, 7, and Benthien, *Skin*, 253.
14. Skin tone also functioned as one element of difference among many in the ancient world. Ancient Egyptian pictorial art regularly represented skin tone and features associated with inhabitants of sub-Saharan Africa, but written representations offered virtually no accounts of stable or generalizable skin tone: the strikingly large number of words used to describe skin tended to emphasize brightness or dullness rather than hue and to be picked out as relative positions rather than as absolute qualities. The same Arabs who would describe themselves as "black" in contrast to the "red" Persians might describe themselves as "red" (or even "white") in relation to sub-Saharan Africans. For the ancient Greeks and Romans, complexion was the consequence of environment, but the crucial lines of distinction—between civilized

and barbarian or, alternatively, between citizen and slave—were understood to be contingent rather than hereditary, accidents of birth rather than their consequences. Likewise, slaves tended to be prisoners of war, rather than distinct phenotypical or family groups (Wheeler, *The Complexion of Race*, 2).

15. The distinction between humoral and anatomical medicine I lay out here, designed to throw into relief the aspects of anatomical medicine that made Kant's conception of race both thinkable and useful, plays down the existence of eighteenth-century models of the body that in retrospect come to appear "transitional." I am thinking in particular of "vitalism," which understood the body to function systemically, on the model of humoral medicine, even as it differentiated among the types of vitality contributed by each organ. Although the movement toward a vision of the distinct operation of individual organs paves the way for anatomical medicine's model of disease located within distinct, fully autonomous organs, the emphasis within vitalism remains on the interaction of the system. As the French physician Theophile de Bordeu describes, "Every organ being sensible in its own way, and being unable to perform its functions—particularly the most forceful—without making some impression on the entire nervous system, it is evident that each organ must make a particular impression on the on the pulse" ("Recherches sur le pouls par rapport aux crises," in *Oeuvre completes de Bordeu*, 1:421; quoted in Anne C. Vila, *Enlightenment and Pathology: Sensibility in the Literature and Medicine of Eighteenth-Century France* [Baltimore: Johns Hopkins University Press, 1998]). See also Barbara Maria Stafford, *Body Criticism: Imagining the Unseen in Enlightenment Art and Medicine* (Cambridge: MIT Press, 1993); F. N. L. Poynter and K. D. Keele, *A Short History of Medicine* (London: Mills and Boon, 1961); and L. J Rather, *Mind and Body in Eighteenth Century Medicine* (Berkeley: University of California Press, 1965). Thanks to Ann Van Sant for her guidance on the topic of eighteenth-century medicine.
16. For more on this shift in medical authority and its relation to shifting class relations, see Mary Fissell, *Patients, Power and the Poor in Eighteenth-Century Bristol* (Cambridge: Cambridge University Press, 1991).
17. Jonathan Sawday, *The Body Emblazoned: Dissection and the Human Body in Renaissance Culture* (New York: Routledge, 1995), 54.
18. Recently, a variety of clinical and experimental medical practitioners, as well as historians of medicine, have begun to explore the ways in which biological racial difference disrupts the notion of the standard body of anatomical medicine. There have been calls for the production of multiple standards, involving the systematic introduction of racially diverse samples into clinical trials. While this line of thought is largely beyond my purview, it is usefully explored in the recent collection *What's the Use of Race: Modern Governance and the Biology of Difference*, ed. Ian Whitmarsh and David S. Jones (Cambridge: MIT Press, 2010).
19. Regimen's centrality for humoral thinking is explicitly theorized in Galen's essay "To Thrasyboulos," where the physician begins by asking whether health ought properly to be conceived as a project for medicine or for gymnastics and concludes by determining that, since the concept of regimen provides a framework for understanding the production and preservation of a body capable of going about "the activities of life" to be aspects of a single project, gymnastics and medicine need not be distinguished from one another. While Galen is known primarily for his theorization of the functioning and treatment of the body, what becomes evident in his essay "On Antecedent Causes" is the degree to which, for him, as for Kant, the functioning of

the body is significant for what it reveals about the structure of causation in general. We ought to understand humoral medicine, with its emphasis on the dynamic relation between internal and external forces to be an expression of Galen's philosophical worldview characterized by coequal forms of causation, rather than understanding coequal causation as theorization of the operation of the humoral body. See Galen, *On Antecedent Causes*, ed. and trans. R. J. Hankinson (Cambridge: Cambridge University Press, 2004).

20. Immanuel Kant, *The Conflict of the Faculties*, trans. Mary J. Gregor (Lincoln: University of Nebraska Press, 1992), 179. References to this work are cited parenthetically in the text hereafter.

21. In his only other extended writing devoted solely to the relationship between medicine and philosophy, "De Medicina Corporis, quae Philosophorum est" ("On the Philosophers' Medicine of the Body"), a lecture delivered at the Rektoratsrede in either October of 1786 or October of 1788, Kant elaborates a position somewhat closer to Hufeland's than the one he offers in the final essay of the *Conflict*. In this earlier essay, he outlines a mutually supplementary relation between medicine's and philosophy's respective capacities to control the state of the body. While the art of medicine should not be practiced "mechanically" upon humans in the way that veterinary medicine is practiced on domestic cattle, but instead ought to enlist the powers of the human mind in helping to mend the body, there is a danger in assuming, as Hufeland seems to in the notion of regimen that Kant criticizes in the opening passages of the *Conflict*, that medicine and philosophy act upon the body in the same manner or at the same time, or that they are mutually apprehensible modes. See Immanuel Kant, "On the Philosophers' Medicine of the Body," trans. Mary J. Gregor, in *Kant's Latin Writings: Translations, Commentaries and Notes*, ed. and trans. Lewis White Beck in collaboration with Mary J. Gregor, Ralf Meerbote, and John Reuscher (New York: Peter Lang, 1986), 185–209.

In her introduction to this essay, Mary J. Gregor makes the case for Kant's detailed knowledge of and interest in contemporary medical debates. Thomas De Quincey's "The Last Days of Kant," based on the translation of Christoph Wasianski, likewise argues for Kant's engagement in the medical discourse of the day. See also Marshall Brown "From the Transcendental to the Supernatural: Kant and the Doctors," *Bucknell Review* 39 (1996): 151–69; and Susan Meld Shell, *The Embodiment of Reason: Kant on Spirit, Generation, Community* (Chicago: University of Chicago Press, 1996), esp. the introduction and chapter 10, "Kant's Hypochondria: A Phenomenology of Spirit."

22. While the sense of inaccessibility to the inner workings of one's body was particularly acute during the decades in which the humoral paradigm was in the process of being actively supplanted by an anatomical logic, I want to make clear that the forms of illegibility I am describing are not merely the consequence of the shift in paradigms, but are the consequence of an ongoing dynamic within the theory (and practice) of anatomical medicine itself. See physician Abigail Zuger's *New York Times* essay of 30 September 2008, entitled "Healthy Right Up to the Day You're Not," and David Agus, *The End of Illness* (New York: Free Press, 2012).

23. In the introduction to his translation of Kant's *Anthropology* that Michel Foucault produced as a second doctoral project (*Madness and Civilization* served as the first project), Foucault made the case for the relevance of Kant's correspondence with Hufeland to the composition of the *Anthropology*—in particular, Kant's preoccupa-

tion with what his diminishing intellectual faculties might reveal about the relation of the legibility and knowability of subjects' bodies to themselves and the grounds of his critical philosophy.

24. In her provocative essay "Slow Death," Lauren Berlant examines a related set of issues surrounding "the obesity epidemic" and sovereignty from within a Foucauldian framework of biopower. She promises to "offer a development in the ways we conceptualize contemporary historical experience, especially when that experience is simultaneously at an extreme and in a zone of ordinariness, where life building and the attrition of human life are indistinguishable, and where it is hard to distinguish modes of incoherence, distractedness, and habituation from deliberate and deliberative activity, as they are all involved in the reproduction of predictable life." I engage the incoherence surrounding agency and the process of dying in greater detail in chapter 2. See Berlant, "Slow Death (Sovereignty, Obesity, Lateral Agency)," *Critical Inquiry* 33 (Summer 2007): 754–80.
25. Immanuel Kant, "An Answer to the Question: What Is Enlightenment?," in *What Is Enlightenment? Eighteenth-Century Answers and Twentieth-Century Questions*, ed. James Schmidt (Berkeley: University of California Press, 1996), 60. References to this work are cited parenthetically in the text hereafter.
26. This suppression applies equally, if less dramatically, to the issues surrounding the temporality of perception laid out in Kant's *First Critique*. While Kant argues there that the fact that we experience images or representations of the world successively is made insignificant by the fact of our experience of the unity of the world though time—in experiencing the necessary causal relations of the various elements of the world to one another, we come to know our own unity as subjects—this is only the case insofar as we presume ourselves to live forever.
27. See Stanley Reiser, *Medicine and the Reign of Technology* (Cambridge: Cambridge University Press, 1978) 20.
28. John Locke and Thomas Sydenham, "Anatomie," reprinted in full in Kenneth Dewhurst, "Locke and Sydenham on the Teaching of Anatomy," *Medical History* 2 (1958): 6.
29. BM Montpellier, MS 256, Barthez, "Cours de therapeutique," no date; quoted in L. W. B. Brockliss, "Before the Clinic: French Medical Teaching in the Eighteenth Century," in *Constructing Paris Medicine*, ed. Caroline Hannaway and Ann La Berge, *The Wellcome Institute Series in the History of Medicine* 50 (1998): 80.
30. Quoted in Russell C. Maulitz, *Morbid Appearances: The Anatomy of Pathology in the Early Nineteenth Century* (Cambridge: Cambridge University Press, 1987), 74.
31. Quoted in Brockliss, "Before the Clinic," 80.
32. David Armstrong, "Pathological Life and Death: Medical Spatialisation and Geriatrics," *Social Science of Medicine* 15A (1981): 253.
33. Ibid., 255. This tension between the pathological and the physiological characterized the formal efforts to produce a methodology for the analysis and treatment of old age from their earliest moments of conceptualization, though the various physicians who theorized the dynamic organized the tension in different ways. The earliest articulation is to be found in Jean-Martin Charcot's 1867 *Clinical Lectures on the Diseases of Old Age*, where Charcot classifies healthy bodies as pathological simply because of their old age. This classification at once created a methodological problem for gerontological research and constituted gerontology as a discipline: in Stephen Katz's formulation, how does one separate "senile" and normal pathologies and study the latter in a scientific way? See Stephen Katz, *Disciplining Old Age:*

The Formation of Gerontological Knowledge (Charlottesville: University of Virginia Press, 1996); also Elie Metchnikoff, *The Nature of Man: Studies in Optimistic Philosophy* (New York: G. P. Putnam's Sons, 1903), and I. L. Nascher, *New York Medical Journal*, 21 August 1909, 358–59. Another useful history of the field of gerontology is W. Andrew Achenbaum's *Crossing Frontiers: Gerontology Emerges as a Science* (Cambridge: Cambridge University Press, 1995).

34. Immanuel Kant, "On the Use of Teleological Principles in Philosophy" ["Uber den Gebrach teleogisher Principen in der Philosophie"], trans. Jon Mark Mikkelsen, in *Race*, ed. Robert Bernasconi (Malden, MA: Blackwell Publishers, Ltd., 2001). References to this work are cited parenthetically in the text throughout. Kant's teleology essay is actually the third and final essay he writes on the topic of race, though the only to identify and analyze skin as a particularly salient sign of racial difference. The two earlier, much briefer and more occasional essays are the 1775 "Of the Different Human Races" ("Von der verschiedenen Racen der Menschen"), which functioned as the preliminary announcement for Kant's lectures in the *Physical Geography* (*Physische Geographie*), and the 1785 "Determination of the Concept of a Human Race" ("Bestimmung des Begriffs einer Menschenrasse"), written in response to Herder's denial of race earlier that year in the second part of his *Ideas toward a Philosophy of the History of Mankind*. Both of these earlier works were written during Kant's precritical period and thus are not particularly relevant to the question of the role of a skin-based notion of race in reconciling some of the tensions internal to Kant's critical philosophy. For the history of Kant's writing on race, see Bernasconi. For more on Kant's precritical essays on race, see Ronald A. T. Judy, *(Dis)Forming the American Canon* (Minneapolis: University of Minnesota Press, 1993); Emmanuel Eze, "The Color of Reason: The Idea of "Race" in Kant's Anthropology," in *Anthropology and the German Enlightenment: Perspectives on Humanity*, ed. Katherine M. Faull (Lewisburg: Bucknell University Press, 1995), 200–241; and Charles Mills, *The Racial Contract* (Ithaca: Cornell University Press, 1997), and "Kant's *Untermenschen*," in *Race and Racism in Modern Philosophy*, ed. Andrew Valls (Ithaca: Cornell University Press, 2005), 169–91. The most interesting and sustained reading I've found of "Teleology" is a chapter devoted to Kant in David Bindman's *Ape to Apollo: Aesthetics and the Idea of Race in the Eighteenth Century*. (London: Reaktion Press, 2002).

35. Both Georg Forster and his father, Johann Reinhold Forster, accompanied Captain James Cook on his voyages to the South Seas, and the younger Forster assisted his father in writing his book on the journey, *Observations Made during a Voyage round the World*, ed. Nicholas Thomas (Honolulu: University of Hawaii Press, 1996). For more on the Forsters' journeys, see Bernasconi, *Race*, and Bindman, *Ape to Apollo*.

36. Kant's contemporary, the comparative anatomist Johann Friedrich Blumenbach, best known for his 1776 *De Generis Humani Varietate Nativa* (*On the Natural Varieties of Mankind*), places a similar emphasis on causation. Blumenbach's centrality to the history of racial thinking is usually tied to the abiding influence of his five-race taxonomy (Caucasian, Mongolian, Malayan, Negroid, American). While Blumenbach does not give skin color the exclusive importance that Kant does, he links such visible externals to a system of internal anatomical differences, discernible only by way of autopsy, in which skeletal differences among racial groups are linked to their having used their bodies differently at some point in the past.

37. David Clark has argued, in a very different context, that Kant reconciles the impulses of his empirical and transcendental projects regarding the legibility of the human by positing "alien others"—visitors from another planet—who "at once

mark the boundary between anthropology and a transcendental investigation [at the same time they register] the inevitability of their mutual contamination" ("Kant's Aliens: The *Anthropology* and Its Others," *New Centennial Review* 2 [Fall 2001]: 208).

38. Certainly, Kant's goal is this superimposition and synthesis. The paradox of his formulation articulates its limits as well: the demand that the universality be something that can be experienced and perceived, rather than thought, seems necessarily to transmute it into something not quite universal—a likeness that in being visible here and now, ceases to be everywhere and anywhere, and in that regard occasions the perception of difference. It is the historical fact of this tilt of the paradox off the equilibrium that Kant conceived that has become the familiar and historically pervasive aspects of his legacy of racial thinking, one I will spend the remainder of this book exploring.

39. This tendency has manifested itself more recently in the form of the controversy over full-body medical scans. The technology of the full-body scan was initially sold by private entrepreneurs on the promise of making the interiors of bodies thoroughly knowable while patients are alive, so that nascent diseases can be discovered before they produce symptoms. The knowledge produced by such technology would seem to threaten the fundamental epistemological structure of anatomical medicine, as well as to undermine the exclusivity of physicians' authority. Critics of the technology responded in just the way we might expect, lambasting proponents for marketing directly to lay consumers, who lack the expertise to distinguish harmless anomalies from potentially pathological ones. For these critics, the inaccessibility of our interiors has a diagnostic usefulness, constitutes a form of knowledge in itself, that ought not to be thoughtlessly exchanged for the promise of transparency. In 2008 Gina Kolata reported that, after an initial efflorescence, the private body-scan industry had largely collapsed for lack of sustained consumer demand ("The Pain May Be Real, but the Scan Is Deceiving," *New York Times*, 9 December 2008). For the meantime, the authority of anatomical medicine appears to be intact. But as Kolata reported, even physician-authorized scanning fell prey to the effects of this tension within anatomical medicine: "Scans—more sensitive and easily available than ever—are increasingly finding abnormalities that may not be the cause of the problem for which they are blamed."

40. Locke and Sydenham, "Anatomie," 4. See also David E. Wolfe, "Sydenham and Locke on the Limits of Anatomy," *Bulletin of the History of Medicine* 35 (May/June 1961): 193–220, and R. M. Yost Jr. "Locke's Rejection of Hypotheses about Sub-Microscopic Events," *Journal of the History of Ideas* 12 (January 1951): 111–30.

41. For the importance of the Robert Hooke's development of microscopic technology to eighteenth-century modes of description, see Cynthia Sundberg Wall, *The Prose of Things: Transformations of Description in the Eighteenth Century* (Chicago: University of Chicago Press, 2006), 72–76.

42. Ann La Berge, "Dichotomy or Integration: Medical Microscopy and the Paris Clinical Tradition," in *Constructing Paris Medicine*, ed. Caroline Hannaway and Ann La Berge, vol. 50 (London: Wellcome Institute Series in the History of Medicine, 1998).

43. This is essentially the argument Jonathan Crary advances in *Techniques of the Observer: On Vision and Modernity in the Nineteenth Century* (Cambridge: MIT Press, 1990), where he argues that, in the mid-nineteenth century, the stereoscope marked and helped bring about a fundamental shift from an objective to a subjective conception of perception.

CHAPTER TWO

1. Teresa Mangum catalogs Collins's recurrent interest in the relations between deformed and standardized bodies in "Wilkie Collins, Detection, Deformity," *Dickens Studies Annual* 26 (1998): 285–310. Peter Logan traces a related nineteenth-century transformation in medical models centered less on the structure of the body than on modes of disease transmission in *Nerves and Narratives* (Berkeley: University of California Press, 1997).
2. Indeed, for many nineteenth-century reviewers, the eventfulness of sensation novels—the elaborateness of their plots—is their defining characteristic. In her now-famous 1862 *Blackwood's Edinburgh Magazine* review "Sensation Novels," Margaret Oliphant remarked, "It is only natural art and literature should, in an age which turned out to be one of events, attempt a kindred depth of effect and shock of incident. . . . Sir Walter [Scott] himself never deprived his readers of their lawful rest to a greater extent with one novel than Mr Wilkie Collins has succeeded in doing with his 'Woman in White'" ("Sensation Novels," unsigned review in *Blackwood's Edinburgh Magazine* 91 (May 1862): 564). Oliphant's review is discussed in Lyn Pykett, "Collins and the Sensation Novel," in *The Cambridge Companion to Wilkie Collins*, ed. Jenny Bourne Taylor (Cambridge: Cambridge University Press, 2006), 50.
3. Wilkie Collins, *The Woman in White* (1860; New York, Penguin, 2003), 3. References to this work are cited parenthetically in the text hereafter.
4. Collins's fascination with poisoning trials continued throughout his career. See Douglas MacEachan, "Wilkie Collins and British Law," *Nineteenth-Century Fiction* 5 (September 1950): 121–39.
5. Collins's recollection is cited in the Nuel Davis 1956 biography *The Life of Wilkie Collins* (Urbana: University of Illinois Press, 1956), 211. While Collins does not actually name the specific trial he attended, John Sutherland lays out the case for concluding that Collins was referring to Palmer's trial in "Wilkie Collins and the Origins of the Sensation Novel," in *Wilkie Collins to the Forefront*, ed. Nelson Smith and A. C. Terry (New York: AMS Press), 75–90. Sutherland's piece is devoted almost exclusively to establishing Palmer as Collins's historical source; he spends almost no time, beyond noting the innovative narrative structure, exploring the force of the Palmer case for *The Woman in White*.
6. For Sundeep Bisla, the interchanging of Laura Glyde and Anne Catherick stands as an expression of Collins's anxiety that his texts will be pirated. See Bisla, "*The Woman in White* and Publishing History," *Dickens Studies Annual* 28 (1999): 103–49.
7. John Stuart Mill, *Autobiography* (1874; New York: Houghton Mifflin, 1969), 9, 12.
8. William Whewell, "Criticism of Aristotle's Account of Induction," in *Theory of Scientific Method*, ed. Robert E. Butts (Indianapolis: Hackett, 1989), 311–21.
9. Aristotle, *Poetics*, trans. Richard Janko (Indianapolis: Hackett, 1987), 12. References to this work are cited parenthetically in the text hereafter.
10. Walter underscores the ambiguation of subject and object in Collins's novel several pages later as he sums up his earlier description: "Mingling with the vivid impression produced by the charm of her fair face and head, her sweet expression, and her winning simplicity of manner was another impression, which, in a shadowy way, suggested to me the idea of something wanting. At one time it seems like something wanting in *her*, at another, like something wanting in myself, which hindered me from understanding her as I ought" (53).
11. That the novel holds out the possibility that this aged body may not in fact be

Laura's but might instead be the body of Anne Catherick reinforces the degree to which the novel's epistemological and representational issues are imbricated with its central plot movements, as I argue in detail below.

12. Rachel Ablow has argued that Count Fosco takes advantage of precisely the model of invisibility I am describing here: he disguises himself from other members of the Brotherhood by becoming fat, although his disguise is finally undone by the writinglike (and hence unaging) mark on his arm that is the sign of his never-entirely-former membership. See Rachel Ablow, "Good Vibrations: The Sensationalization of Masculinity in *The Woman in White*," *Novel* 37 (Fall 2003 / Spring 2004): 170. See also William Cohen on the role of the body in the reading experience, including the conjuring of imaginary perceptions in *Embodied: Victorian Literature and the Senses* (Minneapolis: University of Minnesota Press, 2008).
13. Elana Gomel and Stephen Weninger argue that clothes function in the novel as a locus for the instabilities and tensions of gender and class identity. See "The Tell-Tale Surface: Fashion and Gender in *The Woman in White*," *Victorian Institute Journal* 25 (1997): 29–58.
14. Quoted in Ian Burney, "'A Poisoning of No Substance': The Trials of Medico-Legal Proof in Mid-Victorian England," *Journal of British Studies* 38 (1999): 65.
15. For a detailed account of the acrobatics involved in Taylor's efforts to make the case for the authority of the emergent field of medical toxicology even in the face of its failure to turn up chemical evidence of poisoning, see Burney's rich and nuanced article (ibid., 66–77) and also Noel G. Coley's "Alfred Swaine Taylor, MD, FRS (1806–1880): Forensic Toxicologist," *Medical History* 35 (1991): 409–27.
16. See William Baker, *Wilkie Collins's Library: A Reconstruction* (Westport, CT: Greenwood Press, 2002), 155.
17. Alfred Swaine Taylor, *On Poisons*, 2nd ed. (1859), vi.
18. Ibid., 8.
19. "The Approaching Trial of William Palmer," *Lancet*, 29 March 1856, 348.
20. "Poisoning in England," *Saturday Review*, 22 December 1855, 134–35.
21. The marquise de Brinvilliers was convicted in 1676 along with her lover of poisoning her father and brothers in order to secure the family fortune, and Marie Lafarge was convicted in 1840 of poisoning her husband, though she was later pardoned. Both cases were the objects of ongoing public fascination in England and the United States. The story of "Madame Laffarge" was staged in a controversial production in 1840 at London's Adelphi Theater, and ten years later it was still sufficiently part of public consciousness to be alluded to in passing in Susan Fenimore Cooper's closet drama *The Lumley Autograph*, published in *Graham's Magazine* in the first half of 1851. See C. J. Thompson, *Poisons and Poisoners* (London: Harold Shalyter, 1931), and Susan Fenimore Cooper, *The Lumley Autograph* in *Graham's Magazine* 38 (January/June 1851): 31–36, 97–101.
22. This quality of irresolution, to my mind, presents a challenge to two powerful and influential accounts of *The Woman in White* that are predicated upon the novel's constitution of an autonomous and comprehensively knowable world: Walter Kendrick's "The Sensationalism of *The Woman in White*," *Nineteenth-Century Fiction* 32 (June 1977): 18–35, and D. A. Miller's "*Cage aux folles*: Sensation and Gender in Wilkie Collins's *The Woman in White*," in *The Novel and the Police* (Berkeley: University of California Press, 1988), 146–91. For Kendrick, Collins's novel undoes the opposition between "novels of character" and "novels of incident" by offering the internal coherence and comprehensiveness of events' relations to one another as

the grounds for a new kind of contract with the reader. For Miller, the novel produces sensations within the reader that have the effect of revealing to him his place within a more general carceral economy, a world in which even one's innermost and unexpected sensations must be assumed to be inevitably knowable.

23. Critical opinion seems oddly bifurcated on the issue of Fosco's role as a poisoner. Readers seem either to leave entirely uncontemplated the notion that Fosco may have poisoned Marian or to take such a reading as self-evident and hence not warranting argument. Exemplifying the latter position, Ronald Thomas simply positions Fosco the poisoner within an implied long history of scientist-malefactors within Collins's oeuvre. See Ronald R. Thomas, "*The Moonstone*, Detective Fiction and Forensic Science," in Taylor, *Cambridge Companion to Wilkie Collins*, 68.
24. One insight made available by this intertwining of the power to intervene in novels and the power to intervene in bodies is the not particularly surprising notion that historical paradigms and periods move and change unevenly, such that elements of old cultural habits and ways of organizing the world often remain present in unpredictable forms and places even after they have supposedly been supplanted. But the novel seems to offer a more historically specific insight as well: to the degree that the emergence of anatomical medicine and its critical aftereffect of physician-poisoning produce bodies and subjects that act and are acted upon in ways they are only intermittently aware of, then the very possibility of historical allegory becomes untenable. In this context, the action of a subject is less an event than it is an epistemology, a reading of the world effects that assigns events to particular acting subjects.
25. Ann Gaylin links Marian's eavesdropping—"an improper activity on the border between inside and outside, private and public"—to the disruption of gender boundaries throughout the novel. See Gaylin's *Eavesdropping in the Novel from Austen to Proust* (Cambridge: Cambridge University Press, 2002), 113.
26. Collins's openness, or susceptibility, to such a diffuse conception of authorship may be registered in the usual accounts of the shape of his oeuvre. He is generally seen to have produced his best work early in his career. See Jenny Bourne Taylor, "The Later Novels," in Taylor, *Cambridge Companion to Wilkie Collins*, 79.
27. My argument here is apposite with Judith Butler's conception of the linguistic performative, particularly as it appears in her effort to differentiate it from Austin's notion of the performative: "J. L. Austin proposed that to know what makes the force of an utterance effective, what establishes its performative character, one must first locate the utterance within a 'total speech situation.' There is, however, no easy way to decide on how best to delimit that totality" (Judith Butler, *Excitable Speech* [New York: Routledge, 1997], 2). I have been arguing that Collins's narrative, having revealed the tenuousness of the structures we conventionally understand to buttress identity across time—including bodies, names, nationalities, and the legible relations between individuals' acts and effects—offers a literalized language, a language and narrative unfolding independently of no-longer-tenable structures of identity, as the basis for new sorts of events and subjectivities. But where Butler would understand her model of performativity to follow from the nature of language per se, I am arguing that such linguistic literalizing becomes available at a particular historical moment, in the context of the dissolution of the traditional grounding of identity brought about by the revelation of anatomical medicine's internal tensions. Many thanks to James Kuzner for suggesting Butler's relevance to my argument.

CHAPTER THREE

1. John Stuart Mill, *On Liberty*, in *On Liberty and Other Essays* (Oxford: Oxford University Press, 1998), 5. References to this work are cited parenthetically in the text hereafter.
2. I'm here drawing upon the summary by Stephen L. Carter of the history of Lani Guinier's nomination that serves as the forward to Guinier's collection *The Tyranny of the Majority: Fundamental Fairness in Representative Democracy* (New York: Free Press, 1994). References to this work are cited parenthetically in the text hereafter.
3. Kwame Anthony Appiah, *The Ethics of Identity* (Princeton: Princeton University Press, 2005), 6.
4. According to Geoffrey Batchen, at least twenty-four people have laid claim to the title of inventor of photography, beginning in 1839: seven French, six English, six Germans, an American, a Spaniard, a Norwegian, and a Brazilian. Both the plethora of "inventors" and the fact that a desire to reproduce the world via refracted light came well *after* the technical means to do so ought to have been available testifies to the existence of a photographic discourse that is related to a variety of historical contexts without being reducible to those contexts. While I am sympathetic to Batchen's impulse, via a notion of discourse, to connect the emergence of a photographic "desire" to a variety of social, intellectual, aesthetic, institutional, and economic developments, I want to insist upon the significance of both the invention and circulation of actual photographic instruments as well as the category of technology, even as I seek to connect a photographic rhetoric to broader intellectual, social, and aesthetic trends. See Geoffrey Batchen, *Burning with Desire: The Conception of Photography* (Cambridge: MIT Press, 1999). For more on the social and scientific context within which Talbot performed his experiments, see Larry J. Schaaf, *Out of the Shadows: Herschel, Talbot and the Invention of Photography* (New Haven: Yale University Press, 1992).
5. William Henry Fox Talbot, "A Brief Historical Sketch of the Invention of the Art," in *The Pencil of Nature* (London, 1844–46; reprinted New York: Da Capo Press, 1968), unnumbered pages.
6. Nor does Talbot confine his interest in interjecting photography into a history of writing/drawing to a metaphorical register: Talbot's oldest surviving photograph, dated 20 June 1835, is an image of his own handwriting: the twenty-six letters of the English alphabet (Batchen, *Burning with Desire*, 144)
7. The nature's "pencil" metaphor appears frequently in writing about photography at midcentury. In *Framing the Victorians: Photography and the Culture of Realism* (Ithaca: Cornell University Press, 1997), Jennifer Green-Lewis notes that many of the early advocates of photography as an instrument for the natural world's self-representation, celebrated the technology as a mechanism for eliminating dissent. By insisting upon photography's relation to writing as well as drawing, Talbot paves the way for imagining a more equivocal relation between photography and dissent, one I argue Mill explores.
8. In his history of photographic criticism, Joel Eisinger examines how partisans for different aesthetic models of photography invoked different technological (pre) histories in order to claim that their divergent aesthetic practices in fact expressed photography's true nature. See Eisinger, *Trace and Transformation: American Criticism of Photography in the Modernist Period* (Albuquerque: University of New Mexico Press, 1995), 18–19.

9. Friedrich A. Kittler, *Gramophone Film Typewriter*, trans. Geoffrey Winthrop-Young and Michael Wutz (Stanford: Stanford University Press, 1999), 7.
10. The notion that agreement might serve as the ground of civil society is of course made most explicit by the genre of the social contract narrative that comes into its own with the writing of Thomas Hobbes and John Locke. While later writers in the tradition (like Samuel Taylor Coleridge in his 1839 *On the Constitution of Church and State*) emphasize the fictionality of such founding narratives of agreement, these later accounts do not challenge the fundamental principle that the possibility of positing agreement among its citizens is constitutive of the polity. But what I mean to make apparent is the degree to which a logic of agreement structures the argument of even some accounts—like John Stuart Mill's utilitarianism—that do not thematize it explicitly.
11. I want to make clear that I am not arguing that Mill's work takes another ideological turn in his final writings. Rather, I am suggesting that the development of photographic storage techniques of the sort Talbot details in his essays makes Mill's early inchoate ideas technically realizable, and once this happens, Mill is able to envision more coherently how a perceptual abstract might organize new forms of public sociability.
12. John Stuart Mill, *Autobiography*, ed. Jack Stillinger (Boston: Houghton Mifflin, 1969), 81. Mill first drafted the *Autobiography* in 1853, the same year he published *On Liberty*; the work was finally published posthumously in 1873. References to this work are cited parenthetically in the text hereafter.
13. T. B. Macaulay, "Mill on Government," from the appendix "Mill vs. Macaulay" in James Mill, *Political Writings*, ed. Terence Ball (Cambridge: Cambridge University Press, 1992), 272–73. References to this work cited parenthetically in the text hereafter.
14. See Laura Snyder, *Reforming Philosophy* (Chicago: University of Chicago Press, 2006), 300.
15. Ibid., 8.
16. I want to make clear that in making the case for a version of commonness that comes into being at no particular moment, Mill is not arguing for the existence of either an ahistorical polity or timeless values, both of which he associates with the false consolations of intuitionism. Mill's departure from his father's and Bentham's utilitarianism is an attempt to conceive of a model of political culture in which contingent and historically shifting social mores and political institutions can be understood to have been brought into being as instantiations of already existing common social feelings.
17. That the original Millian subject is both genderless and male is a rhetorical convention at once so widespread and frequently analyzed and criticized that it would be of little interest but for the fact that Mill's later introduction of the category of gender into his analysis, which he does in the most sustained way in *The Subjection of Women*, occurs in terms made available by the invention of photography and becomes the occasion for his redefinition of the subject from a laboring subject conceived in terms of his agency to a multisensory subject conceived in terms of his or her perceptions
18. Mill's historicization of tyranny at the opening of *On Liberty* marks the essay's most pointed departure from the deductivist utilitarianism of his father's 1823 "Essay on Government," which analyzed the relative merits and shortcomings of the "Democratical," "Aristocratical," and "Monarchical" governments as types. This opening also

bespeaks the influence of Macaulay's critique on the younger Mill's thinking: we recall Macaulay's remark: "We have here an elaborate treatise on Government, from which, but for two or three passing allusions, it would not appear that the author was aware that any governments actually existed among men" (Macaulay, "Mill on Government," 273)

19. John Stuart Mill, "What Is Poetry?," originally published in *Monthly Repository* (January 1833) reprinted in *Essays on Poetry by John Stuart Mill*, ed. F. Parvin Sharpless (Columbia: University of South Carolina Press, 1976), 5. References to this work are cited parenthetically in the text hereafter.

20. Jonathan Loesberg identifies the same drive toward an autonomous structure of representation in Mill's essay. But where I understand such a structure to engage with *On Liberty*'s politics of institutionalization and its attendant model of historiography, Loesberg reads the move, in ways not incompatible with my own account, as part of Mill's effort to imagine the possibility of free will from within an apparently deterministic associationist philosophy. In Loesberg's reading, as in my own, the autonomy of poetic production breaks down around the effort to communicate poetic feeling, the breakdown signaled by the dubious refiguration of poetic obliviousness to audience as "soliloquy." But because Loesberg sees poetry primarily as a disruption of the deterministic causation of philosophical associationism, within a framework that would assimilate the processes of representation and "storage" entirely within a more general logic of cause and effect, he sees Mill as largely abandoning his poetic project in the pages following the introduction of the figure of the soliloquy. Loesberg is unable to see the ways in which Mill's earlier distinction between "hearing" and "overhearing" might offer a way toward an as yet unrealizable solution. See Loesberg, "In Which a Poet Is Frightened by a Lion: The Philosophical Context of Mill's Poetic Theory," *Victorian Newsletter* 55 (Spring 1979): 26–31.

21. While Mill's vision of a social commonness generated out of an escape from the particularizings of time and space, of the event, might seem to resemble the universalism of Kant's critical philosophy, the fact that Mill envisions commonness as an *escape*—that is, the fact that he understands individuals in social relation to one another to preexist the moment in which they successfully cast off their particular qualities and/or come to recognize their likeness to one another—registers his important differences from Kant. Whether the poet deliberately ignores the assembled audience or is simply absorbed into a state of obliviousness by his poetic efforts, clearly for Mill, individual subjects become the model for commonness only when they withstand the pressure to be like others or to make others like them, to please or persuade.

22. In refusing to decide whether the poet pretends to be unaware of his audience or is genuinely oblivious ("the peculiarity of poetry *appears to us* to lie in the utter unconsciousness of a listener"), Mill strikes a markedly different stand than Diderot, for whom the deliberate performance of unconsciousness is openly acknowledged. See Michael Fried, *Absorption and Theatricality: Painting and Beholder in the Age of Diderot* (Berkeley: University of California Press, 1980), passim. For particularly insightful accounts of the way in which the most celebrated poets of Mill's era differently criticized Mill's position by means of their independent development of what came to be known as the dramatic monologue, see Herbert F. Tucker, "Dramatic Monologue and the Overhearing of Lyric," in *Critical Essays on Robert Browning*, ed. Mary Ellis Gibson. (New York: G. K. Hall, 1992), 21–35, and Isobel Armstrong, *Victorian Poetry: Poetry, Poetics and Politics* (London: Routledge, 1993), chap. 5.

23. Thomas Babington Macaulay, "Milton," in *The Works of Lord Macaulay*, vol. 5 (London: Longmans, Green, 1875), 1–45. References to this work are cited parenthetically in the text hereafter.
24. Not only does this passage insist upon the separability of seeing and hearing, but the very fact of their bifurcation is itself seemingly sufficient, if the unremarked upon shift from earlier singular "listener" to a plural but undifferentiated audience here is any indication, to constitute the audience as a unit, consciousness unified into consensus.
25. As the influence of Friedrich Kittler's writing has made its way into the American literary academy, there has emerged a good deal of interesting work on Victorian notions of sound and their relations to older conceptions of voice in Victorian poetry and narrative. See Yopie Prins, "Voice Inverse," *Victorian Poetry* 42 (Spring 2004): 43–59; Jay Clayton, "The Voice in the Machine," in *Language Machines: Technologies of Literacy and Cultural Production*, ed. Jeffrey Masten, Peter Stallybrass, and Nancy Vickers (New York: Routledge, 1997), 209–32; Ivan Kreilkamp, "A Voice without a Body: The Phonographic Logic of *Heart of Darkness*," *Victorian Studies* 40 (Winter 1997): 211–44; and Jonathan Sterne, *The Audible Past: Cultural Origins of Sound Reproduction* (Durham: Duke University Press, 2003).
26. In insisting that poetry accomplishes what it does to the degree that its effects don't seem to be traceable back to a localizable cause or event—it evokes an already existing sense of commonness rather than bringing about an agreement and hence escapes the pitfalls of politics—Mill seems to operate within a similar analytical framework to that articulated in Shelley's "Defence of Poetry," even as he comes to very different conclusions from Shelley. For Shelley, who famously concludes his essay by declaring poets to be "the unacknowledged legislators of the world," poetry is fundamentally like politics—and essentially revolutionary—insofar as it instantiates causation in the form of the metaphors that are its constitutive representational structure. I'm grateful to Herbert Tucker for suggesting the relevance of Shelley's "Defence."
27. The question of the relation of Mill's theory of poetry to contemporary poetic practice is more complicated than it might initially appear. While Robert Browning famously and explicitly understood the form of his dramatic monologues to illuminate the incoherences of the notion of poetry Mill sets out in "What Is Poetry?"—in particular, the opposition between eloquence and poetry, hearing and overhearing—Mill's account of poetry is not irrelevant to poetic practice. With its particular emphasis on feeling as the grounds of commonness, "What Is Poetry?" draws in obvious ways on romantic poetic practice, as well as the theorization of such practice in Wordsworth's "Preface to *Lyrical Ballads*." But the abstraction and separation of modes of perception I'm arguing Mill gestures toward can be seen to bear some descriptive relation to Tennyson's work. I'm thinking not only of the famously "aural," singsongy quality of that poetry, but also the ways in which, in a poem like "The Lady of Shalott," he offers images—for example, a river that simultaneously surrounds and is surrounded by fields—that are pointedly impossible to visualize, effectively inviting readers to imagine what they cannot see: "On either side the river lie / Long fields of barley and of rye, / That clothe the wold and meet the sky" (lines 1–3). In this regard, Tennyson would seem to be attempting to produce a version of perception markedly disjunct from the medium of writing. Thanks to Jayne Lewis for pressing me on this issue.

28. John Stuart Mill, *The Subjection of Women*, in *On Liberty and Other Essays* (Oxford: Oxford University Press, 1998), 471. References to this work are cited parenthetically in the text hereafter.
29. Indeed, the younger Mill pointedly departed from his father's position on the political status of women. In "On Government," James Mill argues that while a democracy with wider suffrage is preferable to one with narrower voting requirements, this principle need not be understood as making the case for extending the franchise to women, since they, like children, can be adequately represented by the votes of their male heads-of-household. (James Mill, *Political Writings*, 27)
30. It might be objected that I am reading "faculties" more literally than the passage warrants, but I want to argue that both the immediate and the broader contexts of Mill's essay make such a reading available. Mill is clearly interested in how women, by a combination of custom, aptitude, and practice, are likely to move quickly from task to task, engaging many problems in rapid succession, rather than focusing their attention on one problem or set of circumstances for a sustained period of time: "They perhaps have [the capacity to jump from one subject to another] from nature, but they certainly have it by training and education; for nearly the whole of the occupations of women consist in the management of small but multitudinous details, on each of which the mind cannot dwell even for a minute, but must pass on to other things, and if anything requires longer thought, must steal time at odd moments for thinking of it" (540). While the emphasis here would seem to be on realized and discernible acts—doing one thing after another—Mill's initial discussion of faculties in *Subjection* takes up a conception of "faculties" as perceptual (and other) capacities alongside a version that registers by way of externally organized (and externally discernible) activities: "There are extremely few things, dependent only on mental faculties, in which women have not attained the rank next to the highest. Is not this enough, and much more than enough, to make it a tyranny to them and a detriment to society, that they should not be allowed to compete with men for the exercise of these functions?" (525). In this passage, Mill insists that women ought to be allowed both to "compete with men" and to "exercise their faculties," and that their inhibition be understood as both "a detriment to society" and "a tyranny to them."

    By this account, the inhibition of women's activities is detrimental on two fronts. It harms society by stopping useful events from taking place—events that generate useful competition; events that produce valuable effects in and of themselves—and it harms women themselves by preventing them from exercising their capacities fully in ways that allow them to be fully human. This double emphasis is consistent, moreover, with Mill's position in *On Liberty*, where the inhibition of debate is harmful both because it prevents certain positions from being articulated that might ultimately produce better collective decisions and because it interferes with individuals' opportunities to exercise their powers of judgment. Mill's recurrence to this doubleness throughout his oeuvre fully justifies, I think, my decision to read women's propensity for "dividing their faculties" as both a division of attention among different activities and a division of perceptual capacities.
31. This emphasis on the reorganizability of perception I have been teasing out from the *Subjection of Women* is articulated much more explicitly by Mill in his *Examination of Sir William Hamilton's Philosophy* (1865) See Snyder, *Reforming Philosophy*, 129–30.

CHAPTER FOUR

1. Catherine Gallagher, "The Body versus the Social Body in the Works of Thomas Malthus and Henry Mayhew," *Representations* 14 (Spring 1986): 83–106.
2. Thomas Malthus, *An Essay on the Principle of Population*, ed. Phillip Appleman (New York: W. W. Norton, 2004), 15. References to this work are cited parenthetically in the text hereafter.
3. This position was elaborated most systematically by the Italian botanist and mineralogist Giovanni Brocchi in his 1814 work *Conchiologia fossile subapennina con osservazioni geologiche sugli Appenini*. See Phillip Sloan, "The Making of a Philosophical Naturalist," in *The Cambridge Companion to Darwin*, ed. Jonathan Hodge and Gregory Radick (Cambridge: Cambridge University Press, 2003), 31.
4. Charles Darwin, *Notebooks* (D 134–35) quoted in Jonathan Hodge, "The Notebook Programmes and Projects of Darwin's London Years," in Hodge and Radick, *Cambridge Companion to Darwin*, 60.
5. Charles Darwin, *On the Origin of Species*, in *From So Simple a Beginning: The Four Great Books of Charles Darwin*, ed. Edward O. Wilson (New York: W. W. Norton., 2006), 451. References to this work are cited parenthetically in the text hereafter.
6. For Gillian Beer, the most fundamental distinction between Malthus and Darwin is tonal and attitudinal: "To Malthus, fecundity was a danger to be suppressed—particularly by draconian measures among the human poor. To Darwin, fecundity was a liberating and creative principle, leading to increased variability, increased potential for change and development" (Beer, *Darwin's Plots*, 2nd ed. [1983; Cambridge: Cambridge University Press, 2000], 29).
7. As is well known, Darwin rushed *Origin of Species* into print after receiving, in 1858, an unpublished sketch of a very similar theory from the biogeographer and specimen collector Alfred Russel Wallace. See Robert J. Richards, "Darwin on Mind, Morals and Emotions," in Hodge and Radick, *Cambridge Companion to Darwin*, 102–3.
8. As Phillip Sloan has noted, Darwin elsewhere called himself a "philosophical naturalist" in an effort to distinguish his work both from natural historians (like Linnaeus), who saw their task as the systematic ordering of animals and plants in the context of the discovery of new species, as well as from the "natural philosophy" of Descartes and Newton, who organized their work around the discovery of natural laws. Darwin instead drew from the work of investigators of the natural world whose work fell outside these two traditions, including that of Etienne Geoffrey Saint-Hillaire, who developed a comparative anatomy based on ideal forms, and of Charles Lyell, who attempted to integrate comparative anatomy and theoretical geology in an effort to discover structural affinities or "unity of types" among kinds of animals usually thought to be members of widely disparate taxonomic groups (Sloan, "Making of a Philosophical Naturalist," 26).
9. With its emphasis on articulating the precise contours of the relation between the process of data collection and the development of his theory, Darwin's self-accounting seems designed to do more than simply stake his claim to originality. Michael Rose has argued, persuasively to my mind, that *Origin* ought to be seen as profoundly influenced by the contemporaneous "induction" debates over the nature of scientific knowledge engaged in by John Herschel and William Whewell. See Sloan (ibid., 24) and Michael Rose, "Darwin and the Philosophers: The Development and Reception of the *Origin of Species*," in *Biology and Epistemology*, ed. Richard Creath and Jane Maienschein (Cambridge: Cambridge University Press, 2000).

10. The most fully elaborated description of *Origin* as an account of events—and change—without agency is Gillian Beer's now-classic *Darwin's Plots*. Beer is particularly interested in the ways in which this disappearance of agency as the central organizing principle presents Darwin with a series of syntactic challenges to which he responds by ambiguating abstractions and by "invent[ing] phrase[s] on the edge of metaphor" (xviii). Moreover, Beer argues, "Terms like 'selection' and 'preservation' raise the question, 'by whom or what selected or preserved?' And in his own writing Darwin was to discover the difficulty of distinguishing between description and invention" (32). While Beer emphasizes the disappearance of a creative agency and the linguistic problem that attends such a disappearance, in my view Darwin's theory does away with something even more fundamental: not simply an origin but an organizing point of view, and with it the possibility of aligning knowledge with an inhabitable point of view. In part, Darwin insists upon the impossibility of associating knowledge with what can be observed visually, and this particular impossibility helps guide the particularly visual quality of the (racial) symbolization that functions as the solution to—or retreat from—this problem in Darwin's final works. But the force of *Origin* does not lie merely in its refusal of the visual or the empirical as organizing principles, but rather, as I will show, with a rejection of the idea that knowledge can be associated with a thinking subject's location in time and space. See also Robert Young, "Darwin's Metaphor: Does Nature Select?," chapter 4 of *Darwin's Metaphor: Nature's Place in Victorian Culture* (Cambridge : Cambridge University Press, 1985). For a position roughly apposite with Beer's from within a philosophical perspective, see Daniel Dennett, *Darwin's Dangerous Idea: Evolution and the Meaning of Life* (New York: Simon and Schuster, 1995).
11. This insistence on the individual as the fundamental unit of Darwinian natural selection is central to Michael Ghiselin's argument in his now-classic *The Triumph of the Darwinian Method* (Berkeley: University of California Press, 1969), as well as in *The Economy of Nature and the Evolution of Sex* (Berkeley: University of California Press, 1974). In the latter work, Ghiselin argues that evolutionary biologists subsequent to Darwin have overlooked the implications of what he calls Darwin's "radical individualism" by imagining that "organized beings (whether animals, societies, machines)" interact with one another such that "the parts have different roles, or functions, in the activities of the whole" (19). But by characterizing populations in terms of their likeness to individuals—their susceptibility to selection—Ghiselin effectively turns selection into a quality of an organism or system rather than a process. In so doing, he effectively renders opaque both the process and the objects of selection. Most obviously, Ghiselin's understanding of population as being essentially (like) individual(s) leaves him unable to distinguish between species, with their interacting individuals and populations and their interacting kinds. In his account, the category of species effectively becomes subsumed within the more capacious category of population.
12. Jonathan Smith deftly analyzes Darwin's adaptation and alteration of the visual conventions of natural history illustration in *Charles Darwin and Victorian Visual Culture* (Cambridge: Cambridge University Press, 2006). Smith argues that Darwin synthesizes visual and textual modes of representation so as to overcome the limitations of both in representing the fundamentally point-of-view-less natural selection. But in Smith's account, even these modes of synthesis have their limits: what is striking is the *absence* of illustrations in *Origin* in contrast to both Darwin's earlier and later writings (4). The abundance of illustrations in *The Expression of the Emo-*

tions and, to a lesser degree, in *The Descent of Man*, serves to reinforce my claim that Darwin's two final works register a retreat from the epistemological radicalism of *Origin*.

13. Contemporary philosophical debates over the nature of biological species have reproduced this movement toward an essentially synthetic, heuristic model of species. The model of historical kinds is theorized in Ruth Garrett Milikin, "Historical Kinds and the 'Special Sciences,'" *Philosophical Studies* 95 (1999): 45–65 (1999), and Richard Boyd, "Kinds, Complexity and Multiple Realization," *Philosophical Studies* 95 (1999): 66–87. For a very useful overview of the philosophical debate over species (including an excellent bibliography as well), see Mark Ereschevsky, "Species," http://plato.stanford.edu/entries/species/ (July 4, 2002)
14. Certainly, it would be possible to argue that the notion of "fitness" offers a position outside the system by which selection can be perceived to have taken place, but the retrospectivity of the criterion testifies to its essential formalism, its resistance to being located at a particular point of view. We can only know what has counted as fitness once the selection has taken place. I'm grateful to Sarah Winter for asking this question.
15. Michael Pollan, *The Omnivore's Dilemma: A Natural History of Four Meals* (New York: Penguin Books, 2006), 212–13.
16. Sloan, "Making of a Philosophical Naturalist," 26.
17. Charles Darwin, *The Expression of the Emotions in Man and Animals*, in Wilson, *From So Simple a Beginning*, 1261. References to this work are cited parenthetically in the text hereafter. I have learned a great deal from Sarah Winter's essay on Darwin's *Expression* as a kind of precursor text for Saussurian semiotics, "Darwin's Saussure: Biosemiotics and Race in *Expression*," *Representations* 107 (Summer 2009): 128–61. See also Stephen G. Alter, *Darwinism and the Linguistic Image: Language, Race and Natural Theology in the Nineteenth Century* (Baltimore: Johns Hopkins University Press, 1999).
18. To reiterate Darwin's language on habit: "Certain complex actions are of direct or indirect service under certain states of the mind, in order to relieve or gratify certain sensations, desires, &c.; and whenever the same state of mind is induced, however feebly, there is a tendency through the force of habit and association for the same movements to be performed, *though they may not then be of use*." And on antithesis: "Certain states of the mind lead to certain habitual actions, which are of service, as under our first principle. Now when a directly opposite state of mind is induced, there is a strong and involuntary tendency to the performance of movements of a directly opposite nature, *though these are of no use*; and such movements are in some cases highly expressive" (1277, *Expression*, emphasis added).
19. Darwin achieves what is essentially the same instantiation of the fossil record by way of his account of embryological development. Ontogeny recapitulates phylogeny, as we've heard, which is to say that the embryo of any given organism moves through the stages of evolution of organisms from lower to higher over the course of that organism's own development from embryo to fetus to baby animal.
20. Jonathan Smith, *Charles Darwin and Victorian Visual Culture* (Cambridge: Cambridge University Press, 2006), 44–60.
21. "When the sexes exist in exactly equal numbers, the worst-endowed males will ultimately find females (excepting where polygamy prevails), and leave as many offspring, equally well fitted for their general habits of life, as the best-endowed males. From various facts and considerations, I formerly inferred that with most animals,

in which secondary sexual characteristics were well developed, the males considerably exceeded the females in number; and this does hold good in some few cases. If the males were to the females as two to one, or as three to two, or even in a somewhat lower ratio, the whole affair would be simple; for the better-armed or more attractive males would leave the largest number of offspring. But after investigating, as far as possible, the numerical proportions of the sexes, I do not believe that any great inequality commonly exists" (*Descent*, 926). This difficulty Darwin experiences establishing the grounds for a distinctly reproductive scarcity—a scarcity of female reproductive partners—would seem to undermine Grosz's claim for an unambiguous *functional* distinction between a natural selection whose success is measured by the number of offspring produced and a sexual selection whose success is measured in terms of the retention of the right to choose reproductive partners. Grosz seizes upon this freedom she associates with sexual selection in order to make the case for a link between sexual selection and an aesthetic impulse. See Elizabeth Grosz, *The Nick of Time: Politics, Evolution and the Untimely* (Durham: Duke University Press, 2004), 73.

22. Darwin makes explicit that the usefulness of racial signs depends upon their non-comprehensiveness, their selection of a particular point of difference from a whole array of possible points of comparison: "There is . . . no doubt that the various races, when carefully compared and measured, differ much from each other,—as in the texture of the hair, the relative proportions of all parts of the body, the capacity of the lungs, the form and capacity of the skull, and even in the convolutions of the brain. But it would be an endless task to specify the numerous points of structural difference" (*Descent*, 900).

CHAPTER FIVE

1. David Simon and Ed Burns, *The Wire* (HBO), season 1, episode 1. Cited hereafter in the text by season and episode.
2. Caroline Levine, "Infrastucturalism, or the Tempo of Institutions," in *On Periodization: Selected Essays from the English Institute*, ed. Virginia Jackson (Cambridge, MA: English Institute in collaboration with the American Council of Learned Societies, 2010), ACLS Humanities E-Book (http://hdl.handle.net/2027/heb.90047).
3. For some overviews of the relationship between race and the Enlightenment, see George Frederickson, *Racism: A Short History* (Princeton: Princeton University Press, 2002); Ivan Hannaford, *Race: The History of an Idea in the West* (Washington, DC: Woodrow Wilson Center Press, 1996); and Robert Bernasconi, ed., *Race and Racism in Continental Philosophy* (Bloomington: Indiana University Press, 2003).
4. Against a chorus of readers eager to characterize *The Wire* as "Shakespearean" in its characterological complexity, David Simon has repeatedly insisted that his series be seen as Aristotelian rather than Shakespearean, partaking of the formal logic and conceptual universe of Greek tragedy that emphasizes the interrelations of plot, agency, and community over the interiority of character. For a detailed account of the relevance of Aristotle's *Poetics* to a narrative structured around the logic of the anatomical medical body, see chapter 2 of this book.
5. David Simon, introduction to *The Wire: Truth Be Told*, ed. Raphael Alvarez (Edinburgh: Canongate Books, 2010), 23, 20.
6. Simon, prologue to Alvarez, *The Wire: Truth Be Told*.
7. Rebecca Skloot, *The Immortal Life of Henrietta Lacks* (New York: Random House, 2010). Skloot chronicles the effects, across decades and institutions and familial

generations, of the harvesting of a particularly virulent and scientifically productive cell line from a cancer-stricken African American resident of East Baltimore. For a different account of the intimate imbrications of race and medicine in Baltimore, see Katie McCabe, "Like Something the Lord Made," *Washingtonian*, August 1989, 108–11, 226–33. McCabe's article, which was the basis for an HBO movie of the same name starring Mos Def, tells the story of Vivien Thomas, an African American lab assistant who, in partnership with Johns Hopkins heart surgeon Alfred Blalock, pioneered the techniques of open-heart surgery in the 1940s. Thomas's contributions were not officially recognized until decades later.

8. Simon, prologue to Alvarez, *The Wire: Truth Be Told*, 3.
9. In "It's All Connected: Televisual Narrative Complexity," in *The Wire: Urban Decay and American Television*, ed. Tiffany Potter and C. W. Marshall (New York: Continuum Publishing, 2009), 190–202, Ted Nannicelli reads *The Wire*'s narrative structure in terms of its positioning along a "series-seriality" continuum that characterizes the range of forms of episodic television. For Nannicelli's purposes, "series" describes television shows whose characters and setting are recycled, while the story concludes in each episode. He argues that most episodic television can be seen as a hybrid of the two forms but that *The Wire*'s form is notable for its positioning at the "radical" serial end of the spectrum: episodes frequently conclude with no narrative resolution whatsoever, while viewers are required to draw on knowledge gleaned from long-past episodes in order to understand basic plot movements. While Nannicelli's framework seems to me useful, his account overlooks the ways in which the series' early episodes train its viewers into a particular kind of sustained, diachronic attentiveness, the kind of sustained "serial" viewing it requires and rewards. This pedagogy begins with the kind of repetition-with-a-difference that I have been describing, a mode that is gradually replaced by a demand for the linking of increasingly temporally diffuse narrative moments. The movement from greater to lesser narrative redundancy also has the effect of associating the temporality of episodes with the accumulation of knowledge rather than the unfolding of events. See also Marsha Kinder, "Re-Wiring Baltimore: The Emotive Power of Systemics, Seriality, and the City," *Film Quarterly* 62 (Winter 2008): 50–52.
10. For a classical Marxist reading of Stringer Bell's fate, see Jason Read, "Stringer Bell's Lament: Violence and Legitimacy in Contemporary Capitalism," in Potter and Marshall, *The Wire: Urban Decay and American Television*, 122–34.
11. This pedagogical function of *The Wire* has registered in popular critical discourse in the ways in which its status as an object of academic interest is discussed—in marked contrast to the familiar responses of contempt with which academic engagement with popular culture are usually greeted. At a recent gathering of the Modern Language Association, for example, where it was possible to hear papers like "The Unbearable Queerness of Madonna's Boots,", discussions of *The Wire*'s popularity as a topic of professional academic study tended to invoke the fact of academic interest as evidence of *The Wire*'s seriousness and complexity as an aesthetic and social object. For another example, see M. Fairbanks, "Deconstructing 'The Wire,'" *New York Times Educational Supplement*, 3 January 2010, 4.
12. I am grateful to Alyson Bardsley for her enormously helpful observations on this point.
13. That Stringer both prepares for and supplements his movement into legitimate real estate by taking business classes at night school reinforces his sense of the association of the diachronicity of the pedagogical and real estate. The few glimpses we

have of Stringer in school, moments in which he is presented actively engaging the principles being presented, make evident that he does not understand his schooling to be mere credentialing.

14. Only blocks from the McCulloh homes and the corner George McMechen first sought to integrate, McCulloh Street is bisected by McMechen Street. The first known record of this street name was the 1822 "Poppleton Map—Plan for the City of Baltimore," which suggests it was named after David McMechen, a state senator and original shareholder in the company that founded the Bolton Hill neighborhood. George McMechen originally hailed from Wheeling, West Virginia (where a branch of David McMechen's family lived as well), and he came to Baltimore in 1891 in order to be part of the first class of the historically black Morgan College. In 1895, he became Morgan College's first graduate, later attending Yale Law School. In 1944, George McMechen became "the first Negro member of the Board of School Commissioners" (*Baltimore Sun*, 25 February 1961). All information courtesy of the archives of the Maryland Historical Society.
15. Garrett Power, "Apartheid Baltimore Style: The Residential Segregation Ordinances of 1910–1913," *Maryland Law Review* 42 (1983): 289, 310. Subsequent citations relating to the ordinances appear parenthetically in the text, and all page references are to Power.
16. This quality of arbitrariness surrounding political outcomes is underscored by the casting joke of the scene: the most forceful advocate for drug decriminalization is fictional Mayor Royce's director of public health, played by Kurt Schmoke, the long-time actual Baltimore mayor, whose departure from office was hastened by his advocacy of drug decriminalization.
17. A sense of this standardized body is what constitutes the professional knowledge of physicians, born as it is in the repeated exposure to bodily interiors via the practice of dissecting cadavers that is central to modern medical education. Physicians can be said to be educated when they have dissected enough bodies to have an idea of the standard (the "normal") that is distinct from the knowledge garnered by empirical observation of any particular body.
18. Mark Seltzer, in *Serial Killers: Death and Life in America's Wound Culture* (London: Routledge, 1998), has persuasively argued for the relationship between serial killers and standardization: "Murder by numbers is the work of the individual I describe as the statistical person: the serial killer that is, is not merely one of an indeterminate number of others but an individual who, in the most radical form, experiences identity, his own and others, as a matter of numbers, kinds, types, and as a matter of simulation and likeness" (4).
19. Jimmy's obvious literary precursor here, underscoring *The Wire*'s "Dickensian aspect," is John Harmon of *Our Mutual Friend*, who is a guest at his own wake.

INDEX